T0300577

Econophysics and Companies

Econophysics is an emerging interdisciplinary field that takes advantage of the concepts and methods of statistical physics to analyse economic phenomena. This book expands the explanatory scope of econophysics to the real economy by using methods from statistical physics to analyse the success and failure of companies. Using large data sets of companies and income-earners in Japan and Europe, a distinguished team of researchers show how these methods allow us to analyse companies, from huge corporations to small firms, as heterogeneous agents interacting at multiple layers of complex networks. They then show how successful this approach is in explaining a wide range of recent findings relating to the dynamics of companies. With mathematics kept to a minimum, the book is not only a lively introduction to the field of econophysics but also provides fresh insights into company behaviour.

HIDEAKI AOYAMA is Professor of Physics at Kyoto University, Japan.

YOSHI FUJIWARA is Research Fellow at Advanced Telecommunication Research Institute International (ATR), Kyoto, Japan.

YUICHI IKEDA is Senior Researcher at Hitachi Ltd, Hitachi Research Laboratory, Japan.

HIROSHI IYETOMI is Professor of Physics at Niigata University, Japan.

WATARU SOUMA is Associate Professor of Physics at Nihon University, Japan.

Econophysics and Companies

Statistical Life and Death in Complex Business Networks

Hideaki Aoyama

Yoshi Fujiwara

Yuichi Ikeda

Hiroshi Iyetomi

and

Wataru Souma

CAMBRIDGE UNIVERSITY PRESS

CAMBRIDGE UNIVERSITY PRESS
Cambridge, New York, Melbourne, Madrid, Cape Town,
Singapore, São Paulo, Delhi, Tokyo, Mexico City

Cambridge University Press
The Edinburgh Building, Cambridge CB2 8RU, UK

Published in the United States of America by Cambridge University Press, New York

www.cambridge.org
Information on this title: www.cambridge.org/9780521191494

First published 2010

A catalogue record for this publication is available from the British Library

Library of Congress Cataloguing in Publication data
Econophysics and companies : statistical life and death in complex business
networks / Hideaki Aoyama . . . [et al.]. ; [foreword by] Hiroshi Yoshikawa.
    p.   cm.
Includes bibliographical references.
ISBN 978-0-521-19149-4
1. Economics – Methodology.   2. Statistical physics.   I. Aoyama, Hideaki, 1954–
II. Title.
HB131.E268   2010
338.8'7 – dc22   2010018296

ISBN 978-0-521-19149-4 Hardback

Contents

Figures

Tables

About the authors

Hideaki Aoyama Professor of Physics, Kyoto University.

He received his PhD from the California Institute of Technology in 1982 and studied high energy physics at SLAC as a postdoctoral fellow, at Harvard University as a visiting scholar and at Northeastern University as a lecturer. He is an advising council for the Credit Risk Database (Tokyo) and a special advisor on physical sciences for the Renewable Energy Foundation (London).

Yoshi Fujiwara Research Fellow at Advanced Telecommunication Research Institute International (ATR) and Adjunct Lecturer at Kyoto University.

He received his PhD from the Tokyo Institute of Technology in 1992 and studied general relativity and quantum cosmology at the Yukawa Institute as a postdoctoral fellow, and at the Institute of Theoretical Physics, University of California at Santa Barbara as a visiting researcher. He was also engaged in research in econophysics at the Department of Economics, Università Politecnica delle Marche with Professor Mauro Gallegati.

Yuichi Ikeda Senior Researcher at Hitachi Research Laboratory, Hitachi Ltd.

He received his PhD from Kyushu University in 1989 and studied experimental high energy physics at the Institute of Nuclear Science, Tokyo University as a postdoctoral fellow, at Brookhaven National Laboratory as a collaborator on the project on Quark-Gluon plasma formulation. He also studied computational plasma physics at the University of California at Berkeley as a visiting industrial fellow. He worked as a senior researcher at Hitachi Research Institute from 2005 to 2008, and is currently seconded to the International Energy Agency (Paris).

Hiroshi Iyetomi Professor of Physics, Niigata University.

He received his PhD from the University of Tokyo in 1984 and continued to study strongly-coupled plasma physics as an assistant professor there. He worked at Hitachi Ltd as a researcher before moving to his current position. Also he studied condensed matter physics at Argonne National Laboratory as a research associate, at Louisiana State University as a visiting associate professor, and at Delft University of Technology as a visiting fellow.

Wataru Souma Associate Professor of Physics, Nihon University, Research Fellow at Advanced Telecommunication Research Institute International, and Visiting Associate Professor, Institute of Economic Research, Hitotsubashi University.

He received his PhD from Kanazawa University in 1996 and studied high energy physics at Kyoto University.

Hiroshi Yoshikawa (Foreword) Professor of Economics, University of Tokyo.

He received his PhD from Yale University in 1978. He served as president of the Japanese Economic Association in 2002 and is currently a member of the Council on Economics and Fiscal Policy in Japan. Among his several books, the latest is *Reconstructing Macroeconomics – A Perspective from Statistical Physics and Combinatorial Stochastic Processes* (Cambridge University Press, 2007).

Foreword

This book is one outcome of the new field of econophysics, and explains a wide range of recent findings relating to the dynamics of companies. While economics and physics each have long histories of their own, and their methods and purposes are obvious, econophysics, which has only a twenty-year track record, is still unfamiliar to many. Indeed, an emerging interdisciplinary approach in which the economy is studied with the tools of physics may provoke doubts as to whether the methods of a hard science can tell us anything about phenomena in which human beings are essential players. However, economics has in fact mimicked physics since the nineteenth century. This is particularly true of those who developed modern economics, the 'neoclassical' economists. The old masters such as Alfred Marshall and Léon Walras all drew inspiration from Newtonian mechanics. The fundamental concept of 'equilibrium', known to all students of the subject, is, of course, borrowed from physical science.

Thus, a moment's reflection shows us that the relation between physics and economics is long-standing and far closer than is commonly realised. Nevertheless, the recent development of econophysics represents a significant development. While traditional economics learned from classical mechanics, which analyses behaviours such as that of a ball thrown in the air or the motion of a weight at the end of a spring, econophysics looks to the statistical methods of the modern physicist.

Obviously, economic phenomena are constituted from the actions of very large numbers of people and companies. In Japan alone there are over a hundred million people and several million companies, or, in the language of physics, the human population is of order 10^8 and that of companies 10^6. Although these are small numbers in comparison with the everyday quantities of the natural sciences, the Avogadro constant, $\sim 6.02 \times 10^{23}$ for example, it is already impossible to track the movements of all people and companies with any high degree of accuracy. Fortunately for economics, this is not a problem, for while, as individuals, we may be interested in a particular person or a particular firm, economics as a discipline deals with macro phenomena, such as the economy of Japan, or that of Europe as a whole.

In its approach to these macro problems, traditional economics attempts first to analyse the microscopic and then to understand the macro-economy by a process of scaling up. In other words, standard economics regards the macro-economy as a homothetic enlargement of the representative micro-unit. Faced with similar problems in the natural world, statistical physics takes a very different route. Recognising that the micro-agents are too numerous to be followed individually, they simply abandon the attempt to capture micro behaviour in detail, and employ statistical methods instead. This is the fundamental concept advanced by Maxwell, Boltzmann and Gibbs.

Notwithstanding this precedent, some may still wonder whether it can *in principle* be meaningful to conduct statistical analysis on social phenomena arising from the actions of individuals, each with an economic motive and a will. Are sophisticated human beings with brains, on the one hand, and inorganic molecules, on the other, really on an equal footing?

More than seventy years ago, when the majority of researchers were opposed to bringing physics into biology, Dr Torahiko Terada, the major force behind the attempt in Japan, remarked:

When making a statistical analysis of a large number of human individuals we may properly regard it as a mere conglomeration of inorganic material, and altogether neglect individual free will. Indeed, it is now clear that pure physical problems, such as the density of particles in a colloidal matter, may with propriety be compared to statistics of a purely physical nature, such as the 'density' or 'average speed' of persons walking along the street ... It is sheer folly to dismiss such insights as heresy simply because they are incompatible with the dogma that 'living creatures cannot be understood by Physics'. Such absurdities remind us that no ignorant amateur poses so serious a threat to progress as a scientist unaware of the nature and goal of their discipline. Torahiko Terada, 'Groups of animals as inorganic groups', *Journal of Science*, Iwanami Shoten (1933)

The application of physics to biology is now an established discipline, biophysics, and the controversies of the past are quite forgotten. We can confidently expect, not least because of trail-blazing studies such as the current volume, that econophysics will soon seem an equally natural development.

Hiroshi Yoshikawa

Preface

Between their first explorations in econophysics and the writing of this book the authors have travelled a long and sometimes winding road. One of our earliest results was the landmark study of personal income distributions in 2000 (Aoyama *et al.*, 2000), which convinced us that thorough empirical study, or 'phenomenology' as it is called in physics, was essential for an understanding of society and economics.

Since then, we have carried out research with an emphasis on the real economy, that is, people (workers), companies (corporations), banks, industrial sectors and countries. We have also studied the various markets that play a vital role in the activity and prosperity of actual businesses. As a result we began to think of writing a book focused on the real economy and based on the analysis of very large quantities of empirical data. Such work has been largely ignored by economists because that discipline does not, unfortunately, value the empirical search for regularities. Yet, it is this observation-based approach that lies at the root of the success so evident in physics. Kepler's laws of planetary movement, for example, were extracted from the vast quantity of astronomical data collected by Tycho Brahe and others. There is every reason to expect laborious but ingenious analysis of economic data to lead to progress, perhaps not as dramatic as that of Kepler, but progress nonetheless.

We hope that this book will serve as a source-book for people like ourselves who want to move the field of econophysics over to the study of practical economics and companies, rather than the current focus on the application of statistical physics to financial risk.

We shall let our three Tuscans discuss the whole subject in the Prologue and the Epilogue, after giving the following sincere acknowledgements – needless to say, many people assisted in the research behind this book. High-accuracy, high-frequency data are a must for detailed study of various economic agents, and we would like to thank the Credit Risk Database Association and its president, Shigeru Hikuma, for general help and advice on the nature of the database, the Organization for Small and Medium Enterprises and Regional Innovation for help in relation to bankruptcy data, and Tokyo Shoko Research Ltd. for assistance relating to chain-bankruptcy.

Many other collaborators have contributed to this book in direct and indirect ways at various stages of our research. Our thanks to all, particularly to the following:

Masanao Aoki (Los Angeles), Mauro Gallegati (Ancona), Corrado Di Guilmi (Ancona), Hiroyasu Inoue (Osaka), Taisei Kaizoji (Tokyo), Yasuyuki Kuratsu (Tokyo), Makoto Nirei (Tokyo), Hideaki Takayasu (Tokyo), Misako Takayasu (Tokyo), Schumpeter Tamada (Hyogo) and Hiroshi Yoshikawa (Tokyo).

We are also grateful to the Yukawa Institute for Theoretical Physics at Kyoto University for allowing us to use the computing facility for part of our numerical computation.

Thanks also to Nao-san for the illustrations, and to John Constable who has not only read the text in its entirety and brushed up and polished the English of our text, but also made many helpful comments.

Finally, we wish to thank Hitachi Ltd and Hitachi Research Institute, which have provided us with research funding for this project. The authors of a work on economics are perhaps more aware than most of just how important such support can be to labourers in the intellectual vineyard.

Prologue

I have for many years been a partisan of the Copernican view because it reveals to me the causes of many natural phenomena that are entirely incomprehensible in the light of the generally accepted hypothesis. (Galileo Galilei in a letter to Johannes Kepler)

SALVIATI: Greetings, Sagredo, Simplicio, my good friends. I can hardly believe that it was only yesterday that we resolved to meet and talk about this book. How the time drags when I am not in pleasant company such as yours.

SIMPLICIO: Greetings to you, most courteous Salviati, and well met, well met I say. My mind is already racing in anticipation. I have not forgotten, and could not forget, our wonderful discussions with Professor Galileo in Tuscany, and I am convinced that on this occasion too you have found something worth the labour of a *Dialogue* (Galilei, 1632).

SAGREDO: For my part I am also delighted to see you both again. In the company of two such philosophers as yourselves I never fail to find inspiration and illumination. Now, would you care to tell me the nature of the subject, Salviati?

SALVIATI: Certainly, certainly, shall I come to the point: I feel that a change is happening, just as it was when we met with Professor Galileo.

SIMPLICIO: *Change!* Ha!

SAGREDO: Now, now, Simplicio... Let's hear this out. The book is about a change, is it? But I don't understand even the title. What is this econophysics?

SALVIATI: You have gone right to the heart of the matter; econophysics is the name of an academic discipline, a name coined in 1995 by that most learned professor of Boston, Eugene Stanley. He means the word to describe the study of the economy or economics as seen through the eyes or analysed with the tools of exact science.

SAGREDO: Well that helps me a little, but I am still puzzled by the appearance of the word 'physics' in this new name. Can you explain that, Salviati?

SALVIATI: Well, that is simple indeed. The main driving force behind this new discipline is the natural science of physics. For, as you will shortly see, statistical physics has many concepts and principles that can be readily applied to phenomena in economics. That is to say, just as economic systems are composed of many inhomogeneous agents, like people, companies and financial institutions, so the natural world studied so successfully by physicists consists of atoms and molecules in gases and condensed matter. The similarity is obvious, is it not?

SIMPLICIO: Well so you say, but I need hardly remind you that there is already a long-established and well-respected discipline studying these matters, namely economics. You should show a little more respect for that authority, for has not economics constructed an intellectual context in which economic observations can be placed; namely, the optimisation of utility by individual economic agents, the specification of the concept of equilibrium and the detailed delineation of the implications of the equilibrium model? Who needs this so-called econophysics?

SALVIATI: Alas, Simplicio, I fear you have erred in two ways.

SAGREDO: Only two? Simplicio's errors are legion and notorious, for example . . .

SALVIATI: Piano, piano, Sagredo. Firstly, Simplicio, my dear fellow, undue or unconsidered respect for authority is a prison with invisible walls. Secondly, the context to which you refer is, as it turns out, not entirely suitable for the analysis of economic phenomena. Let me put it in this way: the grounding principle of econophysics, and this is much more important than the mere import of certain concepts from physical science, is the scientific approach itself, where hypotheses and possible theories are discussed freely in an open manner, tested against determinable facts and used to make predictions, though not necessarily in that order. And science is really about changing ourselves, our mind, our dearest views, even when we are comfortable and don't wish to be changed, or find alternative views almost impossible to hold in our minds. For example, the quantum theories, or relativistic theories, all of which are beyond our everyday realm – is that not so Simplicio!

SIMPLICIO: I am sure you mean no offence, but there is no need to raise your voice, Sagredo, I am listening carefully, though I am not sure yet that I understand your point.

SALVIATI: Forgive me my dear Simplicio, the subject is of very great importance to me. For you see, the most remarkable thing is that if physicists and economists clear their minds of constraints, they can work together in this discipline, and very fruitfully.

SAGREDO: So, you say that this book is about the scientific study of companies, firms and corporations?

SALVIATI: Yes, yes, the study of the real economy, as it is made up of people, companies, financial institutions – and all this through the lens of exact science. An acquaintance of mine, some sort of poet really, but we need not hold that against him, once said that:

> Science, . . . is the north-west passage
> between cynicism and credulity.

Perhaps it is a little difficult to understand (poets!), but I think on reflection the matter is clear enough. The challenge before us is to find a way between, on the one hand, a credulous belief in the views of the establishment, whether that is the Church or in this case the academy, and, on the other, a bitter nihilism that tells us to abandon our endeavours because knowledge is impossible and the establishment does no more than reflect the structures of political power prevailing in its time. However, and wonderfully, the methods of science can and do break down the endless circular movement of constrained institutional thought, and, in spite of all the difficulties, these methods also build up a body of facts and understanding on which two or more minds can agree.

SAGREDO: Ah yes, I think I can accept this; the method yields understanding without the need to invoke any divine or ultimate foundations to knowledge.

SALVIATI: Precisely, but as yet in economics there is a lack of progress academically.

SIMPLICIO: Well! I'm not sure everyone would agree with that.

SALVIATI: Perhaps not, but you have to admit that economics is not a powerfully predictive or technological science yet.

SAGREDO: That would be difficult to dispute, sadly.

SALVIATI: But we need not despair; this book argues that there is a way through.

SAGREDO: That is most encouraging. I'll make a start straightaway; I hope it isn't too difficult.

SALVIATI: Certainly not. The authors told me that their aim is to speak clearly to a very wide range of readers, not just students of physics or economics, but of other fields too. Indeed they hope for many readers outside the world of universities, people in financial institutions and companies and businesses of all kinds and sizes. Everybody in fact who is interested in or practises economics, and that is, I hazard the guess, almost everybody.

SAGREDO: Is there much mathematics? It seems unavoidable.

SALVIATI: Well, you are right that there must be some, but the authors have designed their argument to make it accessible to those with only a basic mathematical training. Complicated mathematical formulae are placed in mathematical boxes, and these are indicated with the icon $\alpha\beta\gamma$.

SAGREDO: Ah, that will be useful for me; very considerate.

SIMPLICIO: I also notice that there are 'coffee break' boxes marked with the icon ☕, which seem to be tempting digressions from the main subject of the book. These look very interesting, though I still have my doubts about the main thesis of this work.

SALVIATI: Well, that is forgivable since you have yet to read it, and when you do I have no doubt that your mind will throw up many questions as you get to grips with the work. You may find that the dedicated support website for the book, www.econophysics.jp/books/ec, answers some of these. There is a great deal of additional information there, and of course you can contact the authors too.

SAGREDO: Splendid, then let us meet again when we have read the book, and formed our opinions of it. Salviati, Simplicio.

SALVIATI: But first, shall we remind ourselves of the ubiquity of economic activities in our daily lives by dropping in to this pleasant-looking inn and purchasing some refreshment before you return to your studies?

SIMPLICIO: For once, Salviati, you have said something with which I can wholeheartedly and completely agree. I do believe it is my turn, and fortunately I have my wallet with me.

1   New insights

This book argues that the phenomena discussed within economics can be approached fruitfully, arguably more fruitfully than with traditional ideas and methods, by employing the concepts and methodologies of the natural sciences. In the present chapter we will describe the background to this claim, and some aspects of the contemporary situation in economics.

1.1   A scientific approach

What is the approach of the natural sciences, and why is it so powerful?

Descartes, of course, characterised science as the process of making ourselves free from any prejudice and dogma when seeking truth. Certainly, our capacity for thought is limited or distorted by the influence of religion, politics or, indeed, the received wisdom of established academic disciplines.

However, the fundamental principles of natural science warn us against these traps and require us to face natural phenomena without bias, and to resist the temptation to truncate our inquiries prematurely. Instead, we must ceaselessly root out error and improve our understanding. It was this attitude that enabled Galileo and his predecessors to overturn the prevailing Ptolemaic theory, and to provide a vastly improved model of the truth. Centuries of cumulative endeavour later we have a set of scientific views stretching from the imperceptible world of elementary particles right through to cosmology, the science of the universe as a whole. In between there is chemistry, biology and much else besides. The increasingly technological society we see around us is an outcome of the application of science and scientific method, and of ceaseless improvement in our conceptions of the world. But suppose that mankind had rejected the scientific viewpoint and approach and adhered to less disturbing ideas, to the comfortable traditional thought, for example, of those such as Galileo's contemporary Cremonini,[1] who had refused to make observations through a telescope. Man would still be living in comparative intellectual darkness, with much of

---

[1] Cesare Cremonini (1550–1631) was a conservative philosopher, and provided Galileo with the model for Simplicio in his *Dialogue Concerning the Two Chief World Systems*.

the potential of our minds, themselves the products of a long evolutionary process, unexploited.

Of course there is more to the history of science and scientific thought than Galileo, but his case is particularly instructive, and further comparison with the present situation in economics is, we think, helpful. Part of Galileo's revolution came about through the use of novel instruments, telescopes, to record previously unrecorded phenomena and aspects of phenomena. Similarly, students of economic behaviour may now use enormously powerful computing resources, and complex software embodying sophisticated mathematics, to collect, observe and analyse large quantities of economic data. It must be emphasised at this point that natural science is more than mathematics, though it is a wonderfully powerful language with which to describe nature. We do not doubt that mathematics will continue to play a hugely important, perhaps growing, role, but mathematics is just a means, not an end. To study natural or economic phenomena in order to exercise our mathematics is fatally to confuse task and tool. Just as it is in the other sciences, our objective in economics is to construct networks of true propositions that model the phenomena under consideration and extend our understanding of the causal processes at work.

Two goddesses are engraved on the reverse side of the Nobel Prize medal for physics and chemistry. Nature is represented by the goddess Natura emerging from clouds and

 holding a cornucopia in her arm. The veil covering her face is held and being withdrawn by the goddess Scientia, the spirit or genius of science. This allegorical description of the process of science rings true for us. The sciences, the collective intellectual activity of many human generations, are gradually unveiling more and more of the natural world, and of all these research programmes physics is the most rigorous and in some sense the most successful. Bearing in mind the features of economic phenomena, for example their fine-grained and intensely complex character, with micro-causes yielding macro-effects, it is not unreasonable to suppose that the methods of physics may give insight in this field too.

However, individuals are the minimum agents in economic and social phenomena, as consumers and workers, and since our behaviour is controlled by our emotions and thoughts, there is a possibility that we can find no fundamental laws describing these processes. Some may believe that it is impossible in principle to find any law at all. We may recall that Durkheim claimed that social facts can only be explained by other social facts. But science should not, through fear of failure, arbitrarily limit its scope, and in fact physicists have already produced sufficiently valuable findings in economics to justify the expectation of more, and of more general insights. As a consequence there is an emerging and coherent interdisciplinary area, *econophysics*, which, while not being studied in independent academic departments, is the subject of prominent international conferences and workshops.

1.1.1   Science of complex systems

Many readers may have heard of the 'science of complex systems' and have some intuitive understanding of its work (Waldrop, 1992; Gell-Mann, 1995; Holland, 1996, 1998). But what does it really mean in practice, and how does it relate to the subject of this book, the study of economic phenomena? Unsurprisingly, the science of complex systems is difficult to explain briefly, but one way to understand it is to take for a moment a different mental perspective from that of the principal philosophy behind natural science, namely the quest for fundamental laws and simpler and simpler explanations.

That is to say we can now see that many complex phenomena in nature are chaotic. Although the behaviour of such a system is derived from a simple law, it is unpredictable. A living thing, for example, should be regarded as a complex object, not simply as an assemblage of parts constituting atoms. That is, we cannot obtain a full picture of such a system by giving a detailed analysis of the individual system constituents. This concept began to gain ground amongst scientists in the 1980s, and is responsible for the emergence of the discipline now known as the science of complex systems.

This point of view is far from incompatible with that of traditional physics and its search for fundamental laws. These are complementary methodologies, a pair of wheels sharing the same axle, and both are necessary if we are to gain understanding of as broad a swathe of the natural world as we can at this time. This is as true for the investigation of economic phenomena as it is for any other aspect of the world. By combining a microscopic study of individuals and companies, one end of the axle, and a macroscopic study of outcomes of complex interactions among individual agents on the other end, we obtain a viable methodology with which we can make progress.

1.1.2   The emergence of econophysics

Only a decade has passed since the term 'econophysics' was first used, and it is developing rapidly (Mantegna and Stanley 2000; Aoki 2002; Takayasu, 2002, 2004, 2006; Bouchaud and Potters 2003; Aoki and Yoshikawa 2007; Aoyama *et al.* 2009). The pleasure of being involved in such a challenging and creative phase is extraordinary, but for those meeting the field for the first time it can be disorientating. Some reassurance can be gained from a glance back at the history of the relationship between economics and physics, which is in fact long and close.

For example, no less a figure than Léon Walras established the general equilibrium theory on the basis of the mechanical outlook of the world prevalent in 1860. The theory explains the balance between the demand and supply of goods that determines price by comparing this balance with a mechanical system consisting of a weight suspended from a spring. The forces of demand and supply correspond, respectively, to the gravitational force working on the weight and the restoring force induced in the spring, and the price so determined corresponds to the length of the spring in equilibrium. The agents in this theory thus represent consumers and producers of goods.[2]

However, the effectiveness of such an analogical approach is limited by the lack of both breadth and fine graining in its analytic texture. This matters because actual economic phenomena include such macro matters as the business cycle, and consequently we need to bear in mind the causal significance of the heterogeneity of economic agents, on the one hand, and economic fluctuations on the other. General equilibrium theory, which for instance describes a number of consumers via a single representative agent, is not able to account for dynamic effects in economic activity.

The discipline of statistical mechanics in physics offers understanding of macroscopic states of matter by employing microscopic information relating to atoms and molecules. It is a successful and structurally relevant model for efforts within econophysics to bridge between micro- and macro-economics.

1.2   Distributions and fluctuations

According to statistical data gathered over the last ten years, the Japanese economy is home to about 2.5 million companies.[3] Additionally, Japan has approximately 67 million workers[4] and more than a thousand financial institutions including city banks, local banks, credit associations and governmental organisations. It is possible in principle to:

(a) list all of these economic agents,
(b) gain some grasp of the relationships among them,
(c) observe the financial and employment conditions of these companies,
(d) monitor money flow between companies and banks and between banks themselves,
(e) store the entire data in real time.

This is a daunting task, but we now have well-developed computers equipped with superb CPUs, enormous amounts of memory and virtually unlimited data storage space. But would it be worth the effort? Such a database would certainly give us a perfect description of the whole economy, but it would not make sense for us as outside observers because even a careful reading of the recorded data would tell us nothing about the rise and fall of companies, the main theme of this book. Clearly, some other approach is needed.

Let us move towards an alternative by reminding ourselves how companies are active in the production process. Each company buys materials and services from producers,

---

[2] In economics, an agent is a constituent in a model used to solve an optimisation problem. Economic agents include, amongst others, households, companies, central banks and governments.

[3] The total number of companies is based on a census taken by the National Tax Administration Agency. Other censuses by the Ministry of Internal Affairs and Communications and the Ministry of Justice give different numbers. Accurate estimation of the number is said to be very difficult. For example, it may be overestimated by an over-thorough count, which includes inactive companies, or underestimated because the research is too cursory.

[4] This number is based on a census by the Ministry of Internal Affairs and Communications. The database covers workers over fifteen years old and also includes persons with no employment at all.

adds value, perhaps by transforming them into other materials, services or products, and sells them on to other consumers, which can, of course, be other companies. In this process of earning money, the company employs its capital and labour along with its own creative ideas. We can see, therefore, that if we can trace the chain of money flows we will have described a very important aspect of the behaviour of companies.

To this end we can conduct statistical manipulations on the microscopic data relating to the 2.5 million Japanese companies and so extract coarse-grained representations. For instance, we might focus on the number of companies falling in the capital ranges of ¥1 million – ¥10 million, and more than ¥10 million. This kind of macroscopic view of the data in terms of statistical distributions will play a primary role in approaching the dynamics of the rise and fall of companies.

This is an idea akin to the approach adopted by statistical mechanics, but we are not claiming that the methods of this field are straightforwardly transferrable to economic phenomena. To gain understanding of any phenomenon, whether it is natural or socio-economic, we must distinguish between the topic's essential and inessential elements. Otherwise, we shall simply list all the data available, an act which yields little or no insight. Furthermore, we may encounter phenomena which do not lend themselves to that style of analysis. In fact, the rise-and-fall dynamics of companies are not random, and, as we shall demonstrate from real data, certain dynamical patterns can be discerned, one of these being the distribution of corporate magnitude. Indeed, it was Pareto, to whom we shall refer repeatedly in this book, who first pointed to this curious truth.

The first step in getting to grips with this matter is to recognise that the distribution of company size is not bell-shaped, but significantly skewed. The normal (or Gaussian) distribution, familiar from general statistics, is a typical example of bell-shaped distributions, and if company sizes were distributed in the normal form, we would find a majority of companies of average size with a few exceptional companies of very small or very large size. But study of the data shows that, in fact, companies are classified into two groups, a small number of giant companies and a large number of small and medium-size enterprises. If we remove the giants and examine the remaining companies we find that they can classified into two groups, the very large and the rest, a procedure that can be carried out repeatedly. This real-world distribution is characterised by a self-similar hierarchical structure, an aspect of the finding with which some readers may already be familiar. However, a non-trivial point is that the distribution obeys a specific form of distribution, the power-law distribution, details of which are discussed in Chapter 2.

Of course, distributions are just collections of snapshots of living companies. If we are hoping to shed light on the dynamics behind these distributions, we need to analyse any fluctuations, such as variations in capitalisation, which reflect the driving forces of production activity. In a static model where everything is balanced without fluctuations, there would be no dynamism at all, and it would be impossible to understand how a particular pattern is brought about and under what conditions the pattern is destroyed. However, where there are fluctuations, and they are invariably present in real-world cases, they are very revealing, and in Chapter 3 we will show that such fluctuations have a distinctive pattern giving rise to a specific distribution.

 Vilfredo Pareto

 Vilfredo Pareto (1848–1923) was an Italian economist. He was born in Paris to an Italian father and a French mother, and raised in that city before returning to Italy to study mathematics, physics and engineering at the University of Turin. Subsequently he worked as a civil engineer for the Italian state railway company and then for an iron works, of which he was for ten years the director. During this time he became a fierce proponent of free trade and minimal government regulation. This led him to intense political activity, and then to a new career in economic studies.

Under the influence of the neo-classical economist Léon Walras, he became a professor in economics in the University of Lausanne at the age of forty-six. His book *Cours d'économie politique* (1896–7) describes the power law that he both proposed and fiercely defended against criticism. Pareto's power law is one of the central components of the econophysical studies of companies and other agents in the real economy, not to mention many other social and natural systems where self-similarity is observed.

As has been remarked, analyses of real data show that there are clearly visible patterns in the distributions and fluctuations relating to companies, and that these are independent of variables such as country and time. The existence of such universality in such phenomena is extremely surprising from the perspective of economics, and encourages the use of the methodologies of natural science in their analysis. But the difficulty of the problem that faces us should not be underestimated, for as we try get to grips with the dynamics of the growth and failure of corporations, we will find that we are seeking an understanding of the interactions between agents, that is, of an economic network formed by the enormously complicated pattern of relationships among agents.

1.3 Are networks complex?

The power-law distribution, which is observed ubiquitously in nature, is a critically important concept in this book, and has in recent years been used to great effect in network science, a relatively new science dealing with a wide variety of phenomena, ranging from the microscopic, for instance in biology where it discusses gene networks, metabolic networks and the interaction network among proteins, right through to the macroscopic, where the Internet provides us with typical examples (Watts, 1999,

2003; Barabási, 2003; Buchanan, 2003; Caldarelli, 2007). For instance, researchers are also interested in communication networks formed by providers and companies, and the linking structure of web pages, social networking services (SNS), the trackback network of blogs, and so on. Other examples might include co-author relations among researchers and friendship networks among football players.

At first glance it may be difficult to believe that the members of such an apparently heterogeneous collection of networks have any common features, but in fact there are several, a fact that points towards the existence of some *universal law* behind the formation processes of networks. On the other hand, it is also true that each network has its own characteristic features, and one of the challenges confronted by network science is to explain how these facts co-exist.

The application of network science theory to economic phenomena is described and argued for in detail in Chapter 4, but for the time being few readers will object to the claim: 'The economy is a very large network consisting of economic agents directly and indirectly linked to each other.' Interestingly, although such a proposition seems unobjectionable, almost commonplace, the idea of studying economic systems from the point of view of networks is a recent one. For instance, the pioneering book written by economists with this perspective was published only in the 1980s (Piore and Sabel, 1984).

Here we pay special attention to the growth and failure of companies interacting with each other over various kinds of business network. Such intercompany networks underlying the dynamics of companies include mutual shareholding relationships, linkage between companies established by interlocking directorates, transaction relationships between sellers and buyers, and collaborative innovation emerging by means of joint applications for patents.

The authors began their study of business networks around 2000, and at that time, even at international conferences, there were very few presentations on this topic. However, since that time the number of papers on this theme has increased rapidly, and network science is now one of the key terms at such gatherings. This dramatic change is a clear indication of the growing understanding that recent developments in network science are relevant to all fields, with economics being no exception.

Indeed, there are points of very close contact between economics and network science, for example the environment surrounding companies is a rapidly changing one, and accordingly the relationship between companies experiences a dynamic influence. Consequently, it is dangerously misleading to focus our attention exclusively on a single company while neglecting its relationships to other companies. Taking a broader view will reveal new aspects to what is actually happening in the industrial economy, a topic that we will take up in the next section.

1.4   Change in the environment surrounding companies

In recent years industry has made a marked shift from *vertical integration* structures to those characterised by the *horizontal division of work*. As a result, managers and analysts have begun to recognise just how important the formation of networks is for corporate competitiveness. Environmental changes of this kind occurred in the electrical and electronics and automobile sectors, two major industries in Japan, from the late 1980s onwards.[5]

1.4.1   Outline of the Japanese electrical and electronics and automobile industries

By the mid 1980s, conglomerates in the electrical and electronics sector, for example Hitachi, Toshiba and Mitsubishi Electric, had established their positions in the Japanese economy. They produced the whole range of electrical and electronics manufactures. For instance, their product range spanned appliances, electronic components, such as liquid crystal panels and DRAM chips, electric power equipment, such as power generators and power grid systems, computers and system integration, such as a bank's mission-critical systems, to telecommunication equipment, such as routers. Their business strength came from their wide product range, because the phase and period of the business cycle of one kind of product are different from those of another kind. They had grown steadily for a long period without experiencing seriously poor performance. It is well known today that a major origin of high profitability in the 1980s was the export of DRAM chips to the USA.

On the other hand, the automobile industry established a unique strength in production systems through continuous effort for decades. The industry consists of several automobile manufacturers, such as Toyota, Nissan and Honda, and a very large number of auto-parts manufacturers, producing transmissions, brakes, electronic engine controllers and other components. Most of the auto-parts manufacturers are located near the factories of automobile manufacturers. They supply various auto-parts immediately to the factory requesting parts. This supply method brought a very high efficiency to their production system. Automobile manufacturers made various small and medium-sized cars in Japan, and exported them mainly to the world's biggest market, that is the USA.

In the middle of the 1980s Japan came under sharp criticism from the USA for its continuously growing trade surplus. A long sequence of repeated negotiations between the two countries eventually created a new economic context for Japanese industry, and after the Plaza Accord was signed by the economically developed nations, the relative value of the yen increased rapidly, with the consequence that automobile manufacturing plants were relocated to the USA. At the same time, various political schemes were devised to increase domestic demand. After the termination of the Cold War, however, political interventions of this kind were rejected, and were ultimately succeeded by an era of deregulation. This sequence of policy changes had consequences for industrial structure, and business networks are key to understanding these changes.

---

[5] Business environmental changes in the global economy are explained from the viewpoint of the USA in Dertouzos *et al.* (1989) and Berger (2005).

1.4.2   The electrical and electronics industry

In the 1980s Japanese companies survived intense competition from American companies in the manufacture of audio-video equipment such as video recorders and televisions. This was also broadly true for companies making components for personal computers, such as liquid crystal panels and DRAM chips. As a result, the US government accused Japan of dumping DRAM chips, and forced Japan to monitor its export prices by concluding the Japan–USA Semiconductor Agreement (from 1985 to 1995). In the process of increasing the production of liquid crystal panels and DRAM chips, Japanese companies built their plants in Korea and Taiwan, a decision motivated in part by the desire to avoid trade conflict. To reduce possible risks in these projects the Japanese companies asked local companies to invest in the business and in return offered technical expertise. This period of activity overlapped to some degree with that during which the Japan–USA Semiconductor Agreement was effective. The point to emphasise here is that Japanese companies changed their industrial structure from vertical integration to a horizontal division of work by switching from *self-manufactured* components to those *outsourced* through collaboration with companies abroad. It should also be remarked that the distribution of process units also entailed the leakage of production technologies.

Although Japanese companies became front-runners in the 1990s, this golden age did not persist for long, as companies were exposed to aggressive competition from Korean and Taiwanese companies, and a price drop due to overproduction. Furthermore, the Japan–USA Semiconductor Agreement seriously damaged Japanese companies and at present Japan has only one manufacturer of DRAM.

Putting aside the subject of specific components for personal computers, there are other more general problems regarding general environmental or contextual change in the computer manufacturing sector. Until the 1980s the computer world was largely a closed system, in which Japanese companies were able to maintain high-profit business in IBM-compatible mainframe computers for the mission-critical systems of banks and other large financial institutions. This was an age of vertical integration. However, after the end of the Cold War in 1990, a new period of *open systems* emerged, one characterised by personal computers and networks. At that time Japanese companies failed to gain control of the standardisation of the CPU for personal computers, so they had to follow an industry standard determined by companies in the USA. The simple assembly of components and the localisation of software packages were not sufficient to permit Japanese companies to take advantage of cumulative technological development by making further progress, and consequently the superiority of Japanese companies has gradually been eroded.

The explosive development of the Internet led to a coming of age, if not quite maturity, in the late 1990s, and, combined with deregulation policies, has radically transformed the industrial structure of communication equipment businesses from vertical integration to horizontal division of work. The new wave has all but destroyed the industrial cluster consisting of NEC, Fujitsu and Hitachi, once called the 'Denden family', and the Nippon Telegraph and Telephone Public Corporation, NTT, which exerted near complete control over this family, which it also supported. Even Japanese companies which manufacture telecommunications equipment for open systems, such as routers, are being out-competed. In contrast the USA has a number of highly profitable fabless companies[6] such as Cisco, which can respond promptly to market needs by simply switching manufacturer. This remarkable outcome is a clear manifestation of the strong causal relationship between network formation and competitive powers.

In addition, the electric power equipment sector is undergoing drastic changes because of deregulation. The electric power industry is typical, having been government-controlled until the 1990s. Companies making electric power equipment were able to maintain high profit margins via their relations with the power companies. However, deregulation of the energy market, which started around 2000, has begun to change this intimate relationship.[7] Some equipment-makers even have their own power plants to sell electricity to power suppliers, and in future it is expected that the formation of business networks among generators and suppliers will lead to reductions in the price of electricity.

1.4.3 The automobile industry

Like the electrical and electronics sector, the automobile industry has also undergone global reorganisation as a consequence of a trade conflict between the USA and Japan; in particular, Japanese companies were prompted to build manufacturing plant in the USA. However, it was the acquisition of Chrysler by Daimler-Benz that triggered the most important phase of global reorganisation. The fact that size matters for survival was widely recognised, as might be guessed by the coining of the term 'Four Million Club' to refer, somewhat enviously or complacently, to those automobile manufacturers producing over 4 million vehicles per annum.

However, in examining the industrial structures of Japan, we observe no fundamental change that excludes certain of the automobile manufacturers. Similarly, in the USA we observe an industrial system established with the co-operation of the Japanese automobile manufacturers and auto-parts manufacturers. Indeed, Japanese companies have now caught up with US companies in sales numbers in spite of the fact that these American companies retain a strong influence on the market. This is partly because these US companies must incorporate very large welfare costs, including pension and medical payments for retired employees, into the prices of cars. By comparison, Japanese companies enjoy relatively low costs for welfare, in addition to efficient production technologies, and can therefore increase their market share and maintain a healthy profit margin. Concerns with regard to energy security and environmental pollution have provided a tailwind for those Japanese companies excelling in the

---

[6] A fabless company is an equipment manufacturer that does not have its own manufacturing capability for electronic components, which is known as a *fab*.

[7] US experience of the deregulation of electric power is instructive, since it allowed the emergence of Enron, the notorious collapse of which due to a large number of improper transactions was one of the defining corporate scandals of our time, and has focused discussions of corporate governance.

production of economical small and medium-sized cars. By contrast, Korean companies are still in the catch-up stage on this matter.

The key production technology keeping Japanese companies internationally competitive is *just-in-time production* which ensures each process keeps inventory to a minimum (Ōno, 1988). The *kanban system* is key to the realisation of this efficiency, and is used in the following way. A *kanban* delivery slip is transferred by the manufacturer to the post-process stage together with manufactured goods. Once the goods are used in the post-process, the *kanban* is returned to the preceding manufacturing process as a purchase order. Thus, in each process, goods are only manufactured once authorised by a *kanban*, creating a chain reaction of production with minimum inventory.

Just-in-time production is based on a business network, in which vertical integration for key components such engines and automobile bodies co-exists with a horizontal division of work for peripheral components such as electronic parts. Formation of a suitable business network is the key to efficient and flexible production.

1.4.4 Industrial structures and business networks

In the last twenty years, the electrical and electronics industry in Japan drastically changed its shape in ways which will be familiar from the other industry examples discussed above. Instead of self-manufactured components, companies are now using outsourced components to produce computers, telecommunication apparatuses and other types of equipment. This change in industrial structure, together with a move towards an open system on account of deregulation, has confronted electrical and electronics companies with a major alteration in their relationship with other companies in their sector. Generally speaking, this has required companies to regard themselves as parts of the whole economy, not as single entities isolated from the system.

On the other hand, the automobile industry continues to develop business networks in an environment comprising a mixture of the two industrial structures. Broadly speaking, vertical integration is used for autobody and core components such as engines, while horizontal division of work is used for peripherals such as electronic components. However, strengthening of the just-in-time production methods, with the aim of keeping Japanese industries internationally competitive, clearly requires elucidation of the business network structure. Furthermore, a case study of the successful handling of major accidents shows that the business network plays an important role in recovering quickly from disasters.

To shed light on these issues in the industrial economy, we therefore have to elucidate what network is formed by companies through their linkages and how they interact with each other on the network, and it is expected that methods developed for analysing complex networks and agent-based simulations will be very useful, as demonstrated in Chapter 5. Perspectives for possible applications to practical business of the basic insights obtained in previous chapters are given in Chapter 6. Topics such as business strategy development methodology, the management of the propagation of credit risk and the innovation of business models are also explored.

In the following chapters we will explain, using many figures, what analyses of real data and simulations teach us about the statistical life and death of companies, and also the relationships between companies. We are all facing a great new wave of methodological opportunities for the understanding of economic phenomena, and we have designed our book to serve as a messenger of some parts of what we believe will be an intellectual revolution.

 Powers of ten

At many points in our text we use large numbers. In some cases, for example money, our intuitive understanding, of $1 million say, is adequate, but it is not always so, and in some cases the quantitative comparison of two large numbers can be opaque or cumbersome. For example, faced with two numbers it is not always immediately obvious how many times greater one is than another. Using exponent expressions, such as 10^6 dollars, is much more convenient in these cases. Within a Western system properly known as the 'short scale' special names are assigned to large numbers in units of 10^3 as shown below:

$$
\begin{array}{rrl}
\text{thousand} = & 1{,}000 = & 10^3 \\
\text{million} = & 1{,}000{,}000 = & 10^6 \\
\text{billion} = & 1{,}000{,}000{,}000 = & 10^9 \\
\text{trillion} = & 1{,}000{,}000{,}000{,}000 = & 10^{12}
\end{array}
$$

This continues up to a vigintillion ($= 10^{63}$). Interestingly, in the East the basic unit is 10^4, giving, in Japanese, *man* (10^4), *oku* (10^8), *chou* (10^{12}), *kei* (10^{16}) and so forth. *Muryotaisu*, the largest unit for numbers currently used in Japanese is 10^{68}, which makes $10^{72} - 1$ the largest number that can be described by words.

It is curious to note that there are other special names for large numbers, and that these do not form part of a sequence, and therefore cannot be called units in a strict sense. For example, Richard P. Feynman once remarked: 'There are 10^{11} stars in the galaxy. That used to be a huge number. But it's only a hundred billion. It's less than the national deficit! We used to call them astronomical numbers. Now we should call them economical numbers.' He, however, must have meant 'debt' not 'deficit', because the latter is about 5×10^9 (in US dollars, 2008) while the former is about 10^{13} similarly. Thus we propose that:

$$1 \text{ Feynman economical number} := 10^{13}.$$

In the microscopic world, 10^{-13} cm is 1 fermi (*yukawa*), which is approximately the radius of the proton. Therefore, 1 feynman is the inverse of 1 fermi (*yukawa*), so to speak.

Incidentally, there are other names for extremely large numbers, such as googol (10^{100}), centillion (10^{303} or 10^{600}, depending on which side of the Atlantic you are) and googolplex ($10^{10^{100}}$). In physics, a large number we encounter is the total number of protons in the observable universe, which is known as the Eddington number, and is approximately 1.57×10^{79}.

No economist should want to use numbers beyond 1 feynman.

2 Size distribution

By looking at a wide range of companies, rather than individual organisations, a curious and somewhat mysterious pattern becomes evident in the rise-and-fall dynamics.

As a preliminary to examining the dynamics of groups of companies, we will first explain what we mean by the size of a company, and then introduce the important concepts of *flows* and *stocks*, and several tools necessary for examining the distribution of company sizes.

We will find that among 'giant' and 'dwarf' companies, the size distribution of giants obeys *Pareto's law*. We will also see that the same law is also found for flow quantities such as individual incomes, and we will touch upon its connection with inequality in society and how it is linked to macro-economics.

We can now turn to the strange world of company dynamics.

2.1 Preliminaries

2.1.1 Flows and stocks

Companies are economic agents that buy materials and services, create added value by utilising their own resources and earn money by selling the products. Thus, the key to understanding company behaviour is a clear understanding of money flows. Companies raise money, then use this capital to obtain raw materials, employees and facilities, and with these resources add value to products and services, which are then sold to obtain more money.

A company is usually legally obliged to communicate its financial situation to shareholders and creditors through audited accounts and statements, which, by and large, are in the public domain. Such accounts are a valuable source of information about company behaviour, but in using such measurable variables, it is important to recognise that *flows* and *stocks* have very distinct physical dimensions. For example, consider a person's savings account, where both deposits (inflows) and payments (outflows) occur. The current balance is a stock, and is a quantity measured at a point in time and in monetary units (yen, pounds, dollars etc.). On the other hand, the payments made in a particular month constitute a flow and, are measured, for example, in units of yen per month. Stocks and flows are therefore differentiated by time.

While a flow is a change of stock, stock itself is an aggregate of flow in the past. Consequently, there is more to describing the financial standing of a company than examining either stocks or flows on their own. The same is true of a national economy, where GDP (gross domestic product) is a flow and the National Balance Sheet describes stocks. For a company, flow quantities including sales, expenditure and operating profit are shown in the Income Statement, and stock quantities such as capital and debt are shown in the Balance Sheet.

Now, available money is an indicator of the size of a company and can be measured from stocks like capital or debt, or from flows like sales or operating profit. The number of employees is also another good indicator of size. On the other hand, no *single* variable is adequate for determining the size of a company. The company with the largest sales is not necessarily that with the greatest capital.

However, by examining the size of a large number of companies from various angles, we find that the fundamental properties remain the same regardless of the variable used, stocks or flows. This may not be surprising since all these stock or flow variables are induced by the money dynamics of the company.

In order to deal with a group of companies, such as those in a business sector (energy, or food processing, say) or the companies within a nation-state, it is critical to use data that are either as exhaustive as possible or have been obtained from consistent examination of carefully selected samples. Otherwise, the analysis may produce misleading results with regard to the distribution and behaviour of the population (see subsection 2.3.3). Even if the sampling is well planned, it is quite common for only summarised statistics to be published, so that individual data are available only to a limited number of researchers, and consequently the dynamics of companies are hidden. One way round this is to use information from income and corporation taxes, and this is the route that we adopt here.[1]

2.1.2   Size distribution and Pareto's law

If it were possible to obtain all the flow and stock quantities for all companies and individuals at all times, a complete description of these economic agents would be obtained. However, such a description would be almost meaningless, and what we require are statistically sorted facts. That is to say, instead of a complete list of the capital statuses of a million companies, it would be more useful to obtain macroscopic descriptions, such as the number of companies with capital between ¥100 million

---

[1] It may be objected that tax data are potentially prone to error, since actual income and declared income might differ. However, it can be argued, and we think persuasively, that listed companies and high-income individuals will file accurate tax forms since the penalties, both legal and reputational, are considerable. Furthermore, statistical analysis reveals some outstanding phenomenological laws, which may be a reflection of truths of a still deeper nature, and this in itself makes the data worth examining.

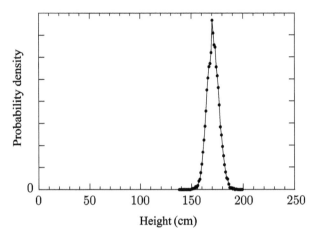

Figure 2.1. Probability distribution of human height (high-school senior male students in Japan).

and ¥1 billion, or how many companies have capital in excess of ¥1 billion. Briefly, distributions are the key to understanding the dynamic properties of the way in which companies rise and fall.

As we have mentioned in section 1.2, this is identical to the methods used in statistical mechanics for analysing microscopic and macroscopic physical states. Since the distribution of company sizes is extremely surprising we will first introduce some appropriate tools for handling these, and make comparisons with other distributions.

The height of male students in the third year of Japanese high school in 2005 is plotted in Figure 2.1. We denote the height by x and the frequency of people with height between x and $x + dx$, where dx is a small number, by $p(x)dx$. For the sake of brevity we will refer to the function $p(x)$ as a *probability density function* (PDF).[2] Figure 2.1 is a histogram with an abscissa graphing the height x, and an ordinate graphing the frequency $p(x)dx$. Adding all the frequencies over the range yields a result of 1, which means that the total area of the histogram adds up to 1.

Note that in this figure most of the individuals are distributed around about 170 cm in height, and in spite of individual differences no-one is 10 cm or 500 cm high. This kind of bell shape, which is centred around a peak and rapidly decreases away from it, is quite common, and the so-called 'normal distribution' is a representative instance. This is a very standard and untroubling distribution.

---

[2] Strictly speaking, the term 'PDF' applies to cases with continuous variables. In this case, since the data are tabulated, the height variable is essentially discrete. The same is true in economics, where the variable x could be money or number of people and hence is often discrete. In such cases, and strictly speaking, the relevant term is 'probability mass function'. However, the difference is not that important and because the scale of the variable is so large compared to the minimum unit, e.g. £1 million compared to 1p, and also because translating all equations and discussions from continuous variables to discrete variables is straightforward. For these reasons we use the terminology for continuous variables throughout this book.

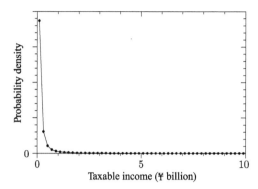

Figure 2.2. Probability distribution of companies' declared income.

Normal distribution

The probability density function (PDF) of a normal distribution $p^{(n)}(x)$ is the following:

$$p^{(n)}(x) = \frac{1}{\sqrt{2\pi}\sigma} \exp\left[-\frac{(x-\mu)^2}{2\sigma^2}\right]$$

(2.1)

Here, μ is the mean and σ^2 is the variance.

By comparison, the distribution of company sizes exhibits striking properties. Take the declared income of companies, an area in which we can get access to data from nearly all the companies with positive income. Figure 2.2 is the PDF plot of the top 78,000 Japanese companies in 2002, presented in a manner similar to that used above for human height. It can readily be seen that this distribution is widely spread. The largest income is the ¥680 trillion of Toyota, which is far too large to be included in Figure 2.2. The smallest income in this data is about ¥20 million. Although there must be companies with an income smaller than this, we can say with confidence that the income of companies varies by at least a factor of 50,000. This makes the distribution in Figure 2.2 right-skewed. A better way to describe this characteristic of the distribution is to say that it has a *long tail*.[3] This is sometimes also called a 'fat' or 'heavy' tail.

The total of income gained by all the domestic companies is finite. Therefore, in view of the fact that there is a huge disparity between companies it may not be surprising that a small number of companies engross a large share of income. However, there is a pattern in this plot. Figure 2.3 is a double-logarithmic version of Figure 2.2. This plot

---

[3] It will be as well to note in passing that the long tail described here is not directly related to the recently popular notion of 'long tail' in business. We will elaborate on this in section 2.5.

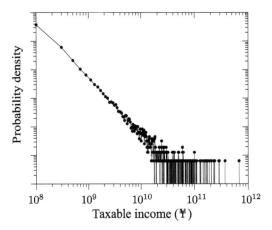

Figure 2.3. Double-logarithmic plot of PDF of companies' declared income.

shows that the PDF can be approximated by

$$\log p(x) = -\alpha \log x + c,$$

where log denotes the natural logarithm and α and c are constants. This approximation is valid in a very wide range, from one billion to several hundred billion yen. The equation above may be rewritten as

$$p(x) = C x^{-\alpha}, \tag{2.2}$$

where $C = e^c$. Thus this distribution obeys a *power law*, and the constant α is the *exponent of the power law*.

   Careful examination shows that the distribution in Figure 2.3 is somewhat shaky in the range $x > 10^{10}$. In making this histogram, we have divided the abscissa x into small equal-sized segments and have counted the number of companies in each segment. As x becomes larger, the size of the segments becomes smaller in proportion and there are many segments without data, causing a rough appearance. *Naively*, it might be supposed that this could be avoided if larger segments were chosen. One might also choose variable-sized segments that become larger as x increases, in order to avoid segments with zero entry. For example, we might choose segments with size equal to $\log x$. However, optimising the choice of segments remains as a technical problem, and the roughness remains no matter what. Moreover, by taking segments of a larger size, we lose some of the information in the original data. These two problems conflict with each other: smaller segments allow us to keep detailed information but lead to roughness in the results, while larger segments lead to a smoother PDF but result in a loss of information. Selecting the right size for the segments, in order to achieve a reasonable balance, is an extremely frustrating technical problem.

We can work around this problem by using a *cumulative distribution function,* (CDF).[4] The CDF $P_>(x)$ is defined by the following:

$$P_>(x) = [\text{The proportion of data with values larger than } x]$$

By this definition, $P_>(\infty) = 0$, and if there is a lower bound x_0 for x, $P_>(x_0) = 1$, as all data have x larger than x_0. It is also evident that $P_>(x)$ is a monotonically decreasing function of x.

The CDF is related to the PDF as follows:

$$P_>(x) = [\text{Total sum of } p(x')dx' \text{ with } x' > x]$$

That is, $P_>(x)$ is an integration of $p(x)$. From this we find from equation (2.2) that the power-law distribution has the following CDF:

$$P_>(x) \propto x^{-\mu} \quad \Longleftrightarrow \quad p(x) \propto x^{-\mu-1} \tag{2.3}$$

The power exponents are related by $\alpha - 1 = \mu$.

 PDF and CDF

The definition of the CDF above can be written as follows as an integral:

$$P_>(x) = \int_x^\infty p(x')dx'.$$

Therefore, the PDF is obtained from the CDF by differentiating it:

$$p(x) = -\frac{dP_>(x)}{dx}.$$

This leads to the relation between the exponents $\alpha = \mu + 1$.

In practice, the CDF of data can be obtained as a *rank-size plot.* Let us say we have n data, $x_1, \ldots, x_n$. We sort them in decreasing order and denote them as $x_{(1)} \geq x_{(2)} \geq \cdots x_{(n)}$. The i-th rank datum is $x_{(i)}$ and there are i items of data with a larger size, $x \geq x_{(i)}$. Therefore, if we plot them with the size x on the abscissa and rank divided by the total number of data n on the ordinate, it yields the plot of the observed CDF.

Or, by simply plotting the rank on the ordinate, we obtain the CDF multiplied by n, $n \times P_>(x)$.

This kind of rank-size plot does not suffer from the problems we encountered in making histograms, so we do not need to worry about the size of the segments, and we get to keep all the information. The rank-size plot is, therefore, an ideal tool for examining these distributions.

---

[4] This is also known as a cumulative distribution or cumulative probability.

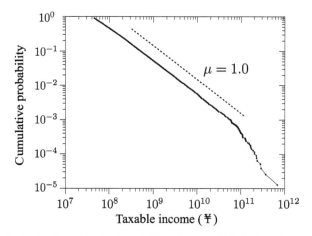

Figure 2.4. Double-logarithmic plot of CDF of companies' declared income.

Sometimes the ordinate indicates the size and the abscissa the rank, with their roles exchanged. Also, the data could be sorted in increasing, rather than decreasing, order. In that case, we would be looking at a variation of the CDF:

$$P_<(x) = [\text{Proportion of data with values smaller than } x],$$

which is related to our original CDF by the following:

$$P_<(x) = 1 - P_>(x).$$

All these approaches are in some sense looking at the same property, but from different angles.

Figure 2.4 is a rank-size plot of companies' declared income. According to this, for the income range from $x = 10^8$, ¥100 million, to $x = 10^{11}$, ¥100 billion, the power law applies with the power exponent very close to $\mu = 1.0$.

A number of natural phenomena obey the power-law distribution, for example the magnitude of earthquakes, the size of craters on the moon, the strength of solar flares and the size of fragments of shattered objects. Among social phenomena, examples might include the size of cities, the number of references to academic papers, the frequency of appearance of words, and individual incomes.

Individual income was first investigated by Vilfredo Pareto in 1896 (see the box in Chapter 1), and his work made a huge impact on the issue of inequality in economics (Pareto, 1896–7). The power-law for the size of cities was first noted by Felix Auerbach (1913), while the size of companies was studied by Herbert Simon and many other researchers. G. K. Zipf's book in 1949 studied long-tailed distributions in a wide variety of social phenomena and human activities and had a considerable influence in the natural sciences and humanities, among the best-known results being Zipf's law concerning the frequency of English words (Zipf, 1949).

However, it is important to be aware that while some phenomena *appear* to obey a power law at first sight, close examination reveals that in fact they do not.

In quite a number of power-law cases the power exponent μ is somewhere between 1 and 3. A smaller value for μ indicates a broader distribution, and thus the existence of larger quantities. In this sense, the power exponent μ is a measure of inequality in the region where the power law applies. We will elaborate on this point in section 2.4.

As is well known, the power law is often called the Pareto–Zipf law, or simply, Pareto's law. In particular, in the case of $\mu = 1$, and in relation to phenomena such as city size or frequency of words, it is commonly referred to as Zipf's law. This is no accident: $\mu = 1$ is one of the most important of power laws, a point we will elaborate in section 2.6.

Hereafter in this book, for brevity we shall refer to the general power law as *Pareto's law*, or as the *Pareto distribution*, and its exponent as the *Pareto index*.

2.1.3 *Other distributions with a long tail*

It should be noted that the term 'Pareto distribution' is based only on the behaviour of the distribution in the asymptotic region, where the variable x is large. Thus it covers a range of distributions, which differ in their functional behaviour in the small-to-medium range, and some of these will be explained in a later section. Thus, the Pareto distribution in this sense is a generic name.

The Pareto distributions are not the only long-tail distributions, a particularly well-known alternative being the log-normal distribution, which is, in essence, a normal distribution in $\log x$. Another important long-tail distribution is the Tsallis distribution (Tsallis, 1988), which has some desirable mathematical properties, although we will not use it in this book.

As we have argued, the Pareto distribution is a class of distribution with a long tail, and is used very extensively for the following reasons:

- power-law behaviour is apparent in a wide variety of data;
- the Pareto distribution has only one (significant) parameter, the Pareto index (Farmer *et al.*, 2005);
- the processes that induce power-law distributions are well understood.

Of course, it is important to make a careful examination of the dynamics behind the phenomenon in question and to determine what kind of distribution is in fact most suitable for understanding its true nature.

2.2 Distribution of personal income

We will digress here to deal with the issue of personal income. This was studied in earlier work by some of the present authors on the basis of a very large Japanese dataset which allowed the discussion of this distribution in detail, with particular emphasis on

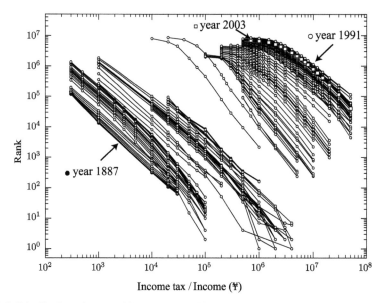

Figure 2.5. Distribution of personal income tax and income.

issues of inequality and their relation to the macro-economic situation (Aoyama *et al.*, 2000). A lack of similar data in other countries seems to have prevented work of similar accuracy before and since (but if any reader knows of comparable data we would very much like to hear of it). Because of its apparently unique status this data has become an important cornerstone of research on the subject of personal income.

While reading this section keep your own income in mind, to put the study into personal perspective.

2.2.1   Income distribution and Pareto's law

Japanese tax returns have been recorded since 1887, giving a very long data series. However, it should be noted that because the tax system has been changed a number of times, there are grounds for caution when comparing data from different periods. However, with this caveat in mind, we can look at the rank-size plots of income distributions from 1887 to 2003 in Figure 2.5, where the abscissa represents the income tax or income.

The leftmost distribution, with filled circles, is for 1887. After this year, the distribution keeps moving to the right and reaches the rightmost curve, with open circles, in 1991. After that it reverses its direction and starts to move to the left, reaching the curve in the middle with open squares in 2003. The gap in the middle of the plot divides the earlier distributions of income tax and the later ones of income. Although the data characteristics are different as such, it is at least true that the plots can be fitted by power-law distributions.

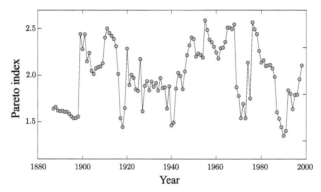

Figure 2.6. Evolution of Pareto index of personal income.

A rough estimate of the Pareto index is given in Figure 2.6, where the abscissa indicates the year and the ordinate the Pareto index. In relation to the inequality of distribution and the macro-economic situation, we observe several things from this plot.

Firstly, the valley-like structure between the 1910s and 1950s: a smaller Pareto index means greater inequality, so a small Pareto index indicates the existence of some people with very large incomes. Therefore, we can see that during this forty-year period, the distribution first became more unequal and then returned more or less to its earlier state. This phenomenon has been described in the economic literature from a different angle, and it is worth pausing to consider just what happened in this period, and what the economic situation was really like.

In 1955 an economist, Simon Kuznets, studied the evolution of the Gini coefficient[5] in the United States, Germany and England, and proposed that in the early stage of economic development inequality in income increases with growth, whilst in countries in an advanced state of economic development the income inequality is reduced and the Gini coefficient becomes smaller, a phenomenon referred to as Kuznets' inverted U-shaped curve hypothesis.[6] In other words, when economic structure is changing rapidly, income inequality grows, but reduces again when conditions stabilise. This might be just what happened in Japan from the 1920s to the 1950s.

Another thing we learn from Figure 2.6 is that income inequality increased in the 1970s. This period was characterised by a real-estate boom, encouraged by the then prime minister Kakuei Tanaka, and the oil crisis, both of which may be behind the income phenomena observed. We can also see in Figure 2.6 that inequality increased again from 1985 to 1998, the so-called 'Bubble Economy' of the Heisei era. We will touch again on this point in subsection 3.2.2.

Examination of recent income distributions using high-frequency data also yields interesting findings. Japanese personal income in 2000 is plotted in Figure 2.7, where

---

[5] We will elaborate on the Gini coefficient in subsection 2.4.1.
[6] The Pareto index and the Gini coefficient moved in opposite directions: greater inequality means a smaller Pareto index and a larger Gini coefficient.

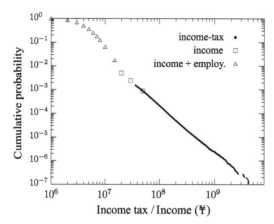

Figure 2.7. CDF of personal income in 2000.

income on the abscissa covers a range from one million to several billion yen.[7] From this plot, we observe that Pareto's law applies to income greater than about ¥20 million. Below this boundary the distribution is different, where we indeed expect the majority of individuals to be on salaries. It is reasonable to expect that these small-to-medium income individuals will exhibit a different distribution to that of the rich, as the latter have income sources other than salary, coming from their investments and other usage of capital.

The relationships between the Pareto index, and two risk capitals, the land-price index and average TOPIX (Tokyo Stock Price Index) are shown in Figure 2.8 for 1980 to 1998. Note that the land-price index is normalised, with the baseline in 1993, and also that the average TOPIX is the average over the year. The solid line in this plot shows the correlation between the land-price index and the Pareto index. We see that from 1980 to 1985 the Pareto index does not change much in spite of the rise in land price. In the next six years, the land price increased rapidly with a decreasing index. The land price peaked in 1991, while the index peaked in 1990, and in 1992, the Pareto index increased significantly, although the land price did not change a great deal. Afterwards, we see a decrease in land price associated with a (mostly) increasing index. This kind of motion is registered as a counter-clockwise rotation in this plot.

The broken line in the plot shows a correlation between the averaged TOPIX and the Pareto index. From 1980 to 1984, we see a moderate increase in the average TOPIX, and an almost constant Pareto index. Then, in the next couple of years, the average TOPIX increases rapidly, while the Pareto index decreases rapidly. The average TOPIX peaks in 1987 and starts to decline later, but the Pareto index continues to decrease

---

[7] This kind of data is obtained from salary income and declared income published by the National Tax Agency, and income tax data for high-income individuals published at local tax offices. The former is in a tabulated form, while the latter is a list of all the people who paid income tax of more than ¥10 million. This covers approximately 80,000 individuals, and thus there are approximately that number of points in this plot. Since anyone with an income of more than ¥20 million must file a tax return, there is an overlapping region between these two kind of data, which allows us to obtain a unified distribution profile.

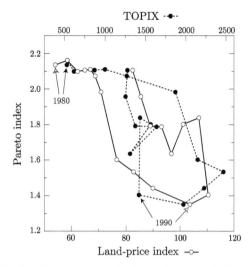

Figure 2.8. Correlation between the Pareto index, land prices and stock prices (TOPIX).

even after 1987 until 1989. It starts to increase rapidly after the bubble of the Heisei era bursts.

As we can see from this kind of study of income distribution, the Pareto index fluctuates around 2, with a strong connection to the macroeconomic situation.

In concluding, it should be recognised that this pattern of income distribution, and the evolution of the Pareto index, is not unique to Japan. We have also looked, though not in so much detail, at income distribution in the United States and Europe, and similar patterns reveal themselves. Connections between the Pareto index, stock prices and land prices are also known to be strong in the United States (Nirei and Souma, 2006). This appears to be a general phenomenon.

 Inspiration in Bali and Kolkata

In the summer of 2002, one of the authors attended an international conference on econophysics at Nusa Dua on the island of Bali. The location was a gorgeous resort hotel on a beautiful sun-drenched beach. The days were filled with excellent presentations on all kinds of economic and social phenomena, the evenings with culinary delights and cabaret. Very nice; but once outside the resort complex, one was painfully aware of the reality of Indonesia: according to a World Bank report, almost half of the Indonesian population has income of less than US $2. And these are dollars which have been adjusted in purchasing power parity, which means that these two dollars indicate money which can buy two dollars worth of goods in the United States. So, this is true poverty.

How can econophysics respond to this situation? One of us was engaged in research relating to high-income people, the results of which are outlined in this section, but he spent a part of his talk drawing attention to the Indonesian problem, a point which was warmly received by the audience. However the kind of data he needed for a detailed study of poverty was beyond his reach and several of the data resources which he could obtain conflicted with each other.

In 2005, an econophysics conference Econophysics-Kolkata I was held in Kolkata, India, and the main theme was income and wealth distribution. Of course, the caste system is still strong in India and there is a huge disparity in income and wealth. One of us got lost in town and wandered around the main and side streets for four hours. The contrasts were memorable, perhaps the most vivid being the sight of a businessman in a clean white shirt, talking on a mobile phone, with at his feet an old homeless woman eating rice and vegetables from a newspaper spread on the road.

At the second Kolkata conference, in 2006, the contrasts were if anything sharper. New Suzuki automobiles were a common sight around the hotel, and mobile phones were visible and their ring tones audible all the time, especially in the conference. On the other hand, the city was filled with homeless people, some of whom did not have even a tent.

India is a growing nation of extremely energetic people, but the effects of globalisation and other macroeconomic phenomena, far from solving the problems, seem virtually to make the inequalities still larger. Standing there in the streets of India, surrounded by frenetic activity and a heat which is not just atmospheric, we began to wonder whether any government can control the situation and improve matters, and whether econophysics, economics or any other academic discipline can make any contribution to this seemingly intractable situation.

2.3   Distribution of companies

2.3.1   Size distribution of companies

In subsection 2.1.2, we used the declared income of companies to explain Pareto's law, but other financial data is also potentially relevant in this context, and may be more informative.

Figure 2.9 depicts the sales of about 450,000 and the profits of about 270,000 companies, ranging from large to small. The potential for data inaccuracy in relation to very small companies should be borne in mind, but information from large companies, those with sales greater than several hundred million yen, is generally regarded as reliable, and the data for profits exhaustive in its detail. In spite of that, it is evident in this plot that large companies obey Pareto's law for these flow quantities. For sales, a rough estimate of the Pareto index in the range from several billion yen ($x \simeq 10^9$ on the abscissa) to several trillion yen ($x \simeq 10^{12}$) is $\mu = 1.05$. Similarly for the profit, in the range between several hundred million yen ($x \simeq 10^8$) and several hundred billion yen ($x \simeq 10^{11}$), the Pareto index is about $\mu = 1.02$.

 The size of cities

The choices made by individuals with regard to where they live, in large or small cities, are certainly influenced by variations in individual life stories and local culture and history. Nevertheless, human societies resemble and often exhibit mysterious and surprising self-organising phenomena. The chart below plots the population of the cities and towns in the northern Japanese island of Hokkaido, based on data obtained from the censuses of 1980 and 2005.

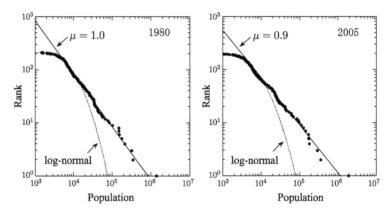

Even though there are only around two hundred points a power law is clearly evident in the tail (the fit to the log-normal distribution is also shown in the figure). Rough estimates of the power exponent would be $\mu = 1.0$ for 1980 and $\mu = 0.9$ for 2005, suggesting that population has become more concentrated in large cities, as a smaller value for μ indicates a greater number of larger cities. As we explain in sections 2.4 and 2.6, a value for μ smaller than 1 indicates the oligopolistic phase.

 Log-normal distribution

The PDF of a log-normal distribution $p^{(\ln)}(x)$ is defined in the range of its variable x from 0 to ∞ as follows:

$$p^{(\ln)}(x) = \frac{1}{\sqrt{2\pi}\sigma} \frac{1}{x} \exp\left[-\frac{(\log(x/a))^2}{2\sigma^2} \right].$$

This is obtained from the normal distribution $p^{(n)}(y)$, which is discussed on page 17, by changing the variable using $y \equiv \log x$:

$$p^{(n)}(y)dy = p^{(\ln)}(x)dx,$$

and then by rewriting it using a new parameter a defined by $\mu \equiv \log a$.

The average of x is not $a\,(= e^{\mu})$ but $ae^{\frac{\sigma^2}{2}}$, and its standard deviation is $ae^{\frac{\sigma^2}{2}}\sqrt{e^{\sigma^2} - 1}$. Further, the median is a and the maximum value of the PDF $p^{(\ln)}(x)$ is at $x = ae^{-\sigma^2}$. The plot below is the log-normal PDF $p^{(\ln)}(x)$ for $\sigma = 0.1, 1, 2$ with the average fixed to 1.

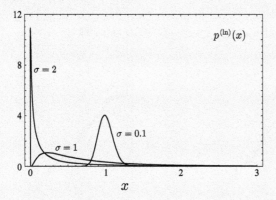

Its CDF, $P_>(x)$, is given by:

$$P_>(x) = \frac{1}{2}\left[1 - \operatorname{erf}\left(\frac{\log(x/a)}{\sqrt{2}\,\sigma}\right)\right],$$

where $\operatorname{erf}(x) \equiv (2/\sqrt{\pi})\int_0^x dt\,\exp(-t^2)$ is the error function.

Thus, the company size distribution has a Pareto index close to 1, a very different result from that obtained for personal income.

If we sort the companies into business sectors we find Pareto distributions for most groups. Figure 2.10 shows the CDF for the following categories: (a) electrical machinery/supplies (b) wholesale (c) retail trade (d) iron and steel/fabricated metal (e) general machinery (f) chemical and petroleum products.

2.3.2 Size of European companies

As we noted before, company size can be measured in terms of either flows or stocks. The question then arises as to whether Pareto's law holds for both.

Unfortunately, it is not generally easy to obtain exhaustive data for companies with, say, total capital greater than a specified value. However, the European electronic

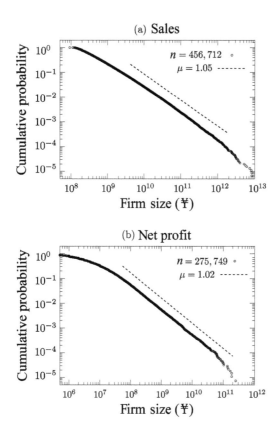

Figure 2.9. CDF of company size, 2002: (a) sales (b) profit.

publishing company Bureau van Dijk offers a comprehensive database, AMADEUS, which covers all companies with either an operating profit greater than €15 million, or a total capital greater than €30 million, or more than 150 employees. This kind of exhaustive listing is ideal.[8]

Figure 2.11 plots the CDF of total capital and sales of French companies, and the number of employees of British companies. We observe in these plots that no matter which quantity we use for measuring company size, we obtain a Pareto distribution. Rough estimates of the index yield values close to the range, $\mu = 0.9-1.0$.

As we will make clear in subsection 2.4.3, $\mu = 1$ is a boundary, or a critical value, where the overall characteristics of the size distribution changes. It should be noted that the values we obtained here for European companies is very close to this critical value.

In this plot of the evolution of the Pareto index, Figure 2.12, the value is stable, staying very close to $\mu = 1$, independently of the measure of size used and the country.

---

[8] The following results were obtained in collaboration with Mauro Gallegati of Ancona, Italy.

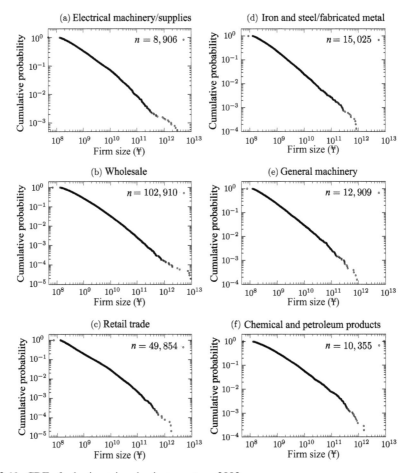

Figure 2.10. CDF of sales in various business sectors, 2002.

2.3.3 A caveat: sample and true distributions

In this section, we will elaborate on a detailed and technical issue. Some readers may want to skip this section and can do so without losing the thread of the discussion.

Although financial data are accessible for quite a number of companies, our experience shows that they are often limited to listed companies, and it is reasonable to fear that statistical analysis which is confined to this subset may yield misleading results. Consequently, in order to get a reliable picture of the character of the whole population of companies, not just the listed ones, we need a consistently planned sample investigation, and if possible, data for all or at least a very large part of the population.

Exhaustive data on declared income was used for Figure 2.3. Restricting ourselves to the listed companies might produce a different result.

Figure 2.13 shows the CDF of the subset comprising listed companies (there are about 2,000) with open circles, while the solid circles represent the CDF of the entire

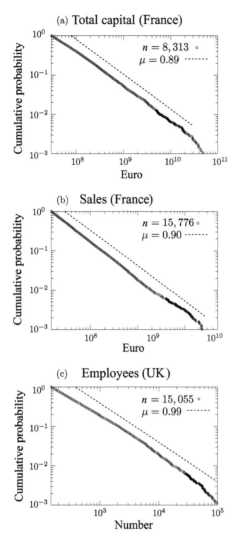

Figure 2.11. CDF of company size, 2001: (a) total capital in France (b) sales in France (c) number of employees in the UK.

set of companies. A best fit, with the log-normal distribution, is given by the solid curve. As we noted before, and as is seen clearly in this plot, the log-normal distribution is quite different from the power-law distribution, even though both of them have long tails.

Figure 2.14 shows the same kind of analysis for the PDF. Both of these plots imply that if one had data only for listed companies, one would conclude that the companies obey the log-normal distribution, in spite of the fact that a completely different distribution, the Pareto distribution, applies to the companies in exactly the same region of declared income.

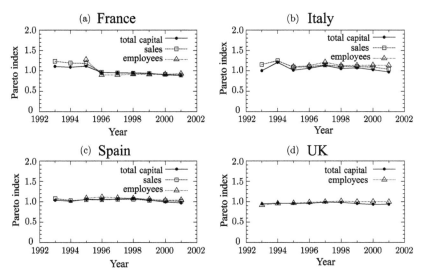

Figure 2.12. Evolution of the Pareto index, 1993–2001: (a) France (b) Italy (c) Spain (d) UK, for total capital, sales and number of employees.

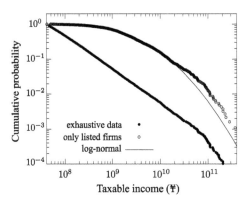

Figure 2.13. CDF for declared company income for all the data (solid circles) and for all listed companies (open circles).

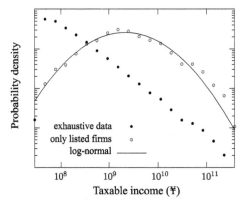

Figure 2.14. PDF for declared company income for all the data (solid circles) and for all listed companies (open circles).

Here we have used data on business tax provided by the National Tax Agency, which made it possible to examine the whole population. But for most financial data such comprehensive coverage is rare. In other less well documented cases we need carefully planned sample investigations of companies, or databases provided by private organisations that specialise in providing information of this kind. Careful preparation of data may lead to reliable statistical conclusions on the population of companies, although sampling of a small number of companies may limit the statistical accuracy.

2.4 Pareto's law

We have seen above that a considerable number of financial quantities for both individuals and companies follow Pareto's law, which, in our view, is essential to an understanding of the economic behaviour of these entities. (See also Steindl, 1965; Ijiri and Simon, 1977; Takayasu *et al.*, 1997 and Axtell, 2001 among a large body of literature.) Pareto's law also manifests itself in many other economic and social phenomena; indeed, it is ubiquitous. As we have stressed in Chapter 1, if one took for granted elementary statistical concepts such as the normal distribution and applied their implications to all these phenomena, serious errors would often arise. This is true for other issues involving fluctuations.[9]

In this section, we will elaborate on several important properties of Pareto's law which are necessary for understanding its further implications.

As we explained in subsection 2.1.3, the term 'Pareto distribution' refers to a group of distributions exhibiting power-law behaviour in the asymptotic region. Therefore, in examining the properties of the Pareto distribution, it is important to distinguish which property is determined by asymptotic behaviour and which property depends on behaviour in the small-to-medium range of the variable. In other words, we need to take care that we select only those properties which are proper to all of the Pareto distributions, not just a few of them.

We note that in referring to the scale of the variable (x), it is relative to a proportional constant in the Pareto distribution: The form of its CDF was given in equation (2.3). Here, we rewrite it as follows by putting its proportional constant in explicit form:

$$P_>(x) \sim \left(\frac{x}{x_0}\right)^{-\mu}. \tag{2.4}$$

This implies that the asymptotic region is the region where x is much larger than x_0 ($x \gg x_0$), since that is the region where $P_>(x)$ is much smaller than 1.

Several Pareto distributions are given in the box below.[10] The PDFs are given in Figure 2.15, while the CDFs are shown in Figure 2.16. All these exhibit $\mu = 1.5$, and show different behaviours for a finite x/x_0, but they approach to the same power function as x/x_0 increases.

---

[9] For example, wind power. It is a problem of fluctuation, and since the normal distribution is not obeyed, naive discussion of averaging is groundless.

[10] Kleiber and Kotz (2003) give several explicit formulae for Pareto distributions, in addition to some of other kinds.

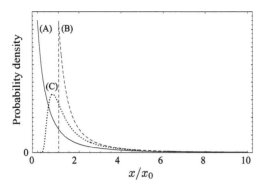

Figure 2.15. PDFs of various Pareto distributions.

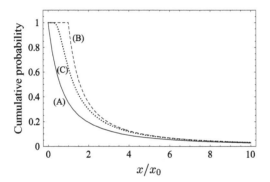

Figure 2.16. CDFs of various Pareto distributions.

When confronted with a distribution, a schoolchild would probably want to know the average, the mean; there is no harm in us doing the same. In fact the mean is finite only for μ larger than 1 and its actual value depends on how the distribution behaves for a finite x. When μ is equal to or smaller than 1, the average is infinite. Therefore, the way in which the average diverges when it approaches 1 from above is common to all the Pareto distributions. It is well known that the average is inversely proportional to $\mu - 1$:

$$\langle x \rangle \simeq \frac{x_0}{\mu - 1}.$$

As it happens, there are a variety of properties to be examined, and in what follows we first examine some well-known and less-known indices in economics, and then generate some of the distributions with simulations and visualise them as a Devil's Staircase. We can then move on to the most important theme, phase transitions, which is in fact our main theme.

For the sake of description, we refer to the stochastic variable x that obeys Pareto's law as 'company size'. Readers may replace it by any other variable.

$\boxed{\alpha\beta\gamma}$ Various Pareto distributions

Some of the Pareto distributions with a simple functional form will be useful for the simulations used later in the book, and we list them here.

As we noted in the main text, the Pareto distribution is defined as a power function in the asymptotic region of its variable x. The CDF $P_>(x)$ has to satisfy $P_>(0) = 1$, so that total probability is 1. But the power-law distribution does not satisfy this property when extended to the finite region of x irrespective of the value of μ. In other words, it cannot be normalised. In order to avoid this problem, we need to modify the behaviour of the CDF for small values of x to obtain a usable probability distribution. (Of course, the CDF is a decreasing function of x by definition, and we must not violate this restriction in such a modification.) Thus, we can obtain an infinite variety of Pareto distributions.

An inverse function of the CDF is needed to conduct a simulation (a point explained in subsection 2.4.2 below). Here are three Pareto distributions whose inverse functions of the CDF are especially simple.

Firstly, we shift the variable x by x_0 in the equation (2.4) to obtain the following:

$$P_>(x) = \left(1 + \frac{x}{x_0}\right)^{-\mu}. \tag{2.5A}$$

This simple function satisfies all the necessary conditions. We refer to this as Pareto distribution (A) and use it for simulations in this book.

Alternatively, if we suppress the divergence of the power function at $x = 0$ we arrive straightforwardly at the following distribution:

$$P_>(x) = \begin{cases} 1 & \text{for } x \le x_0, \\ \left(\dfrac{x}{x_0}\right)^{-\mu} & \text{for } x \ge x_0. \end{cases} \tag{2.5B}$$

This is as simple as the distribution (A), although its PDF is sharply peaked and may not be suitable for some purposes. We call this distribution (B).

It is also possible to invert the variable in the Weibull distribution to obtain the following:

$$P_>(x) = 1 - e^{-(x/x_0)^{-\mu}} \tag{2.5C}$$

This is sometimes called a 'stretched exponential distribution', and we call it (C).

2.4.1   Gini and Robin Hood

At this point it seems appropriate to discuss the *Gini coefficient* and the Robin Hood index, both of which are measures of inequality. The first of these is well known, and while the second is a little more obscure it is based on a unique and intriguing idea.

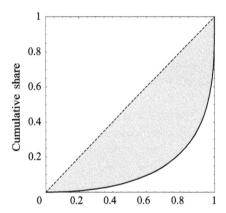

Figure 2.17. An example of a Lorenz curve.

Corrado Gini was an Italian statistician,[11] who in 1912 invented a measure of income inequality, now named after him. The *Robin Hood index* is another measure invented for the same purpose by Edgar Malone Hoover Jr (Hoover, 1936). It is sometimes called the *Hoover index*, and crops up in contemporary literature from time to time, for example in a recent article by Robert Sapolsky (Sapolsky, 2005). It is interesting to look at these indices in relation to Pareto distributions and the Pareto index.

A Lorenz curve is defined by the following. Let us say that we have N companies, and we arrange them in increasing order of size, from small to large, and calculate the proportion of the smallest k companies, which we denote by S_k. Since the total share of all the companies is 1, we have $S_N = 1$. Corresponding to the k-th (smallest) company, we can place a dot on the co-ordinate $(k/N, S_k)$. By definition, such dots stay within a square where both sides are equal to 1. By connecting all these dots, we obtain a graph that goes up from the lower-left corner to the upper-right corner. In actual cases, N is very large and the graph appears smooth. For this reason, it is called a **Lorenz curve**. An example is given in Figure 2.17, where the solid line is the Lorenz curve for the Pareto distribution (B) with $\mu = 1.5$ in the preceding box. If all the companies are of the same size, the Lorenz curve is a diagonal line (the dotted line in the figure), and in general the curve is below that diagonal line.

The Gini coefficient is defined by the area between the Lorenz curve and the diagonal (the shaded region in Figure 2.17), divided by the area of the triangle made by the diagonal line and the sides, which is $\frac{1}{2}$. Therefore, the Gini coefficient is 0 if all the companies are of the same size, and is always between 0 and 1. The larger the Gini coefficient is, the larger the inequality.

Now, the Gini coefficient as defined above depends on the value of μ, as in Figure 2.18 for this distribution. As is seen here, the Gini coefficient increases as μ decreases, which is in agreement with the general property of μ, where smaller values of μ mean the appearance of larger companies and thus higher inequalities.

---

[11] His detailed biography is given in Kleiber and Kotz (2003).

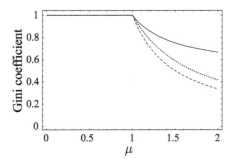

Figure 2.18. The μ-dependence of the Gini coefficient.

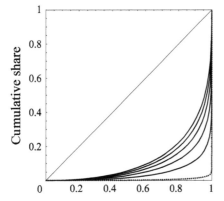

Figure 2.19. Lorenz curves for various values of μ.

Once μ is smaller than 1, the Gini coefficient is *exactly* 1. The Lorenz curve behaves as in Figure 2.19 as μ decreases, where the solid curves are for the values $\mu = 1.5, 1.4, 1.3, 1.2, 1.1$ downwards, ending with the dotted curve for $\mu = 1.01$ at the bottom. It is evident that as μ approaches 1 from above, the Lorenz curve shrinks down to the sides, resulting in the Gini coefficient converging to 1.

The Robin Hood index may be better explained for personal wealth. Let us suppose that we want to create a society where everyone has an equal share of wealth. In order to achieve this goal, we need to move wealth from the rich to the poor in the style of Robin Hood. Firstly we define the boundary between the rich and poor classes. A suitable choice is the person who has the ideal, equal, amount of wealth, a value we can calculate by dividing the total wealth by the number of people. This person is at the place where the Lorenz curve has a gradient equal to 1, as the gradient is the share of wealth of the person at that point (the black dot in Figure 2.20). This may be more easily understood if one recalls that the Lorenz curve has a constant gradient of 1 when complete inequality is achieved. Those above this person in the rank order are rich, and those below are poor.

The proportion of the population which is poor is R, as defined in the figure, while the proportion which is rich is $1 - R$. Therefore, for equality, the poor must have a share of wealth equal to R and the rich $1 - R$. However, the poor's share of wealth is S, while

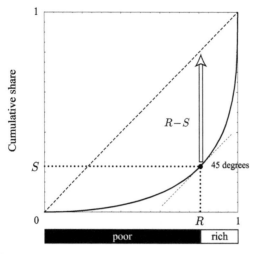

Figure 2.20. Definition of the Robin Hood index.

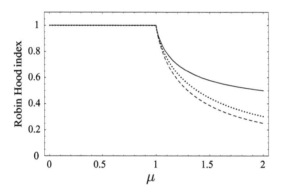

Figure 2.21. μ-dependence of the Robin Hood index.

that of the rich is $1 - S$. Therefore, our task is to move the share equal to $R - S$ from the rich to the poor. This is equal to the largest vertical distance between the Lorenz curve and the diagonal line, and is shown by the arrow in the figure. With this definition, this quantity, known as the Robin Hood index, is larger for larger inequalities, with a maximum value equal to 1.

The μ-dependence of the Robin Hood index for the Pareto distributions (A)–(C) is plotted in Figure 2.21. The Robin Hood index is equal to 1 for $\mu \leq 1$, as is evident from the plot of the Lorenz curve (Figure 2.19).

The behaviour of the Lorenz curve, the Gini coefficient and the Robin Hood index implies that for μ equal to or less than 1 the completely unequal society is realised. Thus the value $\mu = 1$ is a very special point. This is the most important property of Pareto distributions, which we will investigate further.

One note before we proceed: our plots of the Lorenz curve, the Gini coefficient and the Robin Hood index were appropriate for cases where the number of companies was infinite; if the number of companies is infinite, complete inequality is achieved only

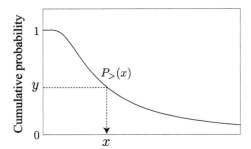

Figure 2.22. The inverse-function method to generate random numbers that obey an arbitrary distribution.

when one company holds 100% of the share. Therefore, the Gini coefficient and the Robin Hood index are close to, but not exactly equal to 1 for $\mu \leq 1$ when the number of companies is finite. Analytical simulation methods can be used to estimate the values of the Gini coefficient and the Robin Hood index for a finite number of companies and values smaller than 1 can be obtained.

2.4.2 Simulation: the inverse-function method

One useful approach to the properties of the Pareto distribution is to simulate them. For example, we can generate random numbers that obey a Pareto distribution and then calculate various quantities of interest. Large numbers of such simulations yield reliable results, a method called **Monte Carlo simulation**, which is perhaps a misnomer since the casinos of that pleasure city seem unlikely to be relying on pure chance.

It is fairly easy to generate a set of numbers that obey a Pareto distribution; it can be done even with standard spreadsheet applications. Of course, such a calculation is meaningful only when repeated a sufficient number of times, which may require abundant resources such as a fast PC or workstation, fast and efficient applications, time, and so on. But as the basic idea for generating Pareto distributions is so simple and is applicable to other distributions, it is worthwhile explaining it here. Readers may note that a Monte Carlo calculation with the familiar normal distribution can be conducted with a combination of the method we describe here and the use of a two-dimensional space, which is called the Box–Muller method.

The first step is to generate (pseudo-)random numbers uniformly distributed between 0 and 1, which we denote by y. The necessary function is available in most applications. We then solve the equation $y = P_>(x)$ to obtain x. Since $P_>(x)$ is equal to 1 at $x = 0$, decreases as x increases, and approaches 0 as $x \to \infty$, the solution x always exists and is unique. By repeating this many times, we obtain a set of solutions for x which obeys the CDF $P_>(x)$. This inverse-function method is illustrated in Figure 2.22. The validity of this method is obvious, given the relation between the rank-size plot and the CDF explained above.

We have listed several examples ((A)–(C)) of the Pareto distribution as equation (2.5). In the following discussion, we use the distribution (B) to examine the essential properties of the Pareto distribution, since it allows a rapid calculation.

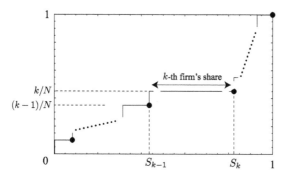

Figure 2.23. How to make a staircase plot. Each dot corresponds to a company.

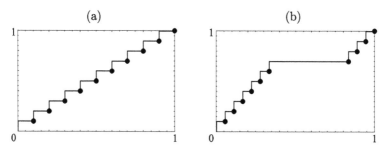

Figure 2.24. Examples of the staircase plot.

2.4.3   *Devil's Staircase*

One intuitively intelligible method to study the properties of a Pareto distribution is a visualisation called a *staircase plot*.

If we order the companies randomly and plot the total share of the first k companies, as S_k, then place a dot for the k-th company at the co-ordinate $(S_k, k/N)$, and finally connect them with lines, a staircase plot emerges, as illustrated in Figure 2.23. Note that although this is similar to the case of the Lorenz curve, here we have a random order and the vertical and horizontal axes are exchanged. In this kind of staircase plot, the flat step of the stair indicates the share of a company, with a wider step indicating a larger share.

Some simple examples will illustrate the method. For example, if there are ten companies and they all have equal shares of 10 per cent, the staircase plot is as shown in Figure 2.24(a). If one company has a 50 per cent share and the other nine companies share the remainder equally, the staircase plot is as shown in Figure 2.24(b). Of course, a random ordering of the companies creates a staircase plot with the wide step located at a different place. In any case, this kind of staircase plot offers a convenient and accessible visualisation of the distribution of the shares.

If the shares are distributed according to a PDF, the staircase has irregular steps throughout its extent. Although the height of the steps is equal to $1/N$ and is constant, the width varies. For a large value of N, the staircase becomes very ragged and would

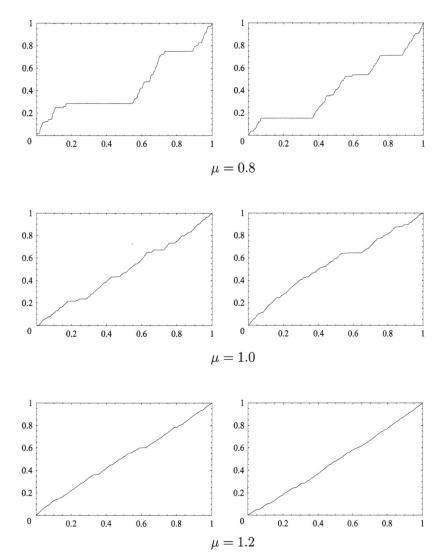

Figure 2.25. Devil's Staircases for $\mu = 0.8, 1.0, 1.2$.

be extremely difficult to climb, which is why it has become known as the *Devil's Staircase*.[12] Mathematically, it is defined as the mapping of a finite interval between real numbers onto another that is almost universally constant.

Figure 2.25 shows Devil's Staircases for several different values of the Pareto index μ. The data were generated by the method explained in the previous subsection and

---

[12] An Internet search for 'Devil's Staircase' yields several mountain trails, among which is a trail up Mount Ngauruhoe in New Zealand, which was the location for the filming of Mount Doom in Peter Jackson's *Lord of the Rings* trilogy, which seems appropriate.

contain $N = 10^5$ companies, but in this figure, we have omitted the dots and just drawn the stairs. We observe that for $\mu = 0.8$ (the uppermost two plots) the stair is quite irregular and ragged, and thus is truly devilish. Generating a large number of staircases for a number of different values of μ, we have found that this raggedness is a common property for $\mu < 1$ and that the smaller the value of μ, the more ragged the staircase is. On the other hand, for $\mu = 1.2$ we observe that the staircase is almost uniform and is like a smooth slope. This is a common property for $\mu > 1$ and the larger the value of μ, the smoother the 'slope'.

Of course it is still a staircase, though the individual steps are not particularly clear since in this case the value of N is large. Closer examination of a selected portion would reveal its detailed features, but we will postpone discussion of this to subsection 2.4.6 which covers fractal dimensions.

At the boundary $\mu = 1$ an intermediate behaviour is observable, part ragged, part smooth. This extent of this variation depends on the (generated) data.

We have learned from these plots that companies with a large share appear for $\mu < 1$. In fact, despite there being a hundred thousand companies the top two or three companies have nearly half of the total. So, these companies are not just large, but huge. While not a monopoly this is obviously an overwhelming oligopoly.

On the other hand, the situation for $\mu > 1$ is quite different. Of course, the size of the companies is not uniform and is distributed more evenly, but the staircase is so smooth that it is almost indistinguishable from the case with equal shares. At least, there is no oligopoly.

This argument is based on casual, or intuitive, observation of the plots, but it can be confirmed by rigorous analysis, which we will consider next.

2.4.4   Oligopoly and monopoly

In the previous subsection, we observed that for $\mu < 1$ a Devil's Staircase with exceptionally large companies appears and an oligopolistic situation arises. Here we will look at the share of top companies in order to obtain a quantitative perspective and increase the accuracy of our discussion.

Let us first look at the maximum size. By this we mean the following situation: Suppose we have N companies in total, with sizes $x_1, x_2, \ldots, x_N$. We can measure and anticipate the maximum of these sizes. In Pareto distributions with a large N and a μ larger than 1, the average maximum size is proportional to $N^{1/\mu}$. This is common to all the Pareto distributions. As stated above, the average size does not have this property. This is a difference arising from the fact that the maximum size is determined by the behaviour of the distribution at large values of x, when N is also large. And this is stronger as N increases. Therefore, the dominant term in the expression of the average of the maximum size for large values of N is determined by the asymptotic behaviour of the distribution, which is common to all the Pareto distributions. We give an explicit formula of the proportional constant in the following box, but here we only note that it diverges as μ approaches 1 from above, in agreement with the fact that the average size diverges at the same time.

 The largest company in a Pareto distribution

When there are N companies, the size of the largest company, when μ is larger than 1 is given by:

$$\langle X^{(\mathrm{max})} \rangle = \Gamma \left(1 - \frac{1}{\mu} \right) N^{1/\mu}.$$

This is common to all the Pareto distributions. Here $\Gamma(z)$ is the gamma function obtained by a suitable analytic continuation of the expression:

$$\Gamma(z) \equiv \int_0^\infty t^{z-1} e^{-t} dt.$$

At $\mu = 1$ and when N is large, its share is

$$\frac{\ln(\ln N) - \gamma_E}{\log N},$$

where $\gamma_E = 2.7799\ldots$ is Euler's constant. The numerator of this expression varies very slowly with N and thus we have elsewhere described it as '*almost* anti-proportional to the logarithm of N'.

For a value of μ less than 1, when N is infinite, the share of the finite-rank company is known analytically. Since it is a complex expression including an incomplete gamma function, we will not go into the details here, but we note that it is somewhat surprising that while a Pareto distribution is defined by such simple power-law behaviour it also yields complex expressions for these quantities through a long series of analytic calculations. This is the joy of mathematics.

Next, we will look at the share of the top companies, which is crucial in determining the overall appearance of the Devil's Staircase.

Figure 2.26 indicates the results of the Monte Carlo calculation and the analytic calculation for the average of the share of the top company. The thick, solid curve denoted with $N = \infty$ is the analytic result for an *infinite* number of companies ($N = \infty$), while the lines above it show the results of the Monte Carlo calculation for 10, 100, ..., and 10 million ($N = 10^7$) companies from top to bottom. As N increases, the results of the simulation converge on the analytic results for $N = \infty$, as they should. (In this simulation, 100,000 data points were generated by the Monte Carlo method for most values of N, except that for $N = 10^7$ 1,000 data points were generated. This was sufficient to guarantee the statistical accuracy of the result.)

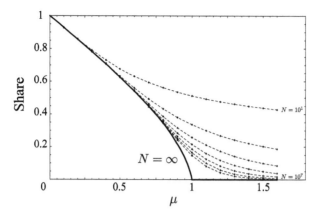

Figure 2.26. Share of the largest company.

As can be clearly seen, the average share of the top company is 0 for μ greater than 1 for $N = \infty$. One might think this is a trivial result: Since there is an infinite number of companies, the share of any company must be zero, but this is a misleading argument.

If one is dealing with distributions that do not have long tails, such as the normal distribution, the above argument is sufficient, but it is not the case for Pareto distributions, which have long tails.

We need to look carefully at what is really happening for Pareto distributions. As we have noted already, the average size is finite for $\mu > 1$. Therefore, the average of the sum of the sizes of all N companies is proportional to N. On the other hand, the average of the maximum size is proportional to $N^{1/\mu}$. The simple ratio of these yields is

$$\frac{N^{1/\mu}}{N} = N^{(1/\mu)-1},$$

which offers an estimate of the average share of the top company. So we find that the exponent of N is $(1/\mu) - 1$, which is negative for $\mu > 1$. Therefore, this ratio goes to zero as N goes to infinity. The behaviour of the average share of the top company in Figure 2.26 for $\mu > 1$ agrees with this estimate.

When μ is smaller than 1 a completely different situation arises. In this case, both the average share and the average of the maximum size diverge when N goes to infinity. Therefore, the simple estimate we made above is not valid,[13] so we need a different calculation for this case. Since it is long, tedious and quite complicated, we will not give the derivation, but simply give the resulting plot in Figure 2.26 with a thick solid curve.

We have seen in the Devil's Staircases that even though there is a large number of companies the top few had major shares. Correspondingly, we see that even when the number of companies is *infinite*, the top company has a finite share. As we noted when

---

[13] This is also understandable, as the above estimate yields infinity for values of μ less than 1, and N also goes to infinity, which is simply wrong because the share must be less than 1 by definition.

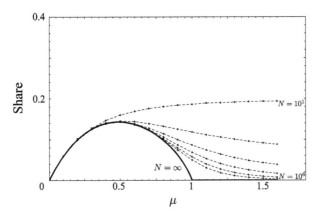

Figure 2.27. The average share of the second-largest company.

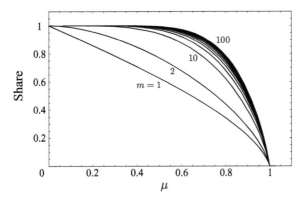

Figure 2.28. Total shares of the top companies.

dealing with $\mu > 1$, this also shows how dangerous it is to apply our naive 'intuition', which has been raised on normal distributions.

To repeat: as soon as μ becomes less than 1, the average share of the top company is finite. In spite of the fact that there is an infinite number of companies, the top company has a finite share. As μ approaches 0, that share approaches 1, in other words, a complete monopoly.

This is, of course, caused by the long tail of the Pareto distributions. The smaller μ is, the longer the tail, and on that long tail we find exceptionally large companies. As soon as μ becomes smaller than 1, the quantitative nature of the size of those extremely large companies changes drastically.

The average share of the second-largest company behaves as in Figure 2.27, where results similar to the top company are observed. The average share is finite for μ less than 1 in spite of the fact that there is an infinite number of companies.

We have also obtained the shares of the top 100 companies for $N = \infty$ and plotted their sum in Figure 2.28. The lowest curve, labelled '$m = 1$', is the share of the top company, the curve above it, labelled '2', is the sum of the shares of the top and

Table 2.1. *Average shares (%) of the top 10, 50 and 100 companies for values of μ close to 1.*

μ	Top 10	Top 50	Top 100
0.90	40.0	49.8	53.5
0.95	24.2	30.5	33.0
0.98	11.8	14.7	15.9

the second companies, and so forth, ending with the sum of the share of the top 100 companies, labelled '100'.

Some of the representative values of the shares of the top companies are listed in Table 2.1, where it is evident that even when μ is less than 1 by a small amount, the oligopoly is severe.

The sum of the shares of the top to the ∞-th company add up to 1 for $\mu < 1$. One might think this is a trivial fact, but it is not that simple, since in calculating the shares we took the total number of companies, N, to be infinite. If we defined N as a finite number and added the shares from the top to the N-th company, it should add up to 1. If we defined N as infinite, distributions without long tails, like the familiar normal distribution, would yield 0 since the share of any company of a finite rank is 0 and 0s add up to 0. This happens for Pareto distributions with values of μ greater than 1. Therefore, it is somewhat surprising, or one might say spectacular, that they add up to 1 for values of μ less than 1.

We can also look at the distribution of the shares, not just their averages. Figure 2.29 illustrates the PDF of the share of the top company for $\mu = 0.2, 0.4, \ldots, 1.4$ and $N = 10, 10^2, \ldots, 10^7$. In all the plots, the leftmost curve is for $N = 10^7$, and N becomes smaller as the peak of the curve moves to the right. Also, for any value of μ, the average share becomes smaller as N becomes larger. So, it should be easy to use this fact to determine which curve is for which N. From these plots, we see that if μ is larger than 1, the distribution is concentrated around the value of the share equal to 0, and as N becomes larger the concentration becomes more intense. This is in agreement with the fact that the average is 0 for an infinite N. On the other hand, if μ is less than 1, the distribution is spread over the whole region from 0 to 1. This shows that in addition to the fact that the average is of order 1, the share of the top company for each dataset could be quite different from the average. That is, the fluctuation of the share of the top company is of order 1.

2.4.5 *Pareto's 80–20 rule*
It is important to distinguish the so-called 'Pareto principle', or 'Pareto's 80–20 rule', from 'Pareto's law'. Some posited instances of the 80–20 rule are:

- 80% of sales are to 20% of consumers
- 20% of time used for a study results in 80% of the conclusions

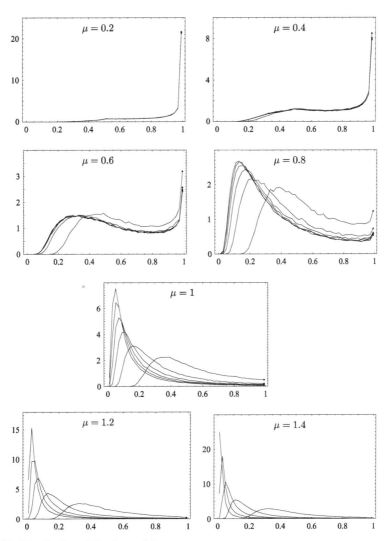

Figure 2.29. Distribution of the share of the top company.

- 80% of crime is committed by 20% of the population
- 80% of happiness in life is derived from 20% of time
- 80% of marriages involve the 20% of the population with divorce histories

Some of these are obviously dubious. Sometimes, they are referred to as being founded on a solid and proven universal scientific law, and the power law is given as justification. This is a rather dangerous trend, bordering on 'pseudo-science'. By looking at this rule using the properties of the Pareto distribution we may be able to shed a more scientific light on it.

For $\mu < 1$, it is easy to see what really happens: even if N is infinite, the top companies have finite shares. Therefore, if we take the top 20% of companies, there is

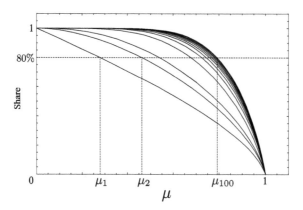

Figure 2.30. The value of μ below which the top n companies achieve a total share greater than 80%.

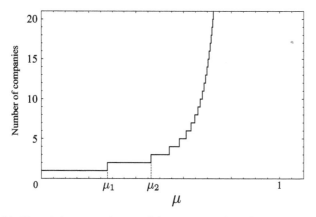

Figure 2.31. The minimum number, n, of the top companies whose total share is greater than 80%.

an infinite number of them and their total share is 100%. The 'Pareto principle' appears to be wrong.

By drawing a line for the share equal to 80% in Figure 2.28, we obtain the rank of those achieving that share plotted in Figure 2.30. We readily see that for $\mu < \mu_1 \simeq 0.28$ the top company has a share greater than 80%, while for $\mu_1 < \mu < \mu_2 \simeq 0.46$ the top and the second company have a total share more than 80%, and so on. Further, for $\mu < \mu_{100} \simeq 0.79$, the top 100 companies have a total share greater than 80%. We have plotted the rank that achieves the 80% share in Figure 2.31, from which one can read the value of μ under which the top twenty companies achieve a 20% share.

On the other hand, if μ is greater than 1, the share of the top 20% of companies is less than 1. But one should be careful in dealing with actual numbers, since this share is not common to all the Pareto distributions, but rather depends on its behaviour in the non-asymptotic region, where its stochastic variable (x) is not large. This returns us to a point of caution raised earlier, namely that the 'Pareto distribution' refers only to its behaviour. To put this another way, it is the name of a class of distributions that

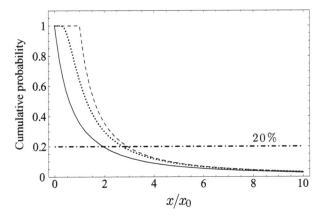

Figure 2.32. Various Pareto distributions and the 20% line.

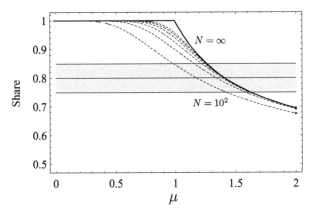

Figure 2.33. Dependence of the share of the top 20% of companies on μ.

approach the power function as the variable x goes to infinity. Each has a different behaviour for small-to-medium values of x. What we have studied above, such as the behaviour of the largest company, depends only on the power aspect for large values of N, and is common to all the Pareto distributions with the same value of μ. But we are now thinking of the top 20% of companies, and their properties are uncommon, no matter how large the total number of companies, N. This can be most easily understood by looking at Figure 2.32. The top 20% of companies are below the horizontal line labelled '20%'. The distribution of their size, x, is given by the curve of distribution, which differs from one distribution to another. Therefore, it is not sufficient to speak casually about using *a* Pareto distribution; we have to specify *which* Pareto distribution we are using.

With this caution in mind, we can use our Monte Carlo method to investigate the Pareto distribution (A) given as equation (2.5A). The result is illustrated in Figure 2.33, where the dots connected by broken lines are the results of Monte Carlo calculation

Table 2.2. *The value of μ at which the top 20% of companies have combined shares of 75%, 80% and 85%.*

N	75%	80%	85%
10^2	1.42	1.18	0.98
10^3	1.58	1.34	1.16
10^4	1.61	1.39	1.22
10^5	1.62	1.40	1.24
10^6	1.62	1.41	1.25
10^7	1.63	1.41	1.26

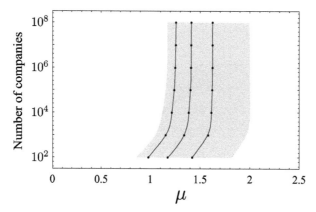

Figure 2.34. The range of μ where the 80–20 rule holds.

with $N = 10^2, 10^3 \dots, 10^8$ from bottom to top respectively, and the thick curve is for $N = \infty$. As we stated above, for values of μ less than 1 a finite number of top companies have a 100% share and therefore the thick curve is exactly 1 for $\mu \leq 1$. The grey area is where the share is between 75% and 85%, so, one might say that when the desired broken line or the thick curve is within this grey area, the top 20% of companies have about 80% of the share. Also, Table 2.2 lists the values of μ where the top 20% of companies have the shares 75%, 80% and 85%. From this we see, for example, that when there are 10,000 companies the top 20% of companies have about an 80% share for μ between 1.2 and 1.6. In Figure 2.34, we have plotted the value of μ where the top 20% of companies have the shares 75%, 80% and 85% with three curves. Further in this plot, we give the range where we did not restrict the proportion of companies to exactly 20% but extended it to the range between 15% and 25%, as denoted by the grey area. From this, as soon as there are a certain number of companies, say 1,000, for values of μ a little greater than 1 and less than 2, the 80–20 rule holds approximately. Of course, this is the result for the Pareto distribution (A), but it is easy to see that a similar result will hold approximately for other Pareto distributions.

As we have seen here, the 80–20 rule is not unconditionally guaranteed by the power law, but it is approximately valid in some regions of μ (and N). Since in practice quite a range of Pareto distributions have a value of μ somewhere between 1 and 3, the 80–20 rule is valid to some extent, and this accounts for its popularity.

Even so, we should be aware that the 80–20 rule is not justified in any precise sense. What is important in practice is to see which kind of distributions the quantity in question obeys, and in what range, and to carry out a correct statistical analysis, including an estimate of the possible range of errors. One may end up with a Pareto distribution, but, equally, the result might well be quite a different kind of distribution. Robust business or governmental strategies can come only from this kind of examination. In other words, 'Pareto's 80–20 rule' belongs only in casual conversation, and could cause real problems if it is allowed to escape into an analysis from which serious consequences may arise.

2.4.6 *The fractal dimension*

The 'fractal' is a mathematical concept discovered by a French-American mathematician, Benoit Mandelbrot. Since his famous book *Fractals: Form, Chance, and Dimension* was published in 1977 the number of scientific papers developing the concept has continued to grow, and now covers a wide range of disciplines. Indeed, fractals are found everywhere in science and technology. There are even industrial applications such as fibres with a strongly water-repellent fractal surface, and fractal antennae that are smaller and more powerful than conventional ones.

It is probably less well known that the concept of the fractal can also be used in the study of complicated behaviours in a market, for example movements in cotton prices, exchange rates and stock values. None of these values obey ordinary, smooth functions; rather they jump about all over the place. They are ragged,[14] and such raggedness is apparent even if we focus on the detail, a property referred to as *self-similarity*. In fact, since real market data has a minimum time-interval the similarity fades as we close in on that minimum interval. Similar structures are commonly seen in nature, a famous and well-studied example being coastlines.

Fractal objects are thus characterised by raggedness and self-similarity, which is measured by their fractal dimension. Think of it like this. The ordinary smooth lines we draw on paper by hand have a dimension of 1. If we draw a circle and fill it in with black ink, we obtain a two-dimensional object. A simple dot has a zero dimension. Turning to the ragged profiles of exchange rates, stock prices and coastlines we might assume that they are one-dimensional since they form lines. But this is not necessarily true. In fact, the length is uniquely determined for ordinary lines, and we can measure it by using a divider. We split the line into segments of the unit length of the divider, and by multiplying the number of segments with the unit length we obtain an approximate value for the total length. By reducing the unit length of the divider, we can get a more

---

[14] In other words, they are 'not universally differentiable'.

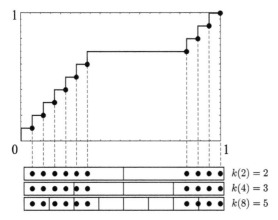

Figure 2.35. How to obtain the fractal dimension of the size distribution of companies.

accurate value. If it approaches a unique value as we reduce the unit length, we define that value as the length of the line.

However, a ragged line may not have that limiting value. Often the measured length becomes longer as the unit length becomes smaller. In such a case, it cannot be regarded as an ordinary one-dimensional line. On the other hand, since the ragged line does not define an area, it is not a two-dimensional object either. The dimension of such a line is somewhere between 1 and 2 and is not an integer; it has a *fractal dimension*. This is basically the condition of calling an object 'fractal'.

In a previous subsection, we visualised the shares of companies $\{S_k\}$ using the Devil's Staircase. This is one example of a fractal.

We will now measure the fractal dimension D, whose definition is illustrated in Figure 2.35. We divide the region $(0,1)$ of the abscissa into small segments of equal size, some of which contain dots and some of which are empty. We denote the number of non-empty segments by $k(n)$ when there are n segments, If the dots cover the region $(0,1)$ then $k(n)$ should be equal to n. For example, consider the set of all real numbers in the region $(0,1)$, which is just a line segment of length 1 and is one-dimensional. (Alternatively, we could select the set of all rational numbers or the set of all non-rational numbers.) In this case, since there are real numbers in any segment of non-zero length, $k(n) = n$. On the other hand, if the set is made with only a point in $(0,1)$, its dimension is 0 and $k(n)$ is always equal to 1 independently of n. From this, we assume the following relationship between $k(n)$ and n:

$$k(n) \propto n^D.$$

The exponent D is the fractal dimension. If D is between 0 and 1, that set is fractal. If D is close to 1, it is a line-like object, whilst if D is close to 0 it resembles sparsely distributed points.[15]

---

[15] We note that there are a variety of 'fractal dimensions'. What we have explained here is the 'box dimension', sometimes called the 'entropy dimension' or 'capacity dimension'. We have used this here because it is easy to measure (Alligood *et al.*, 1997; Falconer, 2003).

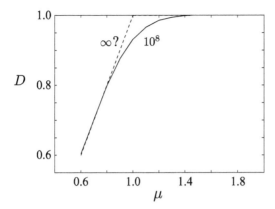

Figure 2.36. Fractal dimension of the Devil's Staircase.

Figure 2.36 charts the results of the Monte Carlo calculation of the fractal dimension D for various values of the Pareto index μ. Since the fractal dimension is obtained more accurately for large numbers, we used data for some 10^8 companies. One possible conclusion from this result is that the accurate value depends on μ as indicated by the broken line denoted by '∞?'. This line is divided at $\mu = 1$: for $\mu > 1$, we find that $D = 1$, and that the distribution is dense, while for $\mu < 1$ we find that D is smaller than 1, and that fractality manifests itself in a Devil's Staircase.

 Golden ratio, silver ratio and self-similarity

Both the golden and silver ratios have long been associated with powerful aesthetic effects.

The golden ratio, sometimes called the golden mean, has been observed in numerous places: for example, in structures such as the Parthenon, and in paintings such as the *Mona Lisa*. The silver ratio is said to be hidden in the pagoda of the famous Horyuji temple in Nara, Japan, and in images of the faces of Buddha.

The actual value of the golden ratio is $1 : \frac{1+\sqrt{5}}{2} \cong 1 : 1.618$, and of the silver ratio, $1 : \sqrt{2} \cong 1 : 1.414$. Both of these have a close connection with the self-similarity which is essential to the fractality.

We show below various rectangles whose sides have these ratios. The slim rectangle on the left has a ratio equal to the golden ratio, while the larger one on the right has that of the silver ratio.

If we delete the leftmost square from the left rectangle, as shown in the illustration, the sides of the remaining rectangle still have the same ratio, the golden ratio. A similar operation on this smaller rectangle yields another rectangle with the golden ratio. This can go on and on infinitely, always resulting in a rectangle with the golden ratio – a variety of self-similarity. Inversely, if we impose this kind of self-similarity on a rectangle, it automatically has the golden ratio.

On the other hand, if we fold a rectangle with the silver ratio in half we again obtain a rectangle of silver ratio. Folding in half again, we obtain a silver ratio again and this can go on infinitely – yet another variety of self-similarity. Incidentally, this property is used for the international standard (ISO 216) for paper size: A0 paper is a rectangle of area equal to 1 m^2 whose sides have the silver ratio. Halving it we obtain the A1 size, halving A1 is A2, and so on.

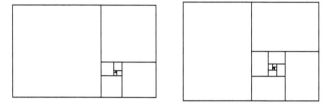

Is the infinite self-similar layer the source of beauty? Many artists and philosophers have supposed it must be, and there is a large literature on the subject. We do not know the answer, but we are very wary of explanations that try to unite very diverse phenomena on slender grounds. Is there really any reason for thinking that there will be one fundamental causal factor behind aesthetic phenomena as apparently diverse as colour combinations, facial characteristics, landscape, sculpture, music and literature? Perhaps not. However, it may well be that self-similarity is peculiarly attractive and rewarding for the human mind, and accounts for *some part* of some of those experiences which we categorise together, in spite of their diversity, as aesthetic.

2.5   Side story: 'long-tail phenomena'

Chris Anderson, the editor-in-chief of *Wired* magazine,[16] learned of an empirical law of sales by using statistics from a digital jukebox company. This empirical law is quite different from that familiar in relation to mega-hits (Anderson, 2006). A CEO of the company asked 'What percentage of the top 10,000 titles in any *online* media store (Netflix, iTunes, Amazon or any other) will rent or sell at least once a month?' Knowing Pareto's 80–20 principle, described in section 2.4.5, Anderson estimated that 80 per cent of the sales come from 20 per cent of the products, and so guessed at about 50 per cent. His mental image was 10,000 books at a large bookstore and 10,000 CD albums at Wal-Mart, half of which are left unsold. However, the answer from this CEO was that '99 per cent' of those top titles sold at least once a month!

In a world where the cost including packaging and storage is negligible and instant search and download is possible, consumers behave in a certain pattern: demand is

---

[16] It is interesting to the present authors that he too comes from a background in physics, has a degree from George Washington University and did research at Los Alamos Laboratory before starting his career in publishing.

unlimited in its variety. Consequently, Anderson became interested in what endless demand and unlimited supply could bring to business and found similar phenomena in iTunes music and Amazon books.

In particular, he made a rank-size plot of one month's downloads of about 1 million titles from an online music company and found a long tail of albums that did not sell much, but whose aggregate contribution to sales is comparable to mega-hits. He described his finding in his book entitled *The Long Tail*, which made a great impact on Net business.

There is a difference in perception here. The long tail we have so far discussed was concerned with a few giants, mega-hits, while Anderson's 'long-tail' is about dwarves and their sum total.

An average American cinema needs to have at least 1,500 customers during a two-week period in order to stay in business, but online distributors, which do not need a millimetre of shelf-space, are apparently quite different.[17]

This 'long-tail' phenomenon can be understood by using the CDF, with its variable x being the sales of goods or downloads as the property not of the tail that extends to the *right* of the plot,

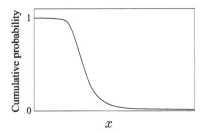

but of the region of small values of x to the extreme *left*. The behaviour is revealed in the following plot:

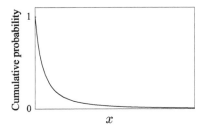

It is interesting to ask whether the power law is obeyed in the region of small values of x.

This sort of new business model is now attracting considerable attention, and is crossing over from the academy into the world of business. For instance the well-known

---

[17] It is worth noting that well before the age of the Internet, some retailers like Sears were launching a business model with an unlimited supply.

micro-economist Hal Varian of the University of California at Berkeley (Varian, 1992) is also a chief economist at Google. We think it is important that a wider range of companies becomes interested in new ways to examine various economic data. The mere plotting of distributions is just a start. New insights into the long tails caused by elementary processes, such as the sales of individual items, whose distributions and fluctuations are not modelled yet, may result in still more routes leading to fresh business models. For instance, with improved knowledge of the distribution of growth rates we may be able to achieve scientific risk management of the sales of goods.[18]

Neither Pareto nor Gibrat could have anticipated modern Internet business with all its new distributions, but their work is intensely relevant, and has prepared the way for a new world of research, bringing academics into partnership with businesses producing very large and valuable datasets. Certainly, the present authors would welcome contacts from any enterprise interested in this kind of collaborative work.

2.6 $\mu = 1$ and phase transition

As we have seen in this chapter, the value $\mu = 1$ of the Pareto index is very special. Let us now look back at what we have found and think about its meaning.

We have seen that in various countries, such as France, the United Kingdom, Italy, Spain and Japan, several quantities used to measure company size, such as total capital, sales and the number of employees, exhibited a Pareto index very close to 1, with only a small fluctuation around this value from year to year. This is radically different from personal income, the Pareto index of which fluctuated between 1.3 and 2.6 (Figure 2.6). This may seem unsurprising when we recall that people tend to be more equal than companies. In mature capitalism, companies are engaged in an unremitting struggle for survival. If defeated, a company may become bankrupt or be subject to merger or acquisition. By contrast, while individuals try to achieve more prosperity, they rarely try to eliminate other people financially. Therefore, it is natural to expect that people are more equal than companies, resulting in a larger Pareto index.[19] If this is the case, why does the Pareto index of companies stay close to 1, rather than falling below this value?

We have examined the property of Pareto distributions in section 2.4 using the staircase plot as a guide to, and a visualisation of, inequality. We have seen that for $\mu < 1$ the staircase became quite ragged, indeed devilish, making the inequality of the society manifest even to a casual observer. On the other hand, for $\mu > 1$, the staircase is disguised by the slope and the inequality is hidden behind its smoothness.

This has been quantified by the calculation of the relative shares. For values of μ smaller than 1, even if there is an infinite number of companies, the finite number of top companies have a finite share. This is the emergence of oligopoly, which would not occur under a normal distribution. On the other hand, nothing like this happens for

---

[18] We are a bit ahead of our story here: we will elaborate on growth rate in detail in the next chapter, where Gibrat's law will play an essential role.

[19] However, it should be noted that several studies of business sectors where governmental control is tight, such as the electric power industry, have shown the distribution to be far from a Pareto distribution, namely $\mu = 1$.

$\mu > 1$. At $\mu = 1$, a somewhat intermediate situation is realised. In fact, the average top share is almost inversely proportional to the logarithm of the number of companies, N, and very slowly goes to 0 as N diverges. Further, in this case, the shape of the Devil's Staircase is sometimes smooth and sometimes rough, varying a lot from dataset to dataset. We also saw that both the Gini coefficient and the Robin Hood index showed that oligopoly does occur for $\mu < 1$, and that a self-similar fractal appears for $\mu < 1$. All these show that the Pareto index $\mu = 1$ is the very boundary between the oligopolistic state and other more equal states, which we might call *pseudo-equal* states. Borrowing terms from modern statistical physics, this kind of point may be called a *transition point*, or a *critical point*.

The majority of economists and business people know little of contemporary physics and its analytical tools and modelling methods. We think that this is a pity, not least because, as we discussed earlier, history tells us that the disciplines of physics and economics have long been connected. But the real value is that even a modest grasp of physics may yield substantial improvements in understanding of the character of economic and social states.

Let us consider heating water at a location close to sea level. If we fill a kettle with water and start to heat it, the temperature rises. As it approaches 100 degrees C., the water will start to boil. Further heating at this stage does not raise the temperature, but only results in more vapour. The water molecules in the vapour obtain their kinetic energy from the heat and are able to exit the liquid state. So any additional heat is used to make vapour, and is carried away by those molecules. However much more energy you put into the water the temperature of the water does not rise further.

In cases such as this the water molecules may exist in a liquid state, water, or in a gaseous state, vapour (or a solid state, ice). Each state is a *phase*. The liquid state is the 'liquid phase' and the gaseous state the 'gaseous phase'. A change from water to vapour, or vice versa, is called a *phase transition*.

The point $\mu = 1$ for Pareto distributions is the critical point between the *oligopolistic phase* and the *pseudo-equal phase*. The economic society of companies is, so to speak, boiling at this critical point. There are two forces that drive the economic society of companies towards this critical point, $\mu = 1$. Companies, especially large companies, try to grow and to obtain large profits at the expense of their competitors. This drive towards yet larger companies forces the value of μ to decline. On the other hand, the oligopolistic phase is in some senses undesirable, as it obstructs free competition and may distort the market. Antitrust laws exist in many countries to suppress this kind of economic state, and in the worst cases, large companies are split into smaller companies. There are a number of other governmental measures to suppress oligopoly and monopoly. All these work to push up the value of μ, but only up to 1, as above $\mu = 1$ oligopoly essentially vanishes. Therefore these two competing pressures enforce $\mu = 1$, as illustrated in Figure 2.37. This is why the actual Pareto index in mature capitalistic countries hovers around $\mu = 1$.

When heating water, thermal energy is transferred to the kinetic energy of the water molecules. Those molecules collide with each other, which results in the exchange

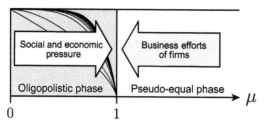

Figure 2.37. Two forces that besiege $\mu = 1$.

of a part of their kinetic energy. As a result, the kinetic energy of a water molecule obeys an exponential distribution called a *Boltzmann distribution*. Since molecules keep colliding with each other, the kinetic energy of each molecule fluctuates. But as the number of molecules is very large, the group of molecules as a whole obeys the Boltzmann distribution and other elegant statistical laws.[20]

Many readers will be thinking of the connections by now: 'molecules'... 'companies'?; 'collisions'... 'business transactions'? That, in a nutshell, is the analogy between boiling water and companies. Since all the agents that compose a society, individuals, companies, banks, markets and government agencies, are diverse and differ considerably in their functions, one might think it would be impossible to find any law to describe them all. However, there are so many agents, each influencing the others through trade, stock exchange and other financial transactions, the exchange and sharing of personnel, and so forth, that a single economic society is the result, just as the myriad of interactions among water molecules produces a phenomenon susceptible of scientific explanation. We suggest that some statistical laws are indeed valid for the whole, and in this chapter we have tried to show that there are some statistical laws governing the group of all companies.

Water molecules interact with each other in three-dimensional continuous space. In contrast, heterogeneous economic agents interact with each other in a network, such as a transaction network, a stock-holding network or a personnel-sharing network. Economic society is made of layers of these various networks overlapping with each other. Our next task, then, is to look at these network structures and the interaction between companies, and so to arrive at a scientific vision of modern-day economic society.

---

[20] We note that Aoki and Yoshikawa (2007) contains a theory that predicts the productivity distribution to be a Boltzmann distribution, which was further developed in the framework of superstatistics by Aoyama *et al.* (2008).

3   Company growth as fluctuations

In the preceding chapter we examined the statistical laws and patterns observed in distributions of company sizes, and it was noted that the tails of the distributions of flow and stock variables quantifying company size both obey Pareto's law.

Indeed, as was mentioned in subsection 2.1.2, Pareto's power law is commonly found in many phenomena observed within the natural sciences, as well as the social and economic sciences. Most researchers in these fields would accept that there is no single mechanism giving a universal explanation for all these phenomena, but rather that different mechanisms would be found for each of a variety of classes of phenomena.[1]

Company size obviously changes over time: last year's sales are not equal to this year's; the previous quarter's total assets are different from those in this quarter; and debt increases or decreases according to levels of borrowing from financial institutions or from investors. Thus we can see that observations on the distribution of company size are a snapshot of the state of a collection of companies, each of which is individually subject to *fluctuations*.

Our analysis is now being led towards the examination of temporal change in company size in terms of flow and stock variables, with a view to providing an account of the appearance of size distributions seen as a consequence of fluctuations. Therefore, our next step is to understand fluctuations in company size, in other words the growth or contraction of companies.[2]

This chapter's focus on the temporal change of flow and stock variables relating to company size is structured as follows.

Firstly, we show that another factor called *Gibrat's law* is phenomenologically valid by examining it in large datasets for European and Japanese companies. In the course of this work we reveal a remarkable fact, an effect which we will call *detailed balance*, which represents a sort of stability in the growth of companies, and is key to relating

---

[1] Mechanisms explaining the origins of power laws in natural and social sciences have been uncovered for more than a dozen classes of phenomena. See Sornette (2004) and references therein.

[2] The importance of understanding fluctuations in terms of heterogeneous interacting agents is well covered in recent studies (Aoki, 2002; Aoki and Yoshikawa, 2007; Delli Gatti *et al.*, 2008).

Gibrat's law (dynamics) to Pareto's law (statics). In addition, we discuss an important statistical method, namely the *copula* method, which can be employed as an alternative to growth rate when measuring the correlation between variables.

Secondly, we will make a detour through the subject of personal income distribution, and reconsider Pareto's original finding, his famous law, in conjunction with Gibrat's law, and both in the light of 'detailed balance'. Interestingly, we will find the same dynamical structure that is apparent in company growth, but more importantly, it will be shown that those laws can break down under abnormal situations in a nation's economy, such as the collapse of the Japanese 'bubble economy' in 1990.

So far, our story has been concerned with, and applies to, large companies, which are dominant in the aggregate of sizes and fluctuations. On the other hand, small and medium-sized companies prevail in overall number. Fortunately, the financial institutions responsible for credit risk management in Japan have recently accumulated and published very large datasets concerning small and medium-sized companies, enabling us to study distributions and fluctuations in this area and reveal phenomena not covered by Pareto's law. Indeed, we shall find a distinctive boundary between large and small companies based not on the legal regulations or arbitrary definitions of what are large and small companies, but instead on quantitative differences in the statics and dynamics. This observation is our third major point.

Fourthly, in contrast to 'growth', it is possible for a company to pass into a state of 'death'. Recall that a company's activity is aimed at the profit anticipated from sales over and above expenses such as labour and financing, and thus that the profit will be determined *a posteriori* by several factors such as sales fluctuations, costs, the price of intermediate goods, interest rates and risks due to exchange rates. If the company becomes short of retained earnings because of those factors, it goes into *bankruptcy*, or experiences corporate death.

Finally, it would be of crucial importance in such activity for a company to determine the amount of output by deciding the input of capital (non-human resources) and labour (human resources). How can we understand the collection of those activities in terms of microscopic behaviour, in which each company attempts under various constraints to maximise profit? We discuss this point briefly under the heading *production function* and what we call the *ridge theory* of company growth.

3.1   Gibrat's law and detailed balance

Let us begin by taking a look at real data so as to understand important phenomenological facts concerning the fluctuations of company growth.[3]

---

[3] There exists a huge literature on company, industry and country growth in economics. We refer to Steindl (1965), Ijiri and Simon (1977), Stanley *et al.* (1996), Amaral *et al.* (1997, 1998), Sutton (1997), Takayasu *et al.* (1997), Okuyama *et al.* (1999), Bottazzi and Secchi (2003), Fu *et al.* (2005), Gabaix (2008) and references therein for other aspects and introductions to previous studies.

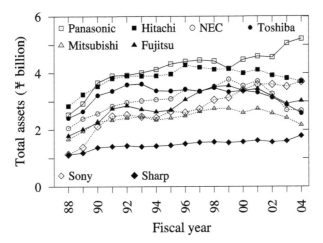

Figure 3.1. Time-series of annual company size for the eight largest electrical and electronics companies (1988 to 2004).

3.1.1 Growth-rate and Gibrat's law

The growth of company size for flow or stock variables can be easily quantified by measuring them at different points in time. To illustrate this, in Figure 3.1, we depict the time-series of annual company size (defined by the summation of assets and debt) for the eight largest electrical and electronics companies (Fujitsu, Hitachi, Mitsubishi, NEC, Panasonic, Sharp, Sony and Toshiba) in Japan, for the fiscal years from 1988 to 2004.[4]

The time-scale here has an annual basis for illustrative purposes; in fact, a quarterly or monthly basis would be adequate. The point is that the dynamics of company growth can only be understood with a time-scale that is longer than that of the activity of the company, typically days and weeks.

In addition, the time-scale should be shorter than that over which macro-economic conditions surrounding the companies are subject to change, say, years and decades. Otherwise, we would not be able to separate the 'fast' variables of company-level dynamics from the 'slow' variables of nation-level macroscopic dynamics.[5]

Let us denote by x_1 and x_2 a company's size at time t_1 and a succeeding time t_2 respectively. We can further define *growth-rate* by

$$R = \frac{x_2}{x_1}.$$

---

[4] The data are on an unconsolidated basis. Companies have slightly different policies in accounting for consolidated and unconsolidated data, so a simple comparison of values of company size might be inappropriate here.

[5] It is not trivial, *a priori*, that such a separation of time-scales is possible. Some abnormal situations, caused by a global shock, for example, may not allow one to distinguish between time-scales in this way. It would, nevertheless, be reasonable to assume that it is possible in ordinary instances, and thus to observe consequences which can be tested against empirical facts *a posteriori*.

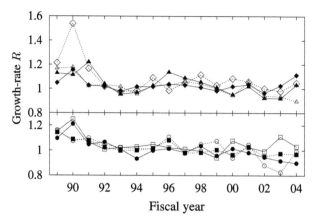

Figure 3.2. Time-series of growth-rates for the eight largest electrical and electronics companies (corresponding to Figure 3.1; 1989 to 2004).

The variable R represents the rate at which a company increases or decreases its size, in terms of, for example, sales or total assets, in the time interval. In addition, we will define the *logarithmic growth-rate* as

$$r = \log_{10} R = \log_{10} x_2 - \log_{10} x_1,$$

where $\log_{10}$ is a logarithm to base 10.[6] If the size does not change, the growth-rate is $R = 1$ and the logarithmic growth-rate is $r = 0$; if the size increases, $R > 1, r > 0$ and if it decreases, $R < 1, r < 0$.

Figure 3.2 shows the annual growth-rates calculated from Figure 3.1. (The upper and lower panels divide the eight companies into two groups of four simply for visual ease.) It can be seen that the growth-rates are diverse across the companies and over time vary around the value 1. If we think of individual companies at the same instant of time as spatially related, we can say that growth-rates fluctuate both in space and time. Since this spatial fluctuation is related to company-size distribution, we can now proceed to investigate the spatial distributions of growth-rates.

We can begin by using the flow variables of companies' declared incomes in the Japanese dataset, the distribution of which was shown in Figure 2.4. This is a suitable set since it is an exhaustive list of incomes for about 57,000 companies covering the region where the power law holds. We can calculate the growth-rate for each company income from 2001 to 2002. Figure 3.3 is the PDF as a histogram for the logarithmic growth-rates r. The magnitudes $r = 0.5$ and 1 correspond to the increase by factors of $3.2 (\approx 10^{0.5})$ and 10, while $r = -0.5$ and -1 represent decreases by factors of $0.32 (\approx 10^{-0.5})$ and 0.1, respectively, in terms of R.

Note that the ordinate has a logarithmic scale. The growth-rate distribution has a strong peak at $r = 0$, and declines as an exponentially decreasing function on each

---

[6] For non-mathematical readers: when $y = 10^x$, one writes $x = \log_{10} y$ by definition. For example, $\log_{10} 1 = 0, \log_{10} 10 = 1, \log_{10} 100 = 2, \ldots$.

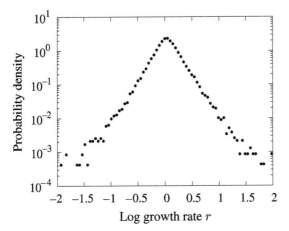

Figure 3.3. Probability distribution for logarithmic growth-rates of company income (2001 to 2002; roughly 57,000 companies).

side for both positive and negative values of r. The number of companies increasing or decreasing in size by a multiple of three ($R = 3$ or 0.3) is approximately 10 per cent of the number of companies with no change ($R = 1$); also the number increasing or decreasing by a multiple of 10 is roughly 1 per cent of the number of unchanged companies. It is intuitively surprising that a company could double or halve in a year, but in fact the data show that this is a quite dramatic observable change.

It is evidently reasonable to ask whether growth-rate is dependent on company size; for example, we might ask whether the growth-rate of a company of size 1 in an arbitrary scale is large when compared with that of a company of size 2? To answer this question we can examine the distribution of sizes in Figure 2.4 again. Let us segregate those companies into categories (or bins) by dividing the size range into five logarithmically equal bins, covering incomes of ¥50 million up to ¥5 billion. In other words, we will divide the interval between two orders of magnitude (from 50 million to 5 billion) into bins by multiples of $10^{2/5} = 10^{0.4} \approx 2.5$; the first bin ranges from 50 million to $10^{0.4} \times 50$ million, roughly 125 million, and similarly for the others.[7]

The resulting bins are then

$$[5 \times 10^{10+0.4\,(n-1)}, 5 \times 10^{10+0.4\,n}] \quad (n = 1, \ldots, 5)$$

We can examine the PDF for the logarithmic growth-rate r by choosing those companies whose sizes fall into each bin. This is called a conditional PDF. Figure 3.4 depicts in a single plot the conditional PDFs thus obtained.

What can we conclude from this plot? Obviously the calculated PDFs overlap and form a single curve as shown in Figure 3.4 (or equivalently as in Figure 3.3). The

---

[7] One could simply split the range into *linearly* equal bins, but since we know that the tail of the distribution exhibits a power law, this would make an inefficient use of the data.

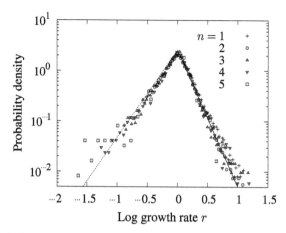

Figure 3.4. Probability distribution for logarithmic growth-rates conditioned by company income size (corresponding to Figure 3.3).

growth-rate does not depend on the selected bin, i.e. it is independent of company size at the outset, as the distribution in the figure shows. In other words, for companies in the regime of Pareto's law, the fluctuation in their rise and fall, as quantified by growth-rate, is statistically independent of the size. This fact looks quite strange at first sight, for one might expect a quantitative difference in the fluctuations for groups of companies with different sizes, a difference that would be responsible for the diversity of company sizes among group. However, our finding is different, and we shall refer to this non-trivial fact as *Gibrat's law*.

3.1.2 Data for Japanese companies

So far, we have examined an exhaustive list of companies from a Japanese company income dataset, and found Gibrat's law. It is interesting to ask whether this law also holds for other quantities that can characterise company activity. For example, we could take the dataset used for our study of company-size distribution, which covers hundreds of thousands of companies, and examine the sales and profits (positive profits, not deficits, are considered here).

Figures 3.5 (a) and (b) show the annual growth-rate for the years 2001 to 2002 for sales (0.34 million companies) and for profits (0.27 million), respectively (corresponding to Figures 2.9 (a) and (b)). The PDFs are conditional, just as they were in Figure 3.4, though the condition here is imposed on the magnitude of sales or profits.

The indices $n = 1, \ldots, 5$ correspond to five logarithmically equal bins, ranging from ¥2 billion to ¥200 billion for sales, and from ¥20 million to ¥2 billion for profits.

We observe that the distribution of growth-rate differs between the two variables. The growth-rate for profit has a larger width in its distribution than that for sales, and

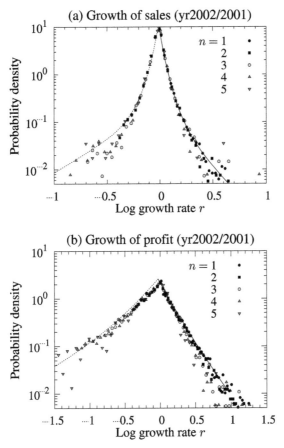

Figure 3.5. Probability distributions for growth-rates: (a) sales (b) profits (years 2002/2001).

a less sharp peak around $r = 0$. We can see, nevertheless, that the PDFs overlap in a single curve irrespective of the chosen bin n. Thus, Gibrat's law also holds for these variables.

3.1.3 Data for European companies
Sales and profits are *flow* variables, as opposed to *stock* variables such as total assets, the number of employees, and others, so we might further ask whether Gibrat's law applies to this latter class of characteristics of company size, and whether it applies in countries other than Japan.

To shed light on these questions we will now turn to several results from datasets for European companies used in subsection 2.3.2. The criterion used for selecting companies for inclusion in the datasets is: profits are larger than €15 million, or total assets exceed €30 million or the company has more than 150 employees; see Fujiwara *et al.* (2004) for details.

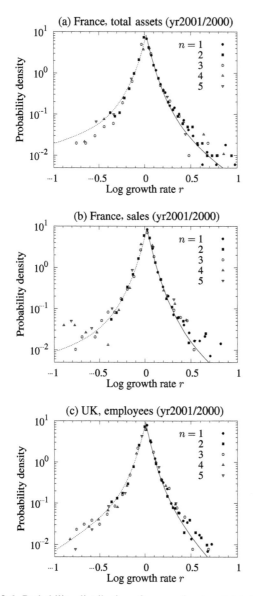

Figure 3.6. Probability distributions for growth-rates: (a) total assets (France) (b) sales (France) (c) number of employees per company (UK) (years 2001/2000).

In Figure 3.6 (a), (b) and (c) are the distributions for annual growth-rates of total assets and sales in France, and of the number of employees per company in the UK, using the same method of conditional PDFs as employed in Figure 3.4.

The bins employed, $n = 1, \ldots, 5$, cover the ranges €30 million to €3 billion for total assets, €15 million to €1.5 billion for sales and 150 persons to 15,000 for the number of employees, in logarithmically equal intervals.

It can be seen that the distributions for different variables have different shapes, and that the width of fluctuation in the number of employees is relatively small compared with that in total assets. The time-scales involved in the fluctuation and dynamics of those variables are different, but, at the same time, we can see that the PDFs give a single overlapping curve whichever bins, n, are observed. Thus we have established that Gibrat's law holds quite universally, irrespective of variables and countries.

 Mathematical expression of Gibrat's law

If the conditional PDF for the growth-rate R of the company size x is denoted by $q(R|x)$, Gibrat's law can be expressed as

$$q(R|x) = q(R),$$

that is, R is independent of x for a certain range of $x > x_0$.

The PDFs shown in Figure 3.4, Figure 3.6 and elsewhere depict the probability distribution function for a logarithmic growth-rate $r = \log_{10} R$, which is related to that for R by the equality of probability, $q(r)dr = q(R)dR$.

3.1.4   Gibrat revisited

Readers in a tearing hurry may want to skip this subsection, where we pause to consider Robert Gibrat (1904–80) a French researcher in economics.

In his seminal treatise, *Les inégalités économiques* (1931), Gibrat proposed a stochastic process which offered the potential for explaining the dynamics of company size. At the time of writing, researchers had found distributions with heavy tails in various of the natural sciences as well as in social and economic sciences, amongst them Jacobus Kapteyn, an astronomer who had discovered the rotation of the galaxy. Kapteyn had suggested a simple process as one of the possible mechanisms that might bring about a highly skewed distribution and, as a result of correspondence with Kapteyn, Gibrat turned his mind to the origin of economic and social inequalities; see Sutton (1997).

The stochastic process is quite simple. Consider a stochastic variable x_t at time t and its growth R_t which is independent of x_t and independent of $R_{t'}$ for a different time t', i.e. at each time the growth simply takes a value drawn from a distribution. He called the basic idea in this stochastic process a 'law of proportionate effect', and actually placed this expression in the subtitle of the treatise.[8] 'Proportionate' refers to the multiplicative nature of the process, that is, the size at the next time-step is

---

[8] The subtitle is long: 'applications: aux inégalités des richesses, à la concentration des entreprises, aux populations des villes, aux statistiques des familles, etc., d'une loi nouvelle, la loi de l'effet proportionnel'. The phrase 'a new law' may be read as a strong claim with regard to his endeavour to explain many social phenomena such as personal income, companies, cities, etc.

determined by a multiplication of the previous size and an independent multiplicative factor; see Redner (1990) for instance. We will call this *Gibrat's process*.

We will later see that if we run a simulation of this stochastic process, the result is a so-called 'log-normal' distribution, one of the classes of skewed distributions well-known in physics and the social sciences; see Aitchison and Brown (1957). One can prove, in addition, that the average and variance of the distribution grow in time. Now, Gibrat employed data of personal income and company size (measured by number of employees, factories, etc.) available at the time of writing, and fitted them with log-normal distributions, claiming the stochastic process as a new finding, a new principle or a law.

Revisiting Gibrat's study with today's high-precision and large-scale data, we immediately notice the difficulties:

- The log-normal distributions do not fit well for the category of the largest firms, putting aside the category of small and middle-sized companies.
- The average and variance do not grow over time.

The data employed in Gibrat's study were not only limited in extent but were presumably to some degree biased, with the result that the apparent fit to the log-normal distribution and its mathematically well-studied model led Gibrat into concluding that the log-normal distribution was what should be considered first. In regard to the second point, Gibrat himself recognised the difficulty and tried, without success, to provide possible solutions; see Sutton (1997).

Let us recall that we denominated as *Gibrat's law* the following property: let the growth-rate of a company i at a point in time be denoted by R_i; if the probability distribution for the collection of growth-rates $\{R_i\}$ is statistically independent of the company size x, then the law holds.

Gibrat's law itself does not lead to Gibrat's process. It will be instructive to exemplify and emphasise this point. Consider an example of Gibrat's process, that is, a multiplicative process as described above. Suppose a company follows this process, then it can continue its business activity however small it may be, because the succeeding multiplicative factors may happen by chance to be small. To avoid such an unrealistic situation, let us assume that there is a threshold for the size of a company, which is interpretable as the minimum level of assets, facilities and number of employees necessary for survival. Also suppose that a company leaves the area of business and is replaced by a newcomer. The new company could start with a minimum size as we have already assumed. This can be conceived of as a 'reflecting barrier', positioned at a small value of company size; the barrier repels companies which shrink down to the threshold and propels them in the direction of growth.

This modifies Gibrat's process slightly, but obviously satisfies the property of Gibrat's law as defined above. Moreover, if we were to run a computer simulation for a collection of companies, each of which follows the modified process, we would find that the distribution for company size follows a Pareto law in the tail. Mathematically, it can be proved that a Gibrat process with a reflecting barrier boundary condition obeys Pareto's law; see Sornette and Cont (1997).

However, we do not claim here that this is a plausible model for explaining the dynamics of companies, at least with respect to Pareto's and Gibrat's laws. Nevertheless, we can now see that Gibrat's law itself does not lead to the Gibrat process, which is just one of the many possible models that satisfy the property of Gibrat's law.

Even so, this observation does not contradict the law of proportionate effect, which we refer to here as Gibrat's law. On the contrary, Gibrat's insight was to focus on the statistical independence of the growth-rate, and this turns out to be correct.[9] The point is that Gibrat's process was simply not an appropriate model to describe real dynamics, as researchers have found with the help of abundant empirical data. We need to find another key to understanding the kinematics of the rise and fall of companies, and this will be attempted in the following section, where we will introduce the concept of 'detailed balance', a concept drawn from statistical physics. Together, these two key concepts – Gibrat's law and detailed balance – solve the long-standing problem of the origin of Pareto's law, eighty years after Gibrat's finding.

3.1.5   Detailed balance

So far, we have been using the variables R and x_1 for the description of growth-rate, but we could also use another equally valid pair, for example x_1 and x_2. A brief glance at the pattern of fluctuation in terms of this pair of variables will illustrate this point.

It will suffice to examine how companies of size x_1 at time t_1 make a transition to a size of x_2 at time t_2. We will take all the companies in the Pareto region, and first plot points for the pair (x_1, x_2), resulting in a so-called scatterplot. Figures 3.7 (a) and (b) are scatterplots which correspond to Figures 3.5 (a) and (b), respectively. Similarly Figures 3.8 (a), (b) and (c) correspond with Figures 3.6 (a), (b) and (c).

Consider, in such a scatterplot, a portion of a rectangle spanning x_1 to $x_1 + dx_1$ and also x_2 to $x_2 + dx_2$, then calculate the number of companies which fall into the rectangle and divide this by the total number in the entire plot. The calculated quantity as a function of the point (x_1, x_2) is called a *joint probability* denoted by $p_{12}(x_1, x_2)dx_1dx_2$. Here dx_1 or dx_2 represents a small interval in the direction of x_1 or x_2.

Even to the naked eye a significant feature is visible, namely that the distribution of points looks almost symmetrical with respect to the diagonal line (running from south-west to north-east). If it is actually symmetrical in a statistical sense,[10] we can say that the following fact holds: companies make a transition from a small interval

---

[9] We will assume that the reader who has followed this discussion is now comfortable with this distinction, though even some professional researchers seem to confuse Gibrat's law with the Gibrat process associated with the log-normal distribution.

[10] While it looks symmetrical, a careful statistical analysis is necessary to check the symmetry, since our eyes easily fail to identify the density of a cloud of points.

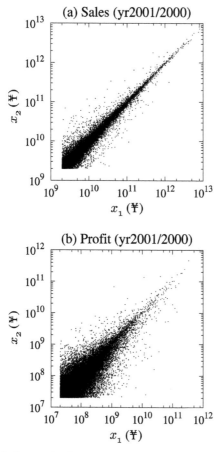

Figure 3.7. Scatterplot for company sizes at successive points in time: (a) sales (b) profits (years 2001/2000).

centring at x_1 in size (state of x_1) to a small interval centring at x_2, and vice versa, from the state of x_2 to x_1. The frequencies of transition of companies from x_1 to x_2, and of the reverse transition are the same. This property is a kind of balance, which holds for any pair of states (x_1, x_2) in the Pareto region.

In the study of the motion of molecules in a gas, and in other cases, statistical physics has a concept for this property, which is called *detailed balance*, a term which we will consequently adopt in this book.

One way to show whether this property holds or not in actual data is to conduct a direct statistical test. Take a scatterplot for $p_{12}(x_1, x_2)$ and flip it so that the x_1 axis is replaced with x_2, and then compare the flipped plot with the original one. The statistical test is to check if the distribution of points in these two plots is indistinguishable merely as two realisations (random samplings) of the same joint probability. A

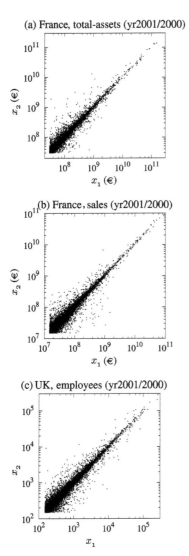

Figure 3.8. Scatterplot for company sizes at successive points in time: (a) total assets (France) (b) sales (France) (c) number of employees (UK) (years 2001/2000).

two-dimensional Kolmogorov–Smirnov test can be used for this.[11] The null hypothesis, namely of symmetry in the scatterplot, survives this test for most datasets.[12]

---

[11] To be precise, one should subtract the overall average in the growth-rate. For example, in Figure 3.2, there are trends at epochs in time, shifting the values of growth-rate to either the positive or negative side. We need to subtract such a shift of the average before conducting the statistical test, because the detailed balance we want to study here is a different property from the effect of a trend.

[12] The profit data in Figure 3.7(b) is an exception, the probable reason being a problem in the dataset itself, as discussed in subsection 2.3.1.

Mathematical expression of detailed balance

Detailed balance can be expressed for the joint probability $P(x_1, x_2)$ as

$$p_{12}(x_1, x_2) = p_{12}(x_2, x_1),$$

that is, the joint probability function is symmetric with respect to the exchange of the two arguments in the function.

The other way to check the validity of detailed balance is, as explained in the next subsection, to compare the data with one of the consequences of detailed balance and Gibrat's law, which we shall call a reflection law.

 Two-dimensional Kolmogorov–Smirnov test

The Kolmogorov–Smirnov test for a one-dimensional distribution is well known and widely used. This is a non-parametric test (no parameters are assumed in the distribution) to check if, in a one-dimensional case, the 'two sets of samples are from the same distribution'. In multi-dimensional cases no non-parametric test is available. Astronomy requires such a two-dimensional test, because researchers want to test whether the distribution of stars differs in two different directions (samples) in a sky (of two dimensions). Empirically, astronomers have found a statistical test which depends only on the correlation coefficient (see the box in section 4.2) for a two-dimensional distribution. See Press *et al.* (1992, ch. 14) and references therein.

It is a surprising fact that such a property holds for the stochastic transitions of company size in competing companies, and we might regard it as a kind of balance or stability. In addition, we should remark that the condition of detailed balance is a law which is independent of Gibrat's law. It is easy to see that in the ecology of growing and shrinking companies, some become dominant and occupy niches vacated by falling companies. However, and this should be emphasised, detailed balance is not a mere balance for the entire population of companies, but a more stringent mathematical statement about the stochastic transitions of companies.

3.1.6 *Relation between Pareto's and Gibrat's laws and the detailed balance*
To sum up: we have so far shown that in the phenomenology of fluctuations, and for a wide range of company sizes, the following hold:

- Pareto's law for the distribution of company size;
- Gibrat's law of the growth-rate of company size;
- detailed balance in the process of growth.

The question that faces us now, is how to relate these three laws to each other? A detailed argument is put in the box below, but we can anticipate the conclusion, by stating that there is actually a provable relation:

> **Under the condition of detailed balance, Gibrat's law leads to Pareto's law as the resulting distribution of company size.**

As a bonus from the proof, it follows that what we call the *reflection law* also holds, which can be written as

$$q(R) = R^{-\mu-2} q(R^{-1}).$$

This equation states that in the PDF for the growth-rate the functional form where $R > 1$ has a mathematical relation to that where $R < 1$, and that the relation depends on the Pareto index μ. Note that this reflection law alone does not determine the shape of the growth-rate's PDF. Actually we have seen that the PDFs for different variables measuring company size take various shapes (see Figure 3.4 for company income and Figure 3.6 for other variables).

It is implied by the reflection law that it is possible to know the distribution of growth-rate for the group of shrinking companies once one knows the distribution for the rest of the (growing) companies. We have actually drawn curves in the PDFs depicted so far by first fitting a non-linear function to the data in the region of positive logarithmic growth-rates ($r > 0$, equivalently $R > 1$) and then calculating the region of negative growth ($r < 0$ or $R < 1$) from the reflection law. Figure 3.4 and Figure 3.6 confirm that the fit is satisfactory, and that the reflection law works adequately.

If you are a practitioner, these laws might appear to be distracting, even boring, mathematics, and certainly far from intriguing. In fact, they have implications for the practice of business. Knowing the details of the distribution of the growth-rate of companies is of value to risk management, since one can perform a quantitative estimation of the risk associated with the growth or decline of companies. It would, of course, be necessary to take into account the consequences of Gibrat's law, that is, the independence of growth from company size. If you make investments in a range of many enterprises, it would be prudent to consider the reflection law relating positive to negative growth-rates, which in turn requires you to have the distribution for growth-rate and also to measure the Pareto index in a statistically reasonable way. That is to say, these points might prove useful in the risk management toolbox.

Proof of the mathematical relation between the laws

It is not difficult to show that Gibrat's law and the detailed balance lead to Pareto's law (Fujiwara *et al.*, 2004).

Since the pair of variables (x_1, x_2) and the pair (x_1, R) are related by $R = x_2/x_1$, one can easily see that the joint probability distribution $p_{1R}(x_1, R)$ is related to the joint probability distribution $p_{12}(x_1, x_2)$ by

$$p_{12}(x_1, x_2) = \frac{1}{x_1} p_{1R}(x_1, R).$$

Now, the conditional PDF, $q(R|x_1)$, for the growth-rate satisfies

$$p_{1R}(x_1, R) = q(R|x_1)\, p_1(x_1),$$

by definition, where $p_1(x_1)$ is the PDF for the size x_1.

Assume that detailed balance holds, then the first equation yields

$$p_{1R}(x_1, R) = \frac{1}{R} p_{1R}(Rx_1, R^{-1}),$$

as readily shown by a simple calculation. Therefore, this equation and the second equation above lead us to

$$\frac{q(R^{-1}|x_2)}{q(R|x_1)} = R \frac{p_1(x_1)}{p_1(x_2)}.$$

Note that this is a consequence of detailed balance alone.

With the additional assumption of Gibrat's law, one can immediately rewrite this equation as

$$\frac{p_1(x_1)}{p_1(x_2)} = \frac{1}{R} \frac{q(R^{-1})}{q(R)}.$$

Note that the left-hand side is a function of x_1 and $x_2 = R x_1$, while the right-hand side is a function only of R. The equality holds if and only if p_1 is a power-law function. (For example, if we expand this equation in terms of R around $R = 1$, we obtain a differential equation that p_1 has to satisfy, one whose solution is the power law and is verified as satisfying the above equation.)

It is also possible to obtain a proof by inserting the power-law function $p_1(x) \propto x^{-\mu-1}$ into the above equation so that the reflection law follows as a consequence.

3.1.7 *Copulas*

Gibrat's law, detailed balance, and so forth have been uncovered by conducting an analysis of the statistical dependence among multiple variables. A powerful method beyond conventional approaches can be applied to such an analysis, and more generally to other analyses regarding correlations, namely the *copula* method.

For two stochastic variables a copula is a function which represents the joint probability function of the variables in terms of cumulative probability functions for each of the variables. A cumulative probability function $P_<(x)$ for a stochastic variable is defined, as explained in subsection 2.1.2, as the probability that the variable takes a value smaller than x. For two stochastic variables the joint cumulative probability function $P_<(x, y)$ is the probability that the first variable is smaller than x *and* the second one is smaller than y. If the two stochastic variables are statistically independent (you cannot predict one from the other), then the probability is simply the product of each variable's cumulative probabilities:

$$P_<(x, y) = P_<(x)P_<(y).$$

The variables are not always statistically independent, however. Yet one is able to show that the joint probability can be expressed by a function of each variable's cumulative probability as

$$P_<(x, y) = C(P_<(x), P_<(y)).$$

The function $C(u, v)$ that appears here is the copula (more mathematically oriented readers may consult Nelsen, 2006).[13]

The word 'copula' is used in linguistics to mean the link between the subject and predicate of a proposition. In statistics, it refers to a link or bond which connects two stochastic variables, and to the method involved in joining them.

Since the copula function has variables consisting of cumulative probabilities $P_<(x)$, it is a multi-variate function with the domain of its argument variables being between 0 and 1. In addition, a copula represents a joint probability, so the value it takes ranges between 0 and 1. Note that copulas are invariant under an appropriate change of scale in the stochastic variables, because the argument variables are cumulative probabilities, not stochastic variables. If the stochastic variable is money, we have the same copula irrespective of how the variable is represented in units of dollars, millions of dollars or the logarithm of a dollar sum. We can even go one step further, and use only the rank (smaller or larger), instead of the value of x. In this sense, therefore, copula is the concept regarding so-called order-statistics. Remember that the concept of the correlation coefficient (see the box in section 4.2), and related concepts, are based on the realm of normal distributions.[14] In contrast, copulas have desirable properties which enable us to describe distributions with fat tails, such as the Pareto distribution, since they do not depend on assumptions for each stochastic variable's distribution (marginal distribution). Copulas can also be used to conduct simulations in multi-variate statistical problems that involve statistical correlations, for example in quantitative finance, risk management, and so forth; see Iyetomi *et al.* (2009b), for example.

---

[13] It is possible to generalise this to more than two stochastic variables, though here we shall focus on pairs of variables.

[14] One can appreciate this simply by noting that a proper definition of a correlation coefficient requires a finite variance, but that in fact our world has enough space for distributions without finite variances.

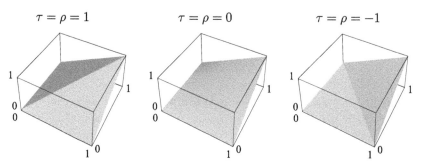

Figure 3.9. Three typical examples of copulas.

Interestingly, the copula function $C(u, v)$ has an upper-bound function and a lower-bound function, as shown in Figure 3.9. In each of these figures, the two axes on the horizontal plane are u and v, the ordinate is the value of $C(u, v)$. The left-hand figure gives the upper bound, while the right-hand one illustrates the lower bound; the middle figure depicts the case of two statistically independent variables. τ and ρ in these figures are to be understood as follows. Kendall's τ is a parameter characterising the copula; it takes a value from -1 to 1, corresponding to the lower and upper bounds of the copula, while it is exactly 0 in the case of statistical independence.[15] Let P_+ be the probability that the relative ordering of the ranks with respect to x is the same as the relative ordering of the ranks with respect to y (the so-called concordant case); and let P_- be the probability that the relative ordering of the ranks with respect to x is opposite to the relative ordering of the ranks with respect to y (the discordant case). Then assuming that there exists no tie, or similar rank in either of x or y, we have

$$\tau = P_+ - P_- \simeq 2P_+ - 1,$$

which indicates the meaning of τ. Suppose, for example, that the variables are company sizes in two consecutive years. If you choose two companies at random, the relative ranking of the two companies in the first year is always the same as the relative ranking in the second year, if $\tau = 1$. And it is fifty-fifty, if $\tau = 0$. If $\tau = -1$, then the rankings are always opposite to each other,

The parameter ρ is conventionally known as Spearman's ρ. This concerns a triplet of companies rather than a pair. Let us be satisfied here with understanding this as (a linear function of) the volume under the surface spanned by the copula function. It is -1 for the lower bound, 1 for the upper bound and 0 in the case of statistical independence.

We will now turn to examine examples of copulas for actual data. Figure 3.10 depicts the copula for Japanese company incomes in the years 2001 and 2002, as studied in subsection 3.1.2. The copula is similar in its functional shape to the upper-bound function shown in Figure 3.9. The parameters of τ and ρ, derived from the real data, are shown in Table 3.1. The value of τ implies that for a randomly chosen pair of

---

[15] This parameter is also called Kendall's rank correlation τ.

Table 3.1. *Parameters of τ and ρ for copulas.*

	τ	ρ
Tax income (Japan): 2001–2	0.59	0.77
Total assets (France): 2000–1	0.86	0.95
Personal income (Japan): 1997–8	0.62	0.72
Tax income and its growth-rate (Japan): 2001–2	0.02	0.05
Total assets and its growth-rate (France): 2000–1	0.03	0.04
Personal income and its growth-rate (Japan): 1997–8	−0.04	−0.05

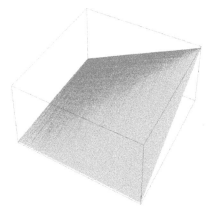

Figure 3.10. Copula for company incomes in the years 2001 and 2002.

companies the probability that the relative ordering of the ranks in the first year is the same as that in the second year is approximately 80 per cent. The various data for European countries have similar copulas. Table 3.1 exemplifies this point from the total assets data for French companies.

For Japanese personal income data the copula has a qualitatively different function from the upper bound (Figure 3.11). In fact, the parameter τ is nearly 0.6, as listed in Table 3.1, which means that for a randomly chosen pair of high-income earners the probability that the relative ordering of the ranks in the first year is opposite to that in the second year is roughly 20 per cent. Some readers will be relieved to hear that this turnover probability does not vanish to 0.

We are also able to test Gibrat's law by using copulas. In the preceding section, the validity of the law was clear from the PDF figures, but it is valuable to quantify the validity in terms of a copula and its parameters. Figure 3.12 shows the copula for the tax income of companies in 2001, and its growth-rate from that year to 2002. It can be observed that the copula function is close to the middle copula of Figure 3.9. Both parameters, τ and ρ, are close to 0. These facts[16] show that Gibrat's law holds with reasonable accuracy, as quantified by the copula and its parameters. A similar result

[16] Calculated for the top 10,000 companies in the year 2001.

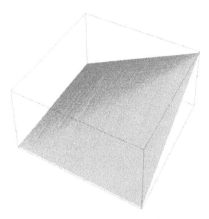

Figure 3.11. Copula for personal incomes in the years 1997 and 1998.

Figure 3.12. Copula for company incomes in the year 2001 and its growth-rates.

is obtained for the total assets data of French companies.[17] In addition, for personal income and its growth-rate, the parameters τ and ρ have small absolute values, as shown in Table 3.1. (The copula figure is omitted here.) Thus we have further evidence for the validity of Gibrat's law.

It should be mentioned here that the copula method will shortly be shown to open the way to a more sophisticated method of performing simulations of multi-variate problems.

3.2   Digression: personal income fluctuation

3.2.1   *Gibrat's law and detailed balance*
Let us make a brief digression away from company growth, and instead consider personal income in relation to Gibrat's law and detailed balance. In doing so, we will show that Gibrat's law and detailed balance, as well as Pareto's law, can break down,

---

[17] Calculated for the top 2,000 companies in this case.

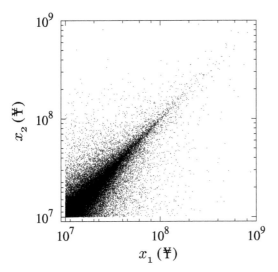

Figure 3.13. Scatterplot for personal incomes (measured by the amount of taxes paid) for two consecutive years (1997 and 1998).

depending on the economic environment (see Fujiwara *et al.*, 2003). We focus, as we have done hitherto, on the high-income region where Pareto's law holds.

Consider, on the one hand, the process by which a person's annual income of ¥20 million doubles in the following year, and, on the other, the doubling process for an initial income of ¥40 million. Do they differ, and if so, how? Alternatively, take the probability of these incomes halving in the following year. At the risk of offending our readers, those with moderate incomes may wrongly guess that fluctuations of this scale are negligible for high-income earners.

We will perform the same analysis of the fluctuation of personal income as we did for company growth. Let last year's annual income be x_1, and this year's x_2. We can calculate from the dataset of high-tax payers *each* person's growth-rate R. How is this possible? From the Japanese datasets in the fiscal years 1997 and 1998, for example, we can identify high-tax paying individuals, and make a list of those persons appearing in both years' data. (See subsection 3.2.3 if you are interested in the story behind this exhaustive Japanese dataset.)

We first show in Figure 3.13 the scatterplot for income tax pairs (x_1, x_2) for these high-tax payers (some 52,000, extracted from 93,000 taxpayers in the fiscal year 1997, and from 84,000 in 1998). The values of x_1 and x_2, respectively, represent the income taxes in 1997 and 1998 (both in yen). The lower limit in the data is ¥10 million, so we are left with the points in the rectangular region $x_1, x_2 > 10^7$. In passing, it should be noted that there are a few extremely high-tax payers towards the north-east, beyond the scope of the figure.

A statistical test for detailed balance gives no ground for the rejection of the null hypothesis that the joint probability distribution is symmetric, so the data is compatible with the property of detailed balance.

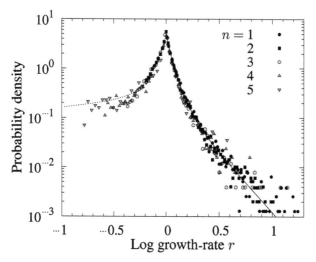

Figure 3.14. Probability distribution for the growth-rate of personal income (1997 to 1998).

Then we proceed to calculate the PDF as a histogram for the logarithmic growth-rate $r = \log_{10} R$ conditioned on the value of x_1, and obtain the result in Figure 3.14. Here the bins $n = 1, \ldots, 5$ are used corresponding to five logarithmically equal intervals from ¥10 million ($x_1 = 10^7$) to ¥100 million ($x_1 = 10^8$). Because numerically $10^{0.2} \simeq 1.58$, these bins are sequentially multiples by 1.58 up to the limit of ¥10 million.

It is clear from the figure that the distribution for the growth-rate collapses into a single curve irrespective of the bins considered, indicating that the growth-rate is statistically independent of the previous year's income tax (Gibrat's law). In other words, for the high-tax payers present in the Pareto region, the transition probability for a doubling or halving of income is independent of initial income. We additionally see in Figure 3.14 that the calculated function of the PDF in the region $r < 0$ by the reflection law from the non-linear fit in the region $r > 0$ yields a satisfactory fit.

We conclude, therefore, that both Gibrat's law and detailed balance hold for personal income, as we conjectured at the beginning of this subsection.

3.2.2 Breakdown of the laws

By taking a close look at the distribution for the growth-rate of personal income in Figure 3.14, we can see that there is a cusp at $r = 0$, around which there is little variation in income, indicating that relatively stable income-earners are dominant. On the other hand, there is a non-negligible percentage of people whose income grows or shrinks by large magnitudes. While the Japanese tax law does not compel the high-tax payers to reveal the sources of their incomes, it is reasonable to assume that they were derived from financial assets and real estate, an assumption that can be verified from Japanese government surveys on family income and expenditure.

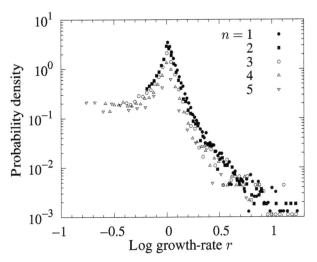

Figure 3.15. Probability distribution for the growth-rate of personal income, 1991 to 1992, corresponding to the Bubble collapse in Japan.

If such high-risk assets as real estate and stocks are prone to large variations in their returns, personal income would obviously be sensitive to such variations, especially for those with high incomes. And, when a macroscopic shock occurs, the laws and balance so far observed can break down, as we shall see shortly.

In the late 1980s, Japan experienced an abnormal rise in the price of real estate and stocks, which peaked during 1990 and 1991 and was followed by a great plunge in the markets. The period is colloquially known in Japan as the Bubble, or the *Heisei* bubble, the name being derived from the term used to describe the reign of the Emperor. A number of high-income earners rose into the Pareto region just before 1991, but after that year, the majority of them disappeared. Hitherto stable high-income earners were also subject to great variations in their risky assets. Examination of the details of two years' data for high-tax payers shows that:

- Pareto's law broke down, and the distribution deviated from a power law;
- Gibrat's law also broke down, as shown in Figure 3.15; and
- detailed balance did not hold.

That is to say, while the laws and balance hold under relatively stable circumstances, they can break down in the presence of drastic changes in the macro-economic environment (see also Aoyama *et al.*, 2004).

This observation completes our description of the phenomenology of fluctuation.

3.2.3 Side story: public notice of high-tax payers, and lost data in Japan
From 1947 to 2005, Japan required a legal public notice of income, in accord with the Income Tax Law, the initial purpose of which was 'to reduce tax evasion through

public notice of high-tax payers' incomes, allowing them to be checked by independent agents'. (Later, publication was justified on the grounds that it gave publicity to those making large contributions to society.) Indeed, for a while after taking effect, information providers who revealed tax-dodgers were offered rewards depending on the amount involved in the tax evasion. The Income Tax Law, Article 233, required that income-earners 'give notice to the public of the names, addresses and amount of income tax of the taxpayers whose income tax exceeds ¥10 million', and also the Ordinance of Enforcement 106 in the Tax Law states that 'the relevant district director must post the notice by displaying it at the posting area in the district or at a public area within the district'.

This law, which was presumably quite unusual in world terms, could potentially have infringed privacy, or assisted criminals in finding targets, since the names, addresses and tax amounts were posted every May in front of tax offices all over the country. After considerable dispute the law was abandoned in 2006, partly because of the weakening of the initial purpose, the prevention of tax evasion, as well as because of the newly passed Privacy Law.

While the problems of privacy encroachment and criminal risk were clear and hardly debatable, the data are, nevertheless, of remarkable intellectual value. Without it, it would not have been possible to reveal the personal income distribution for the entire range of incomes or conduct an investigation of individual growth-rates. Indeed, Japanese economists have benefited significantly from the existence of this and other datasets concerning socio-economic inequality, and when presenting the results at international conferences we have observed that colleagues are as surprised by the existence of the data as they are by the results.

Indeed, in the high-income region the tax data are exhaustive, which is not the case in most datasets examined since Pareto. For example, the well-known economist D. G. Champernowne was advised by J. M. Keynes to study personal income for his thesis, and proposed a stochastic model to explain the distribution, which describes the transition of an individual's income from one moment to another, and thus the growth process (see Champernowne, 1973 for details; also Mandelbrot, 1997, ch. E11). However, to the best of our knowledge, there has been no work that directly observes the process, and such an investigation has been regarded as a formidable task up until the present time.

The Pareto distribution and its index, the distribution of growth-rates, are matters of interest not only for economists examining the skewed distribution of high-income earners and the origin of this phenomenon in terms of growth, but also for tax administrators aiming to maintain government tax revenue and manage the associated risk.

Furthermore, it should be remarked that the data serve as a tool for measuring 'social disparity', since the tail of the Pareto region and its quantification is complementary to the well-known Gini coefficient described in subsection 2.4.1. Let us recall the way in which the long tail of the distribution is stretched towards the high-income side. If we take readily available data published by the Japanese National Tax Authority, as with the tabulated data in other developed countries, we find a single point for the total number of high-income earners (above a few tens of millions of yen in the Japanese case).

One of the present authors raised this issue with a member of the Japanese Government's Tax Commission. Since the abolition of the law requiring the publication of tax data this material is no longer available, and while personal privacy is a critical concern, it should not become an excuse for ceasing to think about the issue. Perhaps the government could have improved the law instead of abandoning it. We can agree that the precise relation between a particular taxpayer and the exact amount of income tax is merely intrusive gossip, but it might be argued that publication and scientific analysis of the stretched long tail of personal income distribution and its changes over time is in the public interest. It would be interesting to know how readers react to this matter.

3.3 Small and medium-sized companies

3.3.1 Large-scale data for small and medium-sized enterprises

We have so far focused only on larger companies in Japan and in Europe, and, as explained in the preceding section, the Pareto region is dominated by a few giant companies forming a large proportion of the aggregated quantities of size, so the dynamics of these firms are obviously important. However, of equal importance are the many dwarfs, the small and medium-sized enterprises, which form the majority of companies.

One of the primary concerns of financial institutions is to determine a reasonable interest rate in financing a large number of small and medium-sized companies. The provision of a quantitative and statistical evaluation of financial risks for such a number of financial entities requires the public availability of a large-scale dataset covering those companies and firms in exhaustive detail.

The Credit Risk Database (CRD) for Japan was founded in 2001 as a membership organisation to collect financial and non-financial data, including default information, on 'small and medium enterprises' (SMEs). In 2005 it was renamed the CRD Association. The purpose of establishing the CRD was to promote the streamlining and efficiency of SME financing by assessing their business conditions on the basis of data gathered by measuring credit risks related to SME financing. As the membership and data collection expanded, the CRD established itself as an infrastructural basis for the gathering and provision of SME data. These data are provided by commercial banks, government-affiliated financial institutions, and the National Federation of Credit Guarantee Corporations, which collects information from more than a million SMEs across the country.

For the purposes of our discussion we accept the definition of SMEs set out in the Small and Medium Enterprise Basic Law. If the company's stated capital or number of employees is less than a threshold specified by the law, the company is said to be an SME, the exact threshold depending on the business sector to which the company

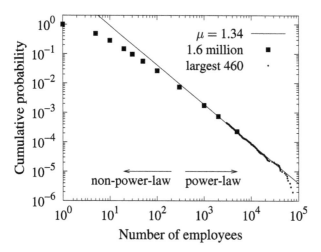

Figure 3.16. Cumulative distribution for company size measured by number of employees (whole range; year 2001).

belongs. For the manufacturing sector, companies with less than ¥300 million of capital or 300 employees are SMEs. For wholesale businesses the level is set at ¥100 million of capital or 100 employees, while for retailers the threshold is ¥50 million or 50 employees. Service industries with less than ¥50 million or 100 employees are classified as SMEs.

Figure 3.16 depicts the cumulative distribution of company size (number of employees) for the whole range where data are available, based on the Establishment and Enterprise Census (Ministry of Internal Affairs and Communications) in the fiscal year 2001, and also on an exhaustive list of the largest 460 companies (provided by a credit research agency). The tail of the distribution will by now be familiar, since it is the Pareto region where a power law applies. A deviation from the power law can be observed in the region of smaller enterprises, with a qualitative change occurring round about the 200 to 300 employee point. The CRD, therefore, covers the non-power-law region as well as the Pareto region, irrespective, for the most part, of the business sector, on which the criterion in the data is dependent. This is ideal for the following study.

3.3.2   Size dependence of growth
At this point we turn to examine the growth-rate and distribution for the stock variables of total assets and debt, and for the flow variable of sales. We can expect the character of fluctuation in the non-power-law region and its transition to the power law, to differ from that considered in section 3.1 where we examined the power-law regime, and our purpose in this chapter is to demonstrate that difference (see Fujiwara *et al.*, 2006a,b for more details).

We will create eight bins, in the same way that we did for large companies in sub-section 3.1.1, divided by logarithmically equal intervals from ¥10 million to ¥1 billion

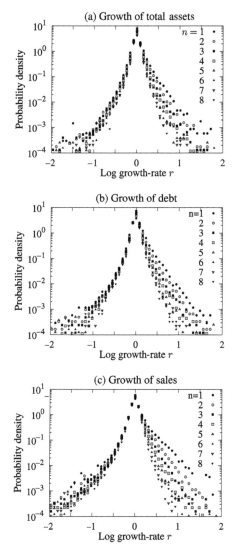

Figure 3.17. Probability distribution for growth-rates of small and medium companies: (a) total assets (b) debt (c) sales (years 2001/2000).

for each of total assets, debt and sales. We can then calculate the PDFs for the logarithmic growth-rate r conditioned by the size of each bin. The results are shown in Figure 3.17.

Immediately, we can see that *Gibrat's law does not hold*, as it is evident that for each of the PDFs the distribution for the growth-rate varies according to the bin or the size. Noting that the indices $n = 1, \ldots, 8$ are numbered in order from smaller to larger sizes, the PDFs show that the typical variation in the growth-rate's distribution becomes smaller, as is plain for the cases of larger companies.

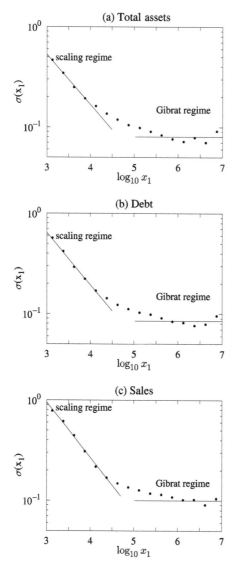

Figure 3.18. Relation between company size and variance of growth-rate for small and medium companies: (a) total assets (b) debt (c) sales (years 2001/2000).

To quantify this fact, we can calculate the variance σ of the growth-rate distribution, which reveals that the initial size x_1 is the controlling variable, as shown in Figure 3.18. This dependence can be expressed quantitatively as a scaling relation:

$$\sigma \text{ is proportional to } x_1^{-\beta}.$$

Here β is a constant whose value is close to 0.5.

It appears that there is a threshold below which the variance in the growth-rate decreases for the larger size of companies, and above which the growth-rate does not change, and Gibrat's law holds. Moreover, the threshold marking the transition of these two phases may differ depending on the variable chosen, i.e. total assets, debt, sales etc.

In summary, we observe from our study of the growth-rate of companies and firms that:

- there is a size below which Gibrat's law does not hold, implying that there is a 'natural kind' of 'small and medium-sized companies', as opposed to a merely legal definition;
- the variance in the distribution for the growth-rate of small and medium-sized companies has a scaling relation with respect to company size, and the scaling relation is of real significance in a quantitative analysis of credit risk management.

3.4 Companies' bankruptcy

3.4.1 Companies' activity and bankruptcy

We so far have talked mainly about the growth of companies, but in fact the activities of companies have, in the abstract, three facets: (1) obtaining finance from financial institutions, markets and investors; (2) investing money to add value to materials and services in anticipation of future return of profit; and (3) collecting the realised profit from the sales minus costs.

However, the flip sides of these activities imply (1) the presence of creditors other than the company's investors; (2) the risk of the loss of invested money; because (3) the profit is necessarily uncertain.

The increase or decrease of stock variables or growth in a company's activities is associated with two aspects of money flow, namely, where the money comes from and goes to, and how it does so.

The idea of double-entry bookkeeping is to describe these aspects of a company's activity (see Pratt, 2008, for example). As is well known, the balance sheet (B/S) describes stock variables, while the profit and loss (P/L) account describes flow variables.[18] The left-hand side (the debit column) records the state of money in terms of where it goes to and how it is used, while the right-hand side (the credit column) describes the cause of an increase or a decrease of money in terms of where it comes from and how it is financed.

The basic ingredients in a B/S are

- *assets* (left): funds in a business which are considered likely to bring about a future increase of the company's fund
- *liabilities* (right): debts which provide a temporary increase of funds at the moment but will cause a future decrease of funds when they are returned to the creditors

---

[18] An additional book describes cash flow, which enables the observer to understand the causes of increase and decrease in a company's money.

- *capital* (right): assets *minus* liabilities, by definition, which is the share of the company's stockholders. This consists of the stockholders' investment and retained earnings arising from the flow of profit.

The ingredients in the P/L are

- *costs* (left): money used to gain profit, including the purchase of intermediate materials and services, labour costs and various other costs
- *profit* (right): revenue *minus* costs
- *revenue* (right): increase of the company's money arising from value added that was generated in the activity of production.

A change in the stock is equal to the flow, and, usually speaking, profit increases the capital as retained earnings. Also, additional investment by stockholders increases the capital. On the other hand, borrowing from financial institutions and markets, such as bonds, increases the liabilities or debts.

Suppose that the company has negative capital, that is the state of debts exceeding assets, then the company will have difficulty in returning the money borrowed from creditors. This is the state of *negative net worth*. A flow of profit can bring about the possible resolution of this critical state, but more probably the company will be plagued with serious funding problems and run out of capital.

Bankruptcy is a general term referring to the process by which a company falls into the state of financial insolvency as a debtor. It is classified by legal and private procedures, namely, suspension of bank transactions, corporate reorganisation and rehabilitation, a procedure for liquidation, etc. Specifically, in Japan, two note-payment defaults made by a company within six months force all transactions of the company to be suspended. More generally, a bankruptcy refers to a malfunction of a company's activities due to a critical problem of funding in one form or another.

3.4.2 Lifetime and debt at bankruptcy

In section 5.3, we will describe the ways in which one can model the dynamics of a balance sheet, but at this point we will pause to examine the phenomenology of the process of bankruptcy, using exhaustive Japanese data (see Fujiwara, 2004 for more details).

Since 1990, the annual number of bankruptcies has varied from 10,000 to 20,000, as shown in Figure 3.19 by the continuous graph (see the right-hand axis), while the total number of companies in Japan is approximately 2 million.[19] Bankruptcy statistics are obtained from the organisation Small & Medium Enterprises and Regional Innovation in Japan (SMRJ). The figure shows bars representing the total debts of bankrupted companies across the country, varying from ¥10 trillion to ¥25 trillion, as shown on the left-hand axis (see also Fujiwara, 2008).

---

[19] The number is from the National Tax Agency's Statistical Survey. There are two other major sources of statistics, the Ministry of Internal Affairs and Communications' Establishment and Enterprise Census, and the Ministry of Justice's records on the entry and exit of companies. These statistics are said to have under- or over-estimation problems arising from, for example, the counting of non-active companies etc.

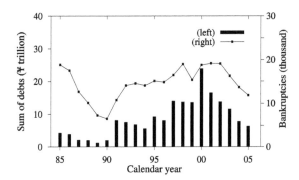

Figure 3.19. Annual number of bankruptcies in Japan and total sum of resulting debts (1985 to 2005; calendar years).

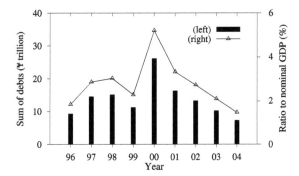

Figure 3.20. Annual sum of debts when bankrupted, and ratio to nominal GDP (1996 to 2004; fiscal years).

From data on the total debt in fiscal years, the quantity of debt involved in each year's bankruptcies is more than 2 per cent of the nominal GDP in the year, as can be seen in the continuous graph in Figure 3.20 (right-hand axis). Of course, not all the debts are lost, since some are partially repaid to creditors, who are eligible to receive a portion of the credit from the bankrupted debtor depending on a ratio determined by the types of bankruptcy and how the creditors are situated. It should, however, be noted that a very large sum of money is at risk every year in Japan; there is no reason to suppose that this is not the case in other countries too.

This point deserves serious consideration, since the distribution for company size when bankrupted, and accordingly that for the amount of debt, has a heavy tail, implying that a giant bankruptcy can occur with a non-negligible probability. Indeed, with the help of an exhaustive list of bankruptcies with debts of ¥10 million or more in the year 1997, essentially covering all the domestic bankruptcies, the distribution for the debt of 16,000 bankrupted companies can be depicted in Figure 3.21.

To assist the naked eye, a dotted line corresponding to the Pareto distribution with index $\mu = 0.9$ is drawn on the figure. The result shows that in the wide range of debt larger than ¥500 million, *debt when bankrupted obeys Pareto's law for the tail of the*

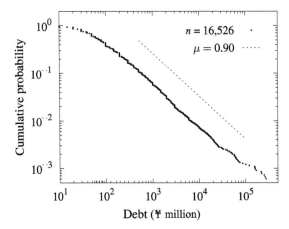

Figure 3.21. Cumulative distribution for debt when bankrupted (approximately 16,000 companies bankrupted with debts larger than ¥10 million in 1997).

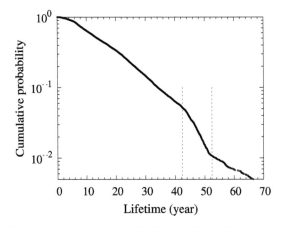

Figure 3.22. Cumulative distribution for lifetime before bankruptcy (approximately 16,000 companies bankrupted with debts larger than ¥10 million in 1997).

distribution. Moreover, for those large bankruptcies, we can calculate the ratio $A = d/s$ between the sales s and the debt d immediately before the bankruptcy. Interestingly, the distribution $p(A)$ is statistically independent of the size s. It follows from this observation that the distribution $p(s)$ for company size s and the distribution $p(d)$ for its debt d are compatible with each other, and obey the Pareto distribution with approximately the same Pareto index. Pareto's laws for company size and for debt when bankrupted are consistent in this sense.

We can also examine the lifetime of a company before bankruptcy, by studying the time elapsing between the establishment of the company and its financial collapse. Figure 3.22 depicts the cumulative distribution of the lifetime, and shows that it is an approximately *exponential distribution*. Note that the abscissa in the figure is linear.

If we were to estimate the typical time before company death from the age at the cumulative probability of 10 per cent (or 10^{-1}), we would arrive at the figure of roughly thirty years. Incidentally, if we look back through the forty-five-year era before 1997, the time-scale involved in the survival process of companies changes drastically within a ten-year period. This corresponds to the dissolution of the corporate-alliances monopoly, a measure enacted during the government of US General Headquarters (from 1945 to 1952), during which a large number of new companies entered the market, as proved by a mathematical argument.

3.5   The production function and ridge theory

3.5.1   The production function
The activities of companies are primarily aimed at earning profits from sales, after spending and investing money on inputs of labour and capital. How do companies determine the amounts of inputs to invest?

Suppose that a company can produce an amount Y from certain amounts of capital K and labour L. The relation between the inputs and the output is the *production function* (see Varian, 2005, for example).

As early as the spring of 1928, the economist P. H. Douglas had analysed a plot of data for capital, labour and production, and got into difficulties. Seeking a reasonable function to fit the data, he discussed with his friend, the mathematician C. W. Cobb, and together they proposed a function of this form:

$$Y = F(L, K) = AK^\alpha L^\beta,$$

which today is known as the Cobb–Douglas production function (Cobb and Douglas, 1928). Here A is a constant of proportionality, and α and β are the selectable parameters. In the special case for which $\alpha + \beta = 1$, the production function can be written as

$$F(L, K) = AL \left(\frac{K}{L}\right)^\alpha = Lf(x), \quad x \equiv \frac{K}{L}.$$

This states that the production function is an *extensive* quantity, to use the terminology of statistical mechanics. That is to say, if a physical system can be analysed by thermodynamics and statistical mechanics then it is possible to calculate its macroscopic state variables. If these state variables do not depend on the system's size they are called *intensive*, while those depending on the size are called *extensive*. Examples of intensive quantities include pressure P and temperature T, while the extensive quantities are internal energy U, volume of the system V, entropy S, and so forth (see Callen, 1985, for example).

Now, managers in companies make decisions on allocating inputs between labour and capital; they could, for instance, purchase new machines for factories and, at the same time, reduce employment. The intention in such a case is to increase efficiency in production by augmenting the reduction of labour with the increase of capital.

Economists often express the allocation between capital and labour as a 'substitution between capital and labour'. The measure used to quantify the extent of this activity is the elasticity of substitution denoted by σ. In the case of the Cobb–Douglas production function, $\sigma = 1$. In fact, there are different views on the substitution between capital and labour. For example, the economist W. Leontief (1941) claimed that there is no substitution between them in company production. This claim amounts to saying that the level of production is determined by the minimum of capital or labour. This corresponds to $\sigma = 0$, which is quite the contrary to the Cobb–Douglas case.

These views might be regarded as too extreme, and, in 1961, the economist K. J. Arrow, with his collaborators, interpolated between the extremes of Cobb–Douglas and Leontief, and proposed a production function called CES (constant elasticity of substitution) (Arrow *et al.*, 1961). In this case $\sigma = 0 \sim 1$. The CES production function includes a special case of perfect substitutes, which is expressed by

$$F(L, K) = A \{\delta L + (1 - \delta)K\},$$

where δ is a constant. The set of all possible combinations of capital and labour which are sufficient to produce a given amount of output is defined simply by linear combinations of K and L.

Yet another new proposal for the production function followed in the literature, suggesting that the elasticity of substitution is a constant for all the cases of Cobb–Douglas, Leontief and CES. Generalisation of this is clearly possible to allow elasticity, and is given by some function of capital and labour. A well-known example of this kind of production function is the one proposed by L. R. Christensen *et al.* (1973) under the name of the transcendental logarithmic production function.

There are still other types than those we have seen so far, but with different numbers of parameters included in the definition of the production function. There is as yet no decisive answer as to which is best, partly because it is trivial to achieve a better fit to data with a larger number of parameters, though one could attempt to obtain an answer by employing some sophisticated technique developed in statistics.

For example, if we take data for about a thousand companies listed in the first sector of the Tokyo Stock Exchange in 2004, we find that the Cobb–Douglas production function has a relatively better fit than others, with the resulting parameters satisfying $\alpha + \beta = 1.02$, which implies that the production function is extensive. For the same dataset we find that $\alpha = 0.121$ and $\log A = 0.081$, so, for our purpose here, we content ourselves by observing the validity of the extensive claim, and adopt the Cobb–Douglas production function in what follows.

3.5.2 *Ridge theory for companies' growth*

The problem now facing us is to explain the behaviour of the population of companies through their attempts to maximise profits. In addressing this matter we shall focus on the production function, as described above, and examine the distribution of companies in the space of (L, K).

We will start by considering profits. A company usually pays for the cost of its capital, K, in various forms, which we summarise here by an interest rate r. Also the company has to compensate for the labour, L, of its employees. Thus the profit Π is given by

$$\Pi = F(L, K) - rK - L.$$

(Here the quantity of labour L is measured in a unit of currency, say dollars, rather than in terms of a number.) Now, the company operates under various constraints in making decisions. This can be revealed by an attempt to maximise the profit in the above equation by choosing the amounts of capital K and labour L. We call this strategy *profit maximisation with respect to all the factors of production*.

In fact, we can prove that profit maximisation with respect to all the factors simply does not work if the production function is an extensive quantity, as shown in the preceding section. Actually, the calculation for the maximisation with respect to all the factors results in an interest rate r which is equal to 20 per cent or so, which is unrealistic by an order of magnitude. That is to say, companies could not in reality accept such high interest rates and gain positive profits. (See the box below on 'Extensivity and maximisation of profit' for further exposition.)

If profit maximisation with respect to all factors is unrealistic, how can the present framework enable us to understand the basic strategy of companies intending to earn profits? An obvious possibility is that, for one reason or another, a company can only change its amount of capital relatively slowly. We could then reasonably ask if it is possible to maximise profit by only changing the labour L, while maintaining a fixed capital K. One can determine, under the validity of an extensive production function, the ratio $x = K/L$, if we assume the interest rate is given by the average for the companies. Clearly, another possibility is that a company may have difficulties in changing the labour input, but can easily control the amount of capital. Also, in this case, the ratio x can be determined by maximisation. (The calculations for these two methods of maximisation is explained in the following box.)

$\boxed{\alpha_\beta^\gamma}$ **Extensivity and maximisation of profit**

As has already been noted, the extensive nature of the production function can be expressed in the way that the function is written as

$$F(L, K) = Lf(x),$$

where $x = K/L$. Putting this into the profit equation, we have

$$\Pi = L(f(x) - rx - 1) \equiv L\pi(x).$$

Here we use the notation $\pi(x) = f(x) - rx - 1$.

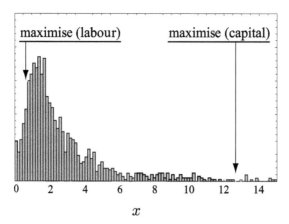

Figure 3.23. Distribution of company's x and two values of x at which profit is maximised under different constraints.

Profit maximisation with respect to all the factors of production implies that the profit Π is maximised with respect to K and also with respect to L. The maximisation for K can be written as

$$0 = \left.\frac{\partial \Pi}{\partial K}\right|_L = \frac{1}{L}\left.\frac{\partial \Pi}{\partial x}\right|_L = \pi'(x).$$

And the maximisation for L can be put as

$$0 = \left.\frac{\partial \Pi}{\partial L}\right|_K = \left.\frac{\partial \Pi}{\partial L}\right|_x + \left.\frac{\partial x}{\partial L}\right|_K \left.\frac{\partial \Pi}{\partial x}\right|_L = \pi(x) - x\pi'(x).$$

To maximise profit with all the factors of production, it suffices to require both of these conditions. As a consequence, it follows that $\pi(x) = 0$, and equivalently $\Pi = 0$, i.e. that the profit is zero at maximum, so is negative elsewhere, a state of deficit. Also, the value for r is determined by two conditions, as noted in the main body of text.

If either L or K is fixed, and the non-fixed variable is changed to maximise the profit, only one of the two conditions is required, so we can avoid the non-sensical solution of vanishing profit. In this case, if we assume the value of r, x can be determined by one of the two conditions. The values are illustrated in Figure 3.23.

Figure 3.23 shows the consequence of our prediction for the ratio x which can be compared with the actual distribution for x. The actual values are concentrated mostly from 1 to 2, with the peak of the distribution located approximately at 1.5. On the other hand, the ratios calculated by maximisation with respect to either capital or labour differ considerably from the peak. A trivial consequence of this observation is that

Figure 3.24. Mountain view with a ridge.

companies fix neither capital nor labour, but change both to some degree in seeking profits, so the actual x values are scattered mostly between the two extremes.

Of course, it must be admitted that this overly rough conclusion gives us little insight into any mathematically useful understanding of company production, even if we understand the properties of the production function. At this point we may wonder whether any further progress is possible in understanding the distribution of x? The answer is yes, but the key to this matter resides in *ridge theory*.

To understand the concept of a 'ridge', think of a mountain climber. A company aiming at larger profits is like a climber attempting to reach a point further up the mountain. Consider the terrain illustrated in Figure 3.24. This terrain includes a ridge or a long area of high land towards the top of the mountain. Suppose you are a climber standing somewhere in this terrain and want to get to a higher place as efficiently as you can. Your best bet is to take the steepest route from the place at which you are standing. Figure 3.25 draws the climber in enlargement. The direction A is the steepest ascent, B and D are two directions with no gradient and C is the steepest descent. The directions A, C are perpendicular to contours, while the directions B, D are tangential to contours. You will walk in the direction A, perpendicularly to contours, so along the steepest-ascent line, and will eventually reach the ridge, along which you will head for the mountain's top. Some climbers may be distracted and deviate from the most efficient path, yet, after a while, all climbers will end up on the ridge.

We can expect from this analogy that the companies will be distributed along the ridge in the terrain of profit. Finding the ridge in our case is a non-trivial task. In the terrain depicted in Figure 3.24 the ridge can be easily identified by eye, but the profit has a gentle terrain, as shown in Figure 3.26. (Note that this figure shows the surface only for a positive profit. The white and flat segment near the axis of L is where the profit is negative and below the horizontal plane, i.e. it corresponds to a state of deficit.) How can we find the ridge in this terrain? The answer is to use a ridge equation, that is

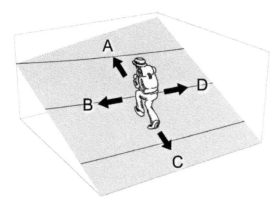

Figure 3.25. A mountain-climber and his or her directions.

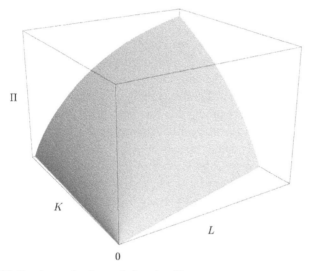

Figure 3.26. Landscape for the profit function Π.

to say an equation which defines the ridge as a curve connecting points, each of which gives the least gradient among the steepest-ascent directions on the contour where the point is located. Details of the equation determining the ridge are given in the box below. By solving the ridge equation, one can find the ridge in any terrain.

The actual solution of the ridge equation for Figure 3.26 is depicted in the contour plot of Figure 3.27, where higher places are represented by a lighter tone, and dashed lines are 'steepest-ascent lines', which an efficient climber would take at each point in the terrain. It is clear that these steepest-ascent lines are perpendicular to the contour lines, and it should also be noted that these lines converge asymptotically into the curve of the ridge, depicted by a dotted line. Our proposition is that the profit-seeking behaviour of companies can be described by this picture.

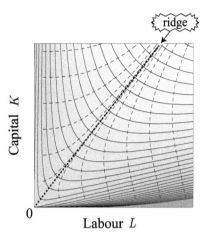

Figure 3.27. Contour lines, steepest-ascent lines and a ridge for the profit landscape of Figure 3.26.

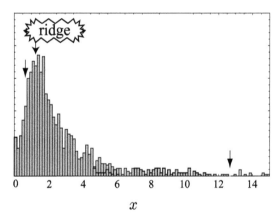

Figure 3.28. Distribution of company's x (Figure 3.23) and the solution of x corresponding to the ridge.

If the production function satisfies the property of extensivity, the ridge equation determines the ratio x. Consequently, the curve of the ridge is actually a line, as shown in Figure 3.27. If we add this value of x to our previous plot for the distribution of x, Figure 3.23, we have Figure 3.28. We can see that the peak in the distribution is located close to the ridge. Of course, the distribution of x is spread around and centred on the ridge, and this can be understood from the fact that the ridge is the place to which the steepest-ascent lines asymptotically approach, but do not cross, and that companies are presumably subject to swings and distracting bounces for various endogenous and exogenous reasons. We conclude, therefore, that one can model such fluctuations in a stochastic formulation, and make a bridging explanation to assist in understanding the distribution of companies.

In conclusion, we have seen in this section that the quantitative analysis of the production function offers considerable insight into the distribution of companies and their strategies, and leads us to a more complete picture of the statistical universe of companies. In the next chapter we will try to add colour to this picture by drawing on the theory of business networks among companies.

αβγ   **Ridge equation**

To write down a ridge equation in a general form, it would be more comprehensive to consider n variables, ϕ_i ($i = 1, 2, \ldots, n$), for the function of profit Π. This is so although what we actually need to consider is the case $(\phi_1, \phi_2) = (L, K)$, in two dimensions ($n = 2$).

In this notation, the ridge equation can be given by

$$\sum_{j=1}^{n} \frac{\partial^2 \Pi}{\partial \phi_i \phi_j} \frac{\partial \Pi}{\partial \phi_j} = \lambda \frac{\partial \Pi}{\partial \phi_i}.$$

Mathematically, this is an eigenvalue equation for the second derivative of Π, and the eigenvalue λ is a parameter on the curve of the ridge solution. That is, for a given λ (in an appropriate range), the solution of the ridge equation gives a set of co-ordinates $(\phi_1, \phi_2, \ldots, \phi_n)$, or a point in the space, the location of which varies by changing the value of λ, resulting in the curve of a ridge.

The above equation can also be interpreted as an extremisation of the length of the gradient vector $(\partial \Pi/\partial \phi)$ under the constraint that $\Pi = $ constant, which is easily proved by the argument of the 'Lagrange multiplier'. From the solutions of the ridge equation we need to choose the minimum of the extreme values in this argument, which correspond to the ridge.

Note that ridge and steepest-ascent line are different concepts. A steepest-ascent line is along the gradient or the direction perpendicular to the contours. In other words, since it is necessarily obtained by requiring that it be parallel to the gradient vectors, a steepest-ascent line is defined by the differential equation:

$$\frac{d\phi_i(s)}{ds} = \frac{\partial \Pi}{\partial \phi_i} \quad (i = 1, 2, \ldots, n).$$

Here s is a parameter on the line of steepest ascent. This is a differential equation with respect to the spatial co-ordinates $(\phi_1, \phi_2, \ldots, \phi_n)$, with an arbitrary choice of initial values for those coordinates. Thus we have an infinite number of steepest-ascent lines for choices of initial values. The dashed lines in Figure 3.27 are drawn by solving this equation for different choices of initial values. See Aoyama and Kikuchi (1992) and Aoyama et al. (1999).

4 Complex business networks

Perhaps everyone has asked themselves whether there is anything in the universe that is perfectly isolated, separate and complete within itself. Some will answer that the universe itself is the only thing, because the universe alone is unique. However, the physics of elementary particles and cosmology suggests the possibility that many universes similar to our universe exist and interact with each other through quantum gravity.

The appearance of a discussion of the universe or universes in a book on economic theory may seem abrupt and even odd, but if we recast the point in terms that are more familiar it will not seem so peculiar. When strangers meet by chance, at a party or on a train for example, it is not uncommon for them to find that they have shared acquaintances. 'It's a small world!', they will exclaim, in genuine surprise. In fact, this happens all the time, so it is not so much the frequency that stimulates our wonder, but the reasons which underlie it, and these are the subject of long-standing and unsolved questions.

In an attempt to shed light on this matter, sociologists have conducted many kinds of experiments, and needless to say this attempt requires an understanding of human networks. However, it is just as important to extend our outlook and to consider the more abstract and far-reaching question: 'What is a network?' In other words, when we cannot solve a problem in a particular and special case, we can sometimes gain insight by generalising. Networks are just such a case.

The history of the train of thought grounded in this viewpoint is not long; indeed, it started only very recently under the name of *network science*, and is making remarkable progress (Watts, 1999, 2003; Barabási, 2003; Buchanan, 2003; Caldarelli, 2007). In the next section, we provide a brief introduction to this new field.

4.1 Introduction to network science

The origin of network science is *graph theory* in mathematics, *social network analysis* in sociology, *statistical mechanics* in physics, and computer science. Historically, graph theory came first, with its origin being Euler's solution of the Königsberg bridge problem in 1736. Subsequently, the theory was developed by various figures of great distinction: Pólya, Erdős and others.

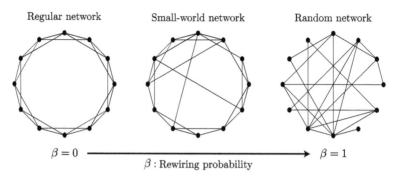

Figure 4.1. Watts–Strogatz β model.

A graph is constructed from *dots* and *lines*. In network science, a dot is called a *node* or a *vertex*, and a line is called an *edge* or a *link*. In this book, we use the terms 'node' and 'link', except in certain special cases. In addition, we use the terms 'graph' and 'network' interchangeably.

The field of graph theory has concentrated its investigation on *regular networks*, *trees* and *random networks*. A regular network has nodes with equal numbers of links, and these nodes are connected in a regular fashion. The left-hand panel of Figure 4.1 shows an example of a regular network. In this figure, each node has four links, and these links connect each node with its two nearest neighbours, both right and left. Hence, in a regular network, every node is equal and there is no special node. A tree is a graph which does not contain *loops*, and its topology is the same as that of trees and rivers in the real world. A random network, on the other hand, is constructed by connecting nodes completely at random. The right-hand panel of Figure 4.1 shows an example of a random network.[1] Graph theory proved various theorems for these networks, but the instances it investigated were quite different from real-world networks, for example social networks.

Social network analysis in sociology has experienced two revolutionary developments, the first in the 1930s, and the second from the 1960s to the 1970s (Freeman, 2004). Between these two revolutionary developments, Stanley Milgram famously tried three times to measure the size of the real social world experimentally (Milgram, 1967), and consequently his name is strongly associated with the terms 'small-world', and 'six degrees of separation'. However, there are many sociologists who do not accept Milgram's interpretation of his experiments, and some sociologists have asked whether the real world is actually small or not. In contrast with graph theory, social network analysis has investigated networks in the real world, but the size of networks considered is comparatively small, not exceeding the order of 10^3.

However, recently, several sets of network data have become available as readily accessed computerised databases, for example, the gigantic network of the Internet

---

[1] Strictly speaking, that shown here is a Watts–Strogatz random network, one of several classes of random networks.

itself, a development which switched the focus of study from small to large networks. It was in this context that Watts and Strogatz published their seminal paper in *Nature*, and so shaped network science as we currently know it (Watts and Strogatz, 1998). The paper introduced the concepts of *averaged path length* and the *clustering coefficient* to characterise networks.

 Milgram's positivism

 Milgram is often thought to be one of the most influential psychologists of the twentieth century, less for 'six degrees of separation' than for the notorious 'obedience to authority' experiment, in which naive subjects were given apparent control over the application of, in fact false, electronic shocks to a third person. The purpose was to investigate our capacity to commit inhumane acts when legitimated by a person in authority.

The result of the experiment suggested that almost all of us, independent of socioeconomic status and sex, are capable of great cruelty if authorised, a result that was contradictory to the preliminary expectations of many psychologists and caused a sensation in 1963 when the paper was published.

As is clear from this experiment, Milgram's approach to science was to proceed *empirically* without relying unduly on plausible but weakly grounded discussion and prejudice. In our investigation of the relation of economy and society, Milgram's attitude will be one of our guiding principles.

The averaged path length is the average number of links which connect a pair of randomly selected nodes by the *shortest path*. Let us denote the number of links which are necessary to connect nodes i and j by the shortest path as l_{ij}. By using l_{ij}, we can calculate, for node i, the mean value of the shortest path, L_i. Thus, the average path length, L, of the network is given by the average value of L_i, i.e.

$$L_i := \frac{1}{N-1} \sum_{j \neq i} l_{ij}, \qquad L := \frac{1}{N} \sum_{i=1}^{N} L_i.$$

where N is the total number of nodes.

If three nodes are connected with each other, e.g. if two of my friends are also friends with each other, this configuration forms a triangle, which we will call a *cluster*. The *clustering coefficient* quantifies the cliqueyness of nodes, and is given by the probability of finding triangles in the network. If the node i has k_i links, the number of possible triangles is given by the number of combinations in which two nodes can be selected from k_i nodes, i.e. $C(k_i, 2) = k_i(k_i - 1)/2$. However, in a real network, only a fraction of these possible combinations is accomplished. The clustering coefficient of node i,

C_i, is defined by dividing the number of actual clusters, E_i, by the number of possible clusters. Thus, the clustering coefficient of the network, C, is given by

$$C_i := \frac{2E_i}{k_i(k_i - 1)}, \quad C := \frac{1}{N}\sum_{i=1}^{N} C_i,$$

i.e. it is the average value of C_i. (See the box below.) By convention, $C_i = 0$ for the trivial cases $k_i = 0$ or 1.

Watts and Strogatz calculated the average path length L and the clustering coefficient C for the collaboration graph of actors in feature films, the electrical power grid of the western United States and the neural network of the nematode worm, *C. elegans* (Watts and Strogatz, 1998). Their results suggested that these networks have both the short average path length that is characteristic of random networks (see the box 'Poisson random network' below) and a large clustering coefficient that is characteristic of regular networks (see the box 'Regular network' below). They referred to networks with this combination of characteristics as *small-world networks* (see the box 'Small-world network' below).

$\boxed{\alpha\beta\gamma}$ **Global clustering coefficient**

We can define another type of clustering coefficient called a global clustering coefficient, which differs from the clustering coefficient defined in the main text. The global clustering coefficient is defined by

$$C_{\text{global}} = \frac{3 \times (\text{number of triangles in the network})}{\text{number of connected triplets of nodes}}.$$

If 'Mr A' has two friends, 'Mr B' and 'Mr C', we refer to this configuration as a connected triplet of nodes, and denote it as 'B-A-C' (or 'C-A-B'). Additionally, if 'Mr B' and 'Mr C' are also friends with each other, we can construct the triangle $\triangle ABC$. This triangle contains three connected triplets of nodes, i.e. A-B-C, B-C-A, C-A-B. The factor of 3 in the above equation makes $C_{\text{global}} = 1$ in this situation.

Incidentally, C_i is explained in the main text as being equivalent to the probability that the friends of node i are also friends with each other, and where C is the averaged value of this probability. On the other hand, C_{global} gives the probability that a randomly selected triplet forms a triangle. C and C_{global} generally have different values (Newman, 2003c). One must be careful which definition of the clustering coefficient is applied in any particular case.

The right-hand panel of Figure 4.1 is an example of a random network, and shows that only a few links connect pairs of randomly selected nodes, and also that there is a low probability of finding triangles. Thus, a random network has a short average path length and a small clustering coefficient. On the other hand, the left-hand panel of Figure 4.1 is an example of a regular network. Contrary to a random network, this figure shows that two randomly selected nodes are connected by many links, and that the probability of finding triangles is high. Hence, a regular network has a long average path length and a large clustering coefficient.

Watts and Strogatz also proposed a so-called β *model*, which aims to answer the *small-world problem*, as discussed in the sociology literature (Watts and Strogatz, 1998; Watts, 1999). Starting from a ring lattice, shown in the left-hand panel of Figure 4.1, we rewire each edge at random with probability β. Thus, the case of $\beta = 0$ is a regular network. By changing the rewiring probability, β, we can reproduce a small-world network. That is to say, a network with $\beta = 1$ would belong to the class of random networks.[2] The β model suggested that the existence of links corresponding to shortcuts is what turns the real world into a small world.

 Poisson random network

The network proposed by Erdős and Rényi (1960) is another example of a random network, this time one where the probability with which two nodes are connected is constant, θ, and independent of the existence of other links. In this case, we can easily see that by definition the probability, $p(k)$, of finding a node with degree k is given by

$$p(k) = C(N - 1, k)\theta^k(1 - \theta)^{N-1-k},$$

where N is the total number of nodes.

If we take the limit $N \to \infty$ under the constant average degree $\langle k \rangle = N\theta =: z$, we have $p(k) \simeq z^k e^{-z}/k!$, where $k!$ is a factorial of k. Thus, the degree distribution is given by $p(k) \simeq z^k e^{-z}/k!$, which is a Poisson distribution, and the network is a Poisson random network.

In a Poisson random network the average path length L_{rand} and clustering coefficient C_{rand} are given by

$$L_{\text{rand}} \simeq \frac{\log N}{\log z}, \qquad C_{\text{rand}} \simeq \frac{z}{N},$$

respectively (see Bollobás, 1985 and Newman, 2003b, for example). The defining characteristic of a random network is that the average path length is proportional to the logarithm of the network size, namely $\log N$. On the other hand, the clustering coefficient is inversely proportional to the size of network, in other words N.

---

[2] The difference between the random network made by rewiring with $\beta = 1$ and that proposed by Erdős and Rényi (1960) is degree distribution.

A little earlier we said that the paper written by Watts and Strogatz was the first paper on network science, but it might be more accurate to say that the paper turned the key of the door to network science without quite opening it. That honour goes to A.-L. Barabási, whose research group at Notre-Dame University wrote a series of papers in 1999 analysing the structure of the World Wide Web (Albert *et al.*, 1999; Barabási and Albert, 1999). They found that the *degree distribution* of that network follows a *power-law distribution*, and they refer to such networks as *scale-free*. Here, the *degree* is defined by the total number of links held by a node (see the box 'Degree distribution and others'). In subsection 4.5.2, we will show that some economic networks are also scale-free networks.

Scale-free phenomena were first observed in the year 1897 when Pareto found the power-law distribution in the wealth distribution of the rich (see Chapter 2). Scale-free phenomena were also observed in the study of *phase transition* and *critical phenomena*, in Mandelbrot's *fractals* and in the study of *complex systems*, all of which have a long history. Many physicists had been fascinated by these phenomena, and had already studied them for some decades before moving smoothly across to the examination of scale-free networks.

$\boxed{\alpha\beta\gamma}$ **Regular network**

As shown in the left-hand panel of Figure 4.1, a regular network is constructed by regularly arranging nodes with equal numbers of degrees, k_0. In a one-dimensional and regularly linked network the average path length L_{reg} and the clustering coefficient C_{reg} are given by

$$L_{\text{reg}} = \frac{N(N + k_0 - 2)}{2k_0(N - 1)} \simeq \frac{N}{2k_0},$$

$$C_{\text{reg}} = \frac{3(k_0 - 2)}{4(k_0 - 1)},$$

respectively. The defining characteristic of a regular network is that the average path length is proportional to the size of network, namely N. On the other hand, the clustering coefficient is completely independent of the size of the network, and is given by $C_{\text{reg}} \simeq 3/4 = 0.75$, when k_0 is comparatively large. In addition, the degree distribution for a regular network is given by Dirac's δ function, i.e. $p(k) = \delta(k - k_0)$.

Subsequently, many concepts and analytical methods were imported into network science from fields such as biology, life science and sociology. Simultaneously, the number of scientists studying network science increased rapidly, and at present the study of networks is interdisciplinary and integrated. It is also practical.

$\boxed{\alpha_\beta^\gamma}$ **Small-world network**

Watts and Strogatz calculated the averaged path length L_{sw} and the clustering coefficient C_{sw} for some real world networks, and found that many have short average path lengths and large clustering coefficients. That is to say, these quantities satisfy

$$L_{sw} \simeq L_{rand} \ll L_{reg},$$
$$C_{sw} \simeq C_{reg} \gg C_{rand},$$

respectively. At present, networks with these characteristics are referred to as the small-world networks of Watts–Strogatz, or, more simply, small-world networks. In the β model of Watts–Strogatz, the degree distribution changes from Dirac's δ function to the Poisson distribution, by changing the rewiring probability β.

One example of the application of network science to the real world is the concept of *hub* and *authority*, which was introduced by Kleinberg (1999) while studying the Internet. Another is the concept of *PageRank* proposed by Brin and Page (1998),[3] a concept responsible for the beginnings of the *Google* search engine.

$\boxed{\alpha_\beta^\gamma}$ **Degree distribution and others**

Degree is the total number of links held by each node. A node with large degree is called a hub. The degree distribution $p(k)$ is the probability that a randomly selected node in the network has degree k.

Sometimes each hub is connected to every other and sometimes not. The *degree correlation* quantifies the correlation between the degrees of two nodes connected by a link. For example, we can study the joint distribution for a pair of degrees, and calculate their correlation coefficients (see the box 'correlation coefficients' below).

If we use qualitative or quantitative characteristics of nodes (for example, race or age) instead of degree, we can examine what kinds of feature affect the existence of links connecting a pair of nodes. That is to say, if we cut links and connect nodes randomly, we lose information embedded in the characteristics of links; therefore, the correlation between nodal characteristics is useful in determining network character. When the probability of constructing a link between nodes with similar characteristics is higher than that of doing so between nodes with

---

[3] Curiously, 'Page' in the word 'PageRank' refers to the name of its discoverer, not a page of a book or a web page.

differing characteristics, we refer to this as *assortativity* (see Newman, 2003c and references therein).

There are other indices characterising networks, for example the correlation between degree and clustering coefficients, *hierarchical structure* (Barabási and Oltvai, 2004), many kinds of *centralities*, *network motifs* (Milo *et al.*, 2002; Shen-Orr *et al.*, 2002), *network spectrum*, and others.

The development of network science also has connections with changing social conditions. The terrible 11 September attacks have had profound consequences, and there is now widespread fear of terrorist networks spanning the world, a previously uncontemplated diversified type of network. Similarly, epidemics such as SARS, bird flu and swine flu, the expanding virtual Internet society and arguably dwindling relations between individuals have drawn attention to the importance of *understanding the world in terms of complex networks*.

At present the concerns of network science are the study of large networks, new *network indices*,[4] fast algorithms for the calculation of network indices, dynamics in networks, mechanisms for the generation of networks, and the visualisation of networks, among others. In addition, how to apply the results of network science to the real world is also an important problem. In the international conference held in Aveiro, Portugal in 2004, one of the organisers, S. Dorogovtsev, referred to the need to move 'beyond Google'. It will take a long time to apply network science to the real world on a broad scale, but the possibility of that outcome is gradually increasing.

4.2   1, 2, 3, . . . , 6 degrees of separation

We earlier referred to Milgram's 'six degrees of separation', and explained that the β model gives an answer to the small-world problem. Here, we explain the method for calculating the average number of nodes within a given number of degrees of separation for both real-world and theoretical networks. This not only gives another intellectual perspective on small-world phenomena, but also includes an important suggestion towards understanding the connection of nodes in a complex network.

We will start with 'one degree of separation', instead of jumping in at 'six'. In short, a node within one degree of separation is a node directly connecting to an arbitrary node with one link. Therefore, the average number of nodes in one degree of separation is equal to the 'average degree', that is the average number of nodes within one degree of separation. In a complete graph, in which every node is connected to every other node, the average number of nodes equals the total number of nodes minus one. On the other hand, in complex networks the average number of nodes is of order 1. Many social or economic networks are huge, and the range of the total number of nodes is

---

[4] An index characterising a network is called a network index. The previously introduce topics of average path length, clustering coefficient and degree are also network indices.

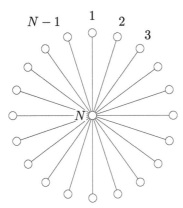

Figure 4.2. A complete graph in which every node is connected to every other within two degrees of separation.

from 10^5 to 10^8 and there is practically no possibility that all nodes can be connected to each other.

Let us now turn to 'two degrees of separation'. In the case of all nodes with an equal degree, k_0, an arbitrary node is connected by k_0 nodes, each of which is connected with $k_0 - 1$ nodes, all except the original node. Thus the number of nodes within two degrees of separation is $k_0(k_0 - 1)$. If we believe that this estimation is correct in the case of a large number of nodes, we might say that the average number of nodes within two degrees of separation is given approximately by

$$\langle k \rangle (\langle k \rangle - 1),$$

by replacing k_0 with the averaged value $\langle k \rangle$. However, this estimation is completely *wrong* as is shown in what follows.

A simple example illustrating this point is shown in Figure 4.2. In this network, the node in the centre of the network is connected to every other node. Thus, the degree of the centre node is $N - 1$, and that of the other $N - 1$ nodes is 1. Hence, the average degree is given by

$$\frac{1 \times (N - 1) + (N - 1) \times 1}{N} = \frac{2(N - 1)}{N} \simeq 2,$$

being approximately equal to 2 for large N. If we substitute this value for our naive estimate for the average number of nodes within two degrees of separation, we get

$$\langle k \rangle (\langle k \rangle - 1) = 2(2 - 1) = 2.$$

However, as is apparent from the figure, all $N - 1$ dead-end nodes are connected with all $N - 2$ dead-end nodes through the centre node within two degrees of separation. (The centre node does not have nodes within two degrees of separation.) Thus, if we calculate the average number of nodes within two degrees of separation, the result is approximately equal to N when N is sufficiently large, which is completely different from the naive estimate obtained above.

Actually, for *general* networks that contain nodes with different degree values, we can calculate the number of nodes within two degrees of separation more precisely. By using the squared average of the degree of nodes $\langle k^2 \rangle$, the result is given by

$$\langle k^2 \rangle - \langle k \rangle.$$

Of course, if the degree of nodes is uniformly k_0, the result is given by $\langle k^2 \rangle = \langle k \rangle^2 = k_0^2$, which agrees with the naive estimate. However, in general, $\langle k^2 \rangle$ is larger than $\langle k \rangle^2$, and the difference between them is given by a variance. Thus, the simple estimation given previously is an *underestimate*. (See Newman, 2003a for an exposition of this fact.)

In fact, in the example of Figure 4.2, because of the existence of the centre node, the magnitude of the squared average of the degree of nodes $\langle k^2 \rangle$ is approximately N. As a result, if we calculate the average number of nodes within two degrees of separation by using the solution stated above, we obtain the correct result, which is approximately equal to N.

From this example, we can see why the average number of nodes within two degrees of separation becomes large:

- Nodes can be connected to many nodes within two degrees of separation through directly connected nodes with a large degree (a hub).
- Nodes with a large degree (hubs) can take such an intermediating role in many cases because they are connected to many other nodes.

To put it simply, the number of your friends is much larger than that which you naively expect, because you have a non-negligible probability of finding a hub amongst your friends. The probability is non-negligible due to the fact that she or he has many friends, and in spite of the fact that the number of such hubs is quite small. The number of your friends' friends is, therefore, much larger than might be expected.

Actually, the real-world networks discussed so far have fat tails and large variance, and the number of nodes within two degrees of separation can be much larger than the above estimate. In fact, the tail of the degree distribution for scale-free networks follows a power-law distribution:

$$P_>(k) \propto k^{-\nu},$$

and therefore, if the power-law exponent ν is less than 2, $\langle k^2 \rangle$ diverges and becomes infinite. (It should be noted that although ν is the same as μ, as defined in subsection 2.1.2, we are introducing the different notation when we refer to the degree distribution.) However, since a divergence of $\langle k^2 \rangle$ occurs in the case of ideal, infinite networks, it is clear, therefore, that such a divergence does not happen in real, finite networks. Precise estimation clarifies that the squared average of the degree of nodes $\langle k^2 \rangle$ becomes the magnitude of the total number of nodes, when the power-law exponent ν is equal to 1.

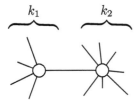

Figure 4.3. Correlation r between degrees of nodes at distance 1.

Thus, in scale-free networks, every node connects with another within two degrees of separation, when exponent ν is equal to 1. However, this is not accomplished in the real world, because actual scale-free networks do not have such a small ν.

$\alpha\beta\gamma$ Correlation coefficients

The correlation coefficient is defined as follows. We suppose that a random variable x has a mean $\langle x \rangle$ and standard deviation,

$$\sigma_x = \sqrt{\langle (x - \langle x \rangle)^2 \rangle} = \sqrt{\langle x^2 \rangle - \langle x \rangle^2}.$$

If we define $\tilde{x} := (x - \langle x \rangle)/\sigma_x$, this new variable $\tilde{x}$ has a mean equal to 0 and a standard deviation equal to 1. For another variable y, we define $\tilde{y}$ in the same way. The average of the product of these two variables

$$r_{xy} := \langle \tilde{x}\tilde{y} \rangle = \frac{\langle xy \rangle - \langle x \rangle \langle y \rangle}{\sigma_x \sigma_y}$$

is called the correlation coefficient of x and y. In addition, the numerator of the last term on the right-hand side of this equation, i.e. the product of the correlation coefficient and the standard deviations of each variable: $\sigma_{xy} := \sigma_x \sigma_y r_{xy}$ is called the *covariance*. It is easily verified that the correlation coefficient r_{xy} necessarily satisfies $-1 \leq r_{xy} \leq 1$.

If we now move to the discussion of three degrees of separation, new evidence is added to the discussion of two degrees of separation and it becomes more interesting, though at this point we will simply display the result. The most effective expression for the number of nodes within three degrees of separation is[5]

$$r \langle k^3 \rangle.$$

r can be referred to as the *correlation coefficient of degrees*, and characterises the correlation between the degrees of two nodes at each end of a link (see Figure 4.3).

---

[5] We here show the equation which is applicable when the clustering coefficient is sufficiently small.

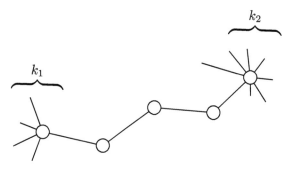

Figure 4.4. Correlation r_4 between degrees of nodes at distance 4.

If the degrees have no correlation, $r = 0$. In scale-free networks, when $v = 1.5$, the average of the cube of degree $\langle k^3 \rangle$ approaches the total number of nodes, i.e. N. Thus, as long as the degree correlation is not equal to 0, every node is connected with every other within three degrees of separation when v is below 1.5. Incidentally, if there is no correlation between degrees, and $r = 0$, every node is connected with another within three degrees of separation when v is below 4/3. From this result, we can see the importance of the correlation between nodes.

Now, if we expand the calculation to the case of six degrees of separation we get a very complicated and long equation, which would need many pages to display.[6] If we pick up the effective part of the equation, which contains the degree correlation coefficient r_4 of nodes connecting within four degrees of separation (see Figure 4.4), we get

$$r_4 \langle k^{17} \rangle^{1/8}.$$

This quantity is of the same order as the total number of nodes when v is less than or equal to 3; therefore the subject of this section, 'six degrees of separation', is realised if v is not over 3. However, in a real network, it sometimes happens that the degree correlation becomes 0 if the separation of nodes is 4. Thus, we simplify the problem by assuming that only the degree correlation coefficient mediated by one link, r, which appeared in the case of three degrees of separation, is not equal to 0, and the degree correlation coefficient mediated by more than two links is equal to 0. In that case we find the term

$$r^2 \frac{\langle k^3 \rangle^2}{\langle k^2 \rangle}$$

is effective to six degrees of separation. Such a result means that this term becomes approximately N when v is less than or equal to 2.4, and all nodes are connected within six degrees of separation.

---

[6] It is impossible to calculate it by hand, so we used the *Mathematica* software for algebraic calculation and a fast PC with 8GB memory; even so, it took over ten minutes to get the result.

In the calculation explained above we ignored the clustering coefficient in cases with three degrees of separation or more. However, this is not likely to happen if the exponent of N is modified by the effect of a clustering coefficient. Additionally, many degree distributions in real-world networks have a fat tail with an exponent in the range from 1 to 3. Thus, for this reason, it is possible to consider that all nodes are connected within the extent of six degrees of separation in the real world, if the network is scale-free.

The calculation of d degrees of separation has an interesting application to the estimation of chains of bankruptcy in a supplier–customer network. As we shall explain in section 6.2, companies connected by supplier–customer relationships to a bankrupted company can also fail. In the range of one degree of separation from a bankrupted company, if there are no other failed nodes, the bankruptcy is isolated. However, if there is another bankruptcy in the range, we can proceed to consider two degrees of separation from the starting bankruptcy. If there is no other failure, then there is a chain of bankruptcies with size two, occurring simply by chance. Proceeding in this way, one can consider chains of bankruptcy of larger sizes in the supplier–customer network, and compare such an estimation of the frequency of 'avalanche' size with what actually happened from a real data. See Fujiwara and Aoyama (2008) for details.

4.3 Networks in the economy

When discussing networks in the economy it is important at the outset to define what we mean by a node in this situation. If we decide that we want this to correspond to the minimum unit which is accepted as an economic entity we might propose the individual person as a candidate. In a future where electronic transactions and IC tags are widespread, and the consumption pattern of an individual and the flows of money and goods are traceable, we will be able to study the network constructed from individuals. However, at present this is impossible.

 Kevin Bacon game

Do you know the 'Kevin Bacon game' which originated from the six degrees of separation theory? Players search for the number of links constituting the shortest path connecting an arbitrarily selected movie star and Kevin Bacon, another actor, by tracing a path through the movie collaboration network. This is called the 'Bacon number'. At the end of 2008, approximately 1 million actors were connected to Kevin Bacon, and the average value of the Bacon number was approximately 2.95. Interestingly, if we calculate the same number for other actors, the actor who has the smallest number, i.e. the centre of the network, is not Kevin Bacon but Dennis Hopper, whose number is equal to 2.74. There are several other numbers of this kind, for example the 'Erdős number' which is defined by the number of links in the collaboration network for the mathematician Erdős.

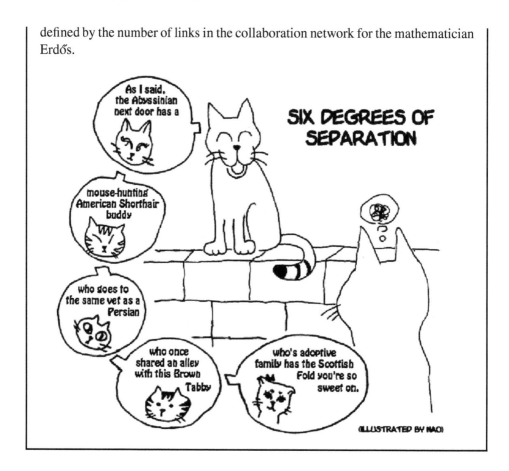

Since, for practical reasons, we need to find another candidate definition of a node it is obvious that we must reconcile ourselves to some degree of *coarse graining*. For example, a node could be defined as a group consisting of several persons, that is to say a company, a local government, a country, and so on. For our purposes in this book we have elected to consider the company as a node.

This decision raises the question of what kind of relationship between companies we should consider as constituting a link. In a company limited by shares, which is the predominant conformation, ownership and management are separated. The shareholders own the company, and each may hold shares in several companies. In listed companies it is frequently found that shareholders are themselves also listed companies. Thus, we can identify for consideration the *shareholding network*, a network in which the nodes are companies and the links are shareholding relationships.

Members of the board of directors are selected at the meeting of shareholders, and the board of directors makes decisions for the management of the company. Sometimes, some members of one board are also members of another board, and so are interlocking directors connecting two or more companies. Thus we can identify the *interlocking directors' network* as another company network.

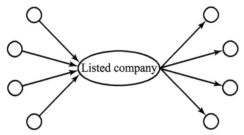

Figure 4.5. Incoming and outgoing links of a listed company in a shareholding or a transaction network.

Under such ownership and management, companies perform many kinds of activity, the most important of which is production. Many companies buy materials and services to make products, and sell these products with value added, so we can on the basis of these relations identify a *transaction network*.

The importance of *innovation* is a much discussed topic, but measuring it is a very difficult problem. Some traction can be obtained by considering patents as if they were innovations, and this is the approach we adopt here. Since companies sometimes apply jointly for a patent, presumably because of previous joint research, we can consider the *network of joint applications for patents* as evidence of an *innovation network*. In what follows we will consider the shareholding network, the interlocking directors' network, the transaction network and the innovation network, in sequence.

4.3.1 The shareholding network
Major shareholder data is useful for studying the shareholding connections among companies,[7] and the data we have used provides the list of top thirty major shareholders for each listed company.

Stockholdings data is also useful for studying the shareholding network. In Japan, we can buy an annual securities report at major bookstores, or read it on the home page of the Electronic Disclosure for Investors' NETwork (EDINET). An annual securities report contains an investment portfolio item in which the details of a company's investment status is reported. In many cases the top ten to twenty major investment companies are reported, but the length of the disclosed list varies from company to company. The list of investment portfolios includes investment trust funds, but here we ignore such funds in our examination of the shareholding network, which is restricted to major shareholder data and stockholding data in 2004.

Figure 4.5 is a conceptual picture of the connection of companies. In this figure, each white circle corresponds to a company. We draw the shareholding network by tracing an arrow from shareholder to company. Thus, major shareholder data corresponds to the left-hand side of Figure 4.5. In this part, each white circle existing on the left-hand side corresponds to a shareholder, and each link describes a shareholding relationship. In other words, major shareholder data is data for links, which come into each listed company. In this way, the link that comes into a node is called an *incoming link*, and

---

[7] Major shareholder data, for example, is commercially available from Toyo Keizai Inc. and Nikkei Data Service Inc.

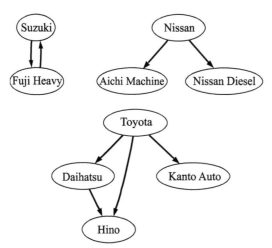

Figure 4.6. Shareholding network in the automobile industry.

the number of incoming links is called the *in-degree* or the *incoming degree*. As stated before, in the case of major shareholder data, the incoming degree is up to thirty.

Meanwhile, stockholding data corresponds to the right-hand side of Figure 4.5. Stockholding data refers to the links that go out from each listed company. A link that goes out from a node is called an *outgoing link*, and the number of outgoing links is called the *out-degree* or the *outgoing degree*. In the case of stockholding data, the outgoing degree differs from company to company.

By using these two kinds of data, i.e. major shareholder data and stockholding data, we get the element shown in Figure 4.5 for each listed company. The shareholding network is constructed by connecting these elements to each other.

For the purposes of the present analysis we will focus on companies concerned with automobile manufacture. According to the classification of industry by NEEDS (Nikkei Economic Electric Databank System), industries concerned with automobile manufacture are separated into automobile (automobile), automobile (auto body and others), automobile (auto parts) and electrical machinery (automobile-related), the terms in brackets corresponding to the sub-classifications of the automobile and electrical machinery industries. We will concentrate on the automobile (automobile) industry, which for simplicity's sake we will refer to as the 'automobile industry'. Thirteen companies belong to this industry, namely Isuzu Motors, Suzuki Motor, Daihatsu Motor, Toyota Motor, Mazda Motor, Aichi Machine Industry, Kanto Auto Works, Mitsubishi Motors, Nissan Diesel Motor, Nissan Motor, Hino Motors, Fuji Heavy Industries and Honda Motor.

The network shown in Figure 4.6 is constructed only from these companies, and is constructed with directed links, so is referred to as a *directed graph* or *digraph*. Sometimes we ignore the direction of links to simplify discussion, and, in addition, there are networks constructed from links which were not originally directed. Unsurprisingly, networks with undirected links are called *undirected graphs*.

Isuzu Motors, Mazda Motor, Mitsubishi Motors and Honda Motor do not appear in Figure 4.6, indicating that these companies are not connected to companies in the same

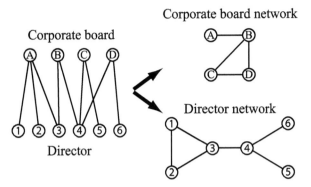

Figure 4.7. The corporate board and directors' network and its reduced graphs.

industry by shareholding relationships. In this case we used major shareholder data and stockholding data, and these data sources list only a limited number of companies. If a complete list of shareholders and stockholders were available there is a possibility that connections between these four companies and other companies belonging to the automobile industry would be revealed. Figure 4.6 also shows that the network is constructed from three *connected components*. Suzuki Motor and Fuji Heavy Industries are connected by a *bidirectional link* meaning that there is a *cross-shareholding*. In addition, both Toyota Motor and Daihatsu Motor are shareholders of Hino Motors.

4.3.2   The interlocking directors' network

The members of the board of directors of a company are selected at a meeting of shareholders, and their names then announced to the public, along with any interlocking directorships they hold. The previous history of members of a corporate board is not necessarily announced to the public. However, for listed companies in 2004, we use data which contains lists of interlocking directorships and the previous history of members of the corporate board.[8]

By employing this data we can conceptually draw an interlocking directors' network and corporate board network as shown in Figure 4.7. This network is constructed from two kinds of nodes, namely directors and corporate boards. A network constructed in this way from two kinds of node is called a *bipartite graph*. If a certain director links many corporate boards and if the director's ideas for the management are frequently adopted, the director's effect is obviously widespread, and so it is natural to consider that such boards are strongly connected by the director. Acting on this consideration we get the upper-right panel of Figure 4.7, which is constructed from just one type of node, i.e. corporate boards. The process by which we reduce a network with two types of node to one with only one type is called *graph reduction*.

Conversely, if we consider that the directors on the same corporate board know each other, we get the lower-right panel of Figure 4.7, which is solely constructed from

---

[8] This data is commercially available from Toyo Keizai Inc.

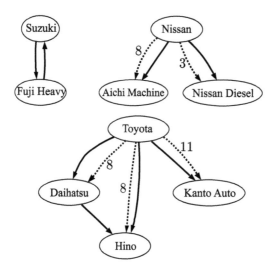

Figure 4.8. The corporate board network in the automobile industry.

directors. Both are interesting, but in this study we will not investigate the director network, and will instead focus on the company (corporate board) network.

Since we can identify interlocking directors and the previous history of directors we can trace links from the previous board of a company to its present board, and from the main corporate board to sub-corporate boards, and then draw these networks as directed graphs.

If we draw the corporate board network alongside the shareholding network shown in Figure 4.6, we get Figure 4.8, with the dotted lines indicating newly drawn links. As before, all the thirteen automobile companies do not appear in this figure, indicating that some companies are not connected in this way with other companies in the same industry. In this figure, the number beside each dotted link corresponds to the number of directors who are either current or former directors of the company at the source of the link. For example, in the case of Daihatsu Motor, eight directors are sent from the board of Toyota Motor or were previously members of the board of Toyota Motor. As with the shareholding network, this network is constructed from three connected components, including the group clustered around Toyota Motor and the group centred on Nissan Motor.

4.3.3   The transaction network

When we talk about friends, we can probably easily and honestly answer the question 'How many friends do you have?' However, if we are asked 'Who are your friends?' we may hesitate, and, even if we attempt an answer, vanity might tempt us to include the name of some well-known person. Something similar happens when a company answers the question 'Which companies are your business partners?'. In general, a company does not have an obligation to disclose the name of business partners, so business data companies get information about suppliers and customers by conducting an interview, and because of the vanity effect the resulting data is considered to be potentially biased.

 Freewares for network analysis

Graph drawing and graph analysis need considerable programming skills, so we might expect that software for graph analysis and graph drawing is expensive; but in fact there is a great deal of free software, for example Graphviz, Pajek and Network Workbench.

Nevertheless, we can gain some insight from this data, and we use two kinds to investigate what we will call the transaction network. One source gives business partner information for 1,404 listed companies, which are non-financial companies listed in the first section of the Tokyo Stock Exchange in 2004.[9] The total number of links in this dataset is 55,348, and therefore each of the 1,404 companies has approximately 80 links. The other gives data for all listed companies in Japan in 2004 and lists the five main suppliers and the five main customers for each company.[10] In our analysis below we synthesise these two datasets, and consider the resulting transaction network.

To draw this network we trace links along the flow of materials and services (which is the reverse of the flow of money), and thus we get part of the network shown in Figure 4.5 for all listed companies, just as we did for the shareholding network. In the case of a transaction network the flow of materials and services defines the direction of the links. Hence, the white circles on the left-hand side of Figure 4.5 correspond to main suppliers, which are located upstream in physical distribution. On the other hand, the white circles on the right of Figure 4.5 correspond to main customers, which are located downstream in physical distribution. The transaction network is constructed by connecting these parts.

We will once again focus on the case of the automobile industry, and superimpose the transaction network on the shareholding and interlocking directors' networks shown in Figure 4.8, thus leading to Figure 4.9. Thin dashed lines are newly added links, and the direction of these links corresponds to the direction of physical distribution. As was the case with the shareholding network and the interlocking directors' network, four companies, Isuzu Motors, Mazda Motor, Mitsubishi Motors and Honda Motor, are not in the transaction network shown in Figure 4.9. The shareholding and interlocking directors' networks are separated into three connected components as shown in Figure 4.8. However, in this case, these connected components are connected into one component as shown in Figure 4.9.

---

[9] This data is provided by Teikoku Data Bank Ltd.   [10] This data is provided by NEEDS.

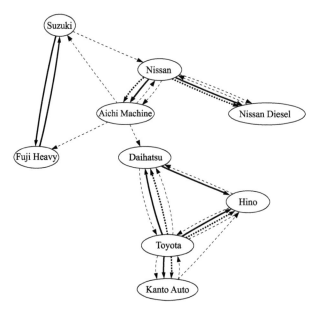

Figure 4.9. Transaction network of the automobile industry.

In Figure 4.9, we can see that there are two groups. One is the group centred on Toyota Motor, and the other is the group centred on Nissan Motor. However, these two groups are connected by the link running from Aichi Machine Industry to Daihatsu Motor. In addition, the links from Aichi Machine Industry to Suzuki Motor and Fuji Heavy Industries play an important part in making one connected component. In this case, Aichi Machine Industry connects different groups, and is called a *gatekeeper*.

In most offices there are well-informed people who may not hold senior posts but play important roles in connecting the various parts of the department. Such persons are gatekeepers. The importance of gatekeepers is characterised by *betweenness centrality*. This index is explained in subsection 4.4.4. In Figure 4.9, we can see that there are many overlaps between shareholding links, the interlocking directors' network and the links of the transaction network.

4.3.4 The innovation network

The patent office publishes information relating to patent applications, and there are several databases derived from that information. For our work we have chosen to investigate cumulative patent data up to 2004. This set contains many items for each patent; for example, citations of scientific papers and patents, main text, classification of technology, applicants, inventors, address of applicants and inventors, etc. Such information is drawn conceptually in the left-hand panel of Figure 4.10. On the basis of this figure we can construct many kinds of network.

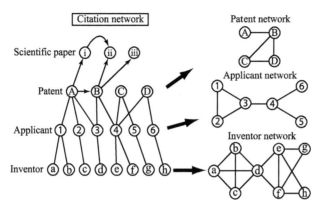

Figure 4.10. Patent network and its reduced graphs.

For example, as shown in Figure 4.10, if we use the citation of scientific papers and patents we can construct a network in which scientific papers and patents or technologies are nodes. In addition, if we extract keywords from the main text and consider them in relation to the citation network, we can construct a conceptual network in which keywords are nodes.

As conceptually shown in Figure 4.10, we can see that patent A and patent B are connected by applicant 3. In addition, we can also see that patents B, C and D are connected by applicant 4. Thus, as shown in the upper-right panel, we can construct a network with patents as nodes. Conversely, applicants 1, 2 and 3 are connected by patent A, and applicants 3 and 4 are connected by patent B. Hence, as shown in the centre-right panel, we can construct a network with applicants as nodes. In many cases, applicants correspond to companies; therefore, we can regard this network as having companies as nodes. In the current study we call this a network of joint patent applications. In addition, we can say that inventors a, b, c and d are connected by patent A, and inventors d, e and f are connected by patent B. Thus, as shown in the lower-right panel, we can construct a network with inventors as nodes.

Just as we did before, we will restrict our analysis to the case of the automobile industry. However, and this is a significant difference, the links in a patent network do not have direction, therefore it is drawn as an *undirected network*. If we draw the patent network alongside that for shareholding and interlocking directors, we obtain Figure 4.11. Undirected and dashed lines represent the connections of joint applications for patents. The number beside each link corresponds to the number of joint applications for patents up to 2004. However, this number suffers from inaccuracy because it is very difficult to identify companies with complete confidence. Different companies sometimes have the same name.

Contrary to the previous examples, this network is constructed from all thirteen companies, and although the Toyota Motor and Nissan Motor groups were evident in the previous networks, they are not evident in Figure 4.11. An interesting point is that Toyota Motor and Nissan Motor are not connected directly, but are connected by an

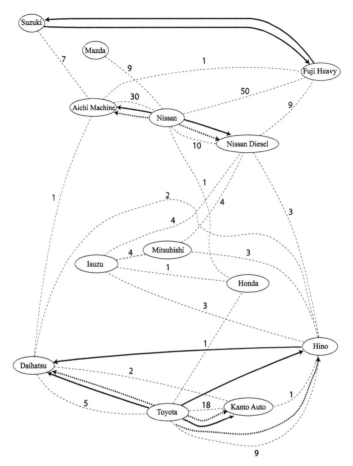

Figure 4.11. Network of joint applications for patents in the automobile industry.

intermediary, Honda Motor. We can also see that there are many overlaps between the links of the shareholding and interlocking directors' networks and those of the joint patent applications network. In addition, companies which are not connected in the shareholding and interlocking directors' network are connected in this case. From this fact, we can infer that for the purposes of innovation, companies are sometimes connected beyond company walls.

We can also investigate the network of joint patent applications constructed from companies belonging to the automobile (automobile) and electrical machinery (automobile-related) sectors. In this case we obtain Figure 4.12. Although there are many companies, the remarkable fact is that there are many joint patent applications between Toyota Motor and Denso Corporation, with the total amounting to 915. There are also many joint patent applications between Honda Motor and Stanley Electric, with the total amounting to 114. On the other hand, there are no joint patent applications between Nissan Motor and companies belonging to the electrical

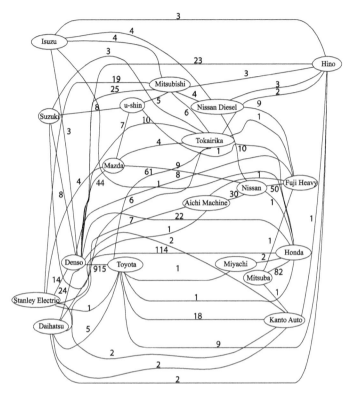

Figure 4.12. Network of joint applications for patents between the automobile and electrical and electronic industries.

machinery (automobile-related) category. Thus, we can infer that Nissan Motor applies for patents with companies belonging to the electrical machinery industry, not the electrical machinery (automobile-related) industry. However, as noted before, there is the possibility that there are missing links, because patent data is not necessarily complete.

4.4 Network indices

At this point we will turn to a discussion of the characteristics of networks through the calculation of network indices. Up to now, we have considered four types of network, i.e. shareholding networks, interlocking directors' networks, transaction networks and innovation networks. As shown above, some companies are connected to other companies with multiple relationships, i.e. *multiple links (multilinks)*. A network with multiple links can be called a *multiple network* or a *multiple graph (multigraph)*.

Now suppose that the weight of every link is equal to 1. Thus, if two nodes are connected by four relationships, we say that these two nodes are connected by one link with weight 4. As explained here, a multiple network is regarded as a *weighted network*. The multiple network and weighted network are here given as an undirected

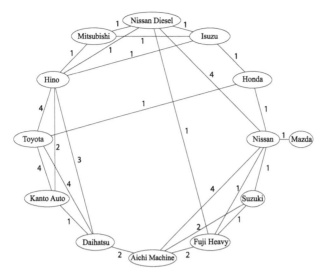

Figure 4.13. Weighted network of the automobile industry.

network because a network of joint patent applications is an undirected network. In the light of this consideration the automobile industry network is drawn as Figure 4.13. The number beside each link represents its weight, and in what follows we will investigate this network by applying the methods of network analysis.

4.4.1   Degree centrality

As stated before, the number of links held by a node is called its degree. In social network analysis in sociology, degree is referred to as *degree centrality*. In this book, we denote the degree of a node i as k_i, where i corresponds to the company's number in the first column of Table 4.1. The second column of this table is the name of the company. The degree calculated for each node of the network shown in Figure 4.13 is given in the third column of the table. From this, we can see that Nissan Motor and Hino Motors have the largest degree value: $k_{10} = k_{11} = 6$. On the other hand, Mazda Motor has the smallest value: $k_5 = 1$.

The sum weight of links attached to each company, which is called the *node strength* or the *vertex strength*, is summarised in the fourth column of Table 4.1. If we denote the weight of a link between node i and node j as w_{ij}, the node strength of node i is defined by

$$s_i := \sum_{j \in \mathrm{adj}(i)} w_{ij}.$$

Here, $\mathrm{adj}(i)$ represents the set of *adjacent* nodes of node i. Thus, $j \in \mathrm{adj}(i)$ states that 'node j belongs to the set of adjacent nodes of node i'. By summing up w_{ij} for j, we obtain s_i. In the case of the network shown in Figure 4.13, Toyota Motor has the largest value for node strength: $s_4 = 13$. On the other hand, Mazda Motor has the smallest

Table 4.1. *Network indices for thirteen automobile companies.*

Number	Name	k_i	s_i	L_i	C_i	C_i^{w}	C_i^{b}
1	Isuzu	4	4	1.92	0.5	0.5	0.03
2	Suzuki	3	4	2.17	1	1	0
3	Daihatsu	4	10	1.75	0.5	0.53	0.11
4	Toyota	4	13	1.92	0.5	0.62	0.05
5	Mazda	1	1	2.5	0	0	0
6	Aichi Machine	4	10	1.83	0.5	0.53	0.111
7	Kanto Auto	3	7	2.17	1	1	0
8	Mitsubishi	3	3	2	1	1	0
9	Nissan Diesel	5	8	1.58	0.4	0.34	0.20
10	Nissan	6	12	1.58	0.27	0.28	0.28
11	Hino	6	12	1.67	0.4	0.4	0.16
12	Fuji Heavy	4	5	1.83	0.67	0.67	0.04
13	Honda	3	3	1.75	0	0	0.09

value, $s_5 = 1$, just as it had for degree value. A consideration of both node strength and degree yields a deep understanding of the characteristics of a network.

4.4.2 Shortest path length

As noted before, path length is also one of the elementary quantities characterising a network. We will here consider the path length in Figure 4.13 in concrete terms. For example, let us take Toyota Motor as the starting point. The company is connected to four companies by one link, these four companies being Hino Motors, Honda Motor, Daihatsu Motor and Kanto Auto Works. In addition, Toyota Motor is connected to five companies by two links, these five companies being Mitsubishi Motors, Nissan Diesel Motor, Isuzu Motors, Nissan Motor and Aichi Machine Industry. Fuji Heavy Industries, Mazda Motor and Suzuki Motor are connected to Toyota Motor by three links. Thus, the average value of links necessary to connect Toyota Motor and the other companies is given by $L_4 = (1 \times 4 + 2 \times 5 + 3 \times 3)/12 = 1.92$. The values of L_i for each company are shown in the fifth column of Table 4.1. From this result, Nissan Diesel Motor and Nissan Motor have the smallest values for shortest path length. In other words, these two companies can easily approach other companies. On the other hand, Mazda Motor has the largest value for shortest path length. Finally, if we calculate average path length for this network, we obtain $\langle L \rangle = 1.897$.

4.4.3 Clustering coefficient

As explained previously, the clustering coefficient is an index which quantifies the cliqueyness of nodes. Taking the network shown in Figure 4.13 we can calculate a clustering coefficient. As in the case of path length, we will take Toyota Motor as an example. Toyota Motor has four links, i.e. companies. Thus, the possible number of combinations to connect these four companies to each other is equal to the number of ways of selecting two companies from four companies, i.e. $C(4, 2) = 4(4 - 1)/2 = 6$. However, as we can see in Figure 4.13, three sets are realised. These are Hino Motors and Daihatsu Motor, Hino Motors and Kanto Auto Works, and Kanto Auto Works and Daihatsu Motor. The clustering coefficient is defined by the ratio of the realised number of combinations to the possible number of combinations; therefore, in the case of Toyota Motor, the clustering coefficient is given by $C_4 = 3/6 = 0.5$.

As we can see in Figure 4.13, Mazda Motor has one link; therefore, the possible number of combinations is $C(1, 2) = 0$. Hence, the clustering coefficient of Mazda Motor diverges. As stated before, the clustering coefficient of a node with one link is defined by 0. The clustering coefficients for each company are shown in the sixth column of Table 4.1. By definition, the clustering coefficient has a value between 0 and 1. As stated above, the clustering coefficient of Mazda Motor is equal to 0 by definition, and although Honda Motor has three links, the clustering coefficient of Honda Motor is also equal to 0. However, the clustering coefficient of Suzuki Motor, Kanto Auto Works and Mitsubishi Motors is equal to 1, because all possible combinations are realised. If we calculate the average value of the clustering coefficient of the network, we obtain $\langle C \rangle = 0.518$. This value is relatively large.

A *weighted clustering coefficient*, that is to say, a clustering coefficient defined by allowing for the weight of links, has also been proposed. There are several definitions of the weighted clustering coefficient, some of them using the weight of links connecting to a node (see Saramäki *et al.*, 2007, for example). Taking the definition of the node strength in subsection 4.4.1, we denote the weight of a link between node i and node j as w_{ij}. In addition, we denote node strength and the degree of the node i as s_i and k_i, respectively. Thus, if node j and node k, which are adjacent to node i, are connected with each other, we define the weighted clustering coefficient as

$$C_i^w = \frac{1}{s_i(k_i - 1)} \sum_{j,k \in \text{adj}(i)} \frac{w_{ij} + w_{ik}}{2},$$

which was originally proposed in Barrat *et al.* (2004). If the weights are equal, this expression reduces to the previously stated formula for the case without weights, as is easily verified.

By using this definition of the weighted clustering coefficient we obtain the results shown in the seventh column of Table 4.1. The weighted clustering coefficient C_i^w has a value between 0 and 1, as in the case of the clustering coefficient C_i. Now, we can compare C_i and C_i^w. As can easily be seen, if C_i is equal to 0 or 1, then C_i^w is also equal to 0 or 1. On the other hand, if C_i has a value between 0 and 1, even if two nodes have the same value of C_i, they may sometimes have different values of C_i^w. For example, as shown in Table 4.1, Isuzu Motors, Daihatsu Motor, Toyota Motor and Aichi Machine Industry have $C_1 = C_3 = C_4 = C_6 = 0.5$. However, by considering a weighted clustering coefficient, we obtain $C_4^w > C_3^w = C_6^w > C_1^w$. In other words, Toyota Motor is responsible for the most tightly connected cluster.

4.4.4   The betweenness centrality of nodes

We can now consider an experiment in which we randomly select two nodes from a network and connect these two nodes by the shortest path. If we repeat this experiment many times, we notice that some nodes and links appear frequently on the shortest path, but others never do so. This characteristic of nodes and links can be quantified by a *betweenness centrality*.

Let us start with nodes and denote the number of shortest paths connecting node i and node j as $\sigma_{j,k}$. Note that we do not consider the length of the shortest path. In addition, we denote the number of shortest paths which pass through node i and connect node j and node k as $\sigma_{j,k}(i)$. The betweenness centrality of node i is defined by

$$C_i^b := A \sum_{i \neq j \neq k \in V} \frac{\sigma_{j,k}(i)}{\sigma_{j,k}}.$$

Note that A is the normalisation factor and V is the set of nodes in the network.

For example, we can consider the case of the connection between Mazda Motor and Kanto Auto Works in Figure 4.13, where we find that the length of the shortest path is equal to 4, and that three paths exist.

- Mazda → Nissan → Nissan Diesel → Hino → Kanto Auto
- Mazda → Nissan → Honda → Toyota → Kanto Auto
- Mazda → Nissan → Aichi Machine → Daihatsu → Kanto Auto

Thus, $\sigma_{5,7} = 3$. In addition, $\sigma_{5,7}(10) = 3$ for Nissan Motor, and $\sigma_{5,7}(i) = 1 (i = 3, 4, 6, 9, 11, 13)$ for Nissan Diesel Motor, Hino Motors, Honda Motor, Toyota Motor, Aichi Machine Industry and Daihatsu Motor, respectively. Thus, $C_{10}^b = 1$ for Nissan Motor, and $C_i^b = 1/3 \, (i = 3, 4, 6, 9, 11, 13)$ for the other six companies, when we ignore the normalisation. Though we are only considering the path between Mazda Motor and Kanto Auto Works, the betweenness centrality is obtained by calculating for every path of every combination of nodes. The eighth column of Table 4.1 is the normalised betweenness centrality of each node. From this result we can see that Nissan Motor has the largest value. This is because, as we can see in Figure 4.13, all companies have to pass Nissan Motor to arrive at Mazda Motor.

4.4.5   Cliques

The clustering coefficient, which was explained earlier, is constructed by regarding a triangle as a cluster, when a *subgraph* forms a triangle. However, we are not limited to triangles and can extend the concept to clusters larger than three nodes. For example, suppose there are four nodes and these four nodes are connected to each other. Such a network is extendable to a network including many nodes, in which all nodes are connected to each other. When every node is completely connected to every other we refer to it as a *complete graph*. Such a complete graph is also referred to as an *n-clique*, where *n* is the number of nodes contained in the network.

Table 4.2. *Cliques among thirteen companies belonging to the automobile industry.*

Clique	Company	Sum of weights
	Hino	6
	Mitsubishi	
	Nissan Diesel	
	Isuzu	
4-clique	Hino	18
	Toyota	
	Kanto Auto	
	Daihatsu	
	Nissan	11
	Aichi Machine	
	Fuji Heavy	
	Suzuki	
5-clique	none	

As we can see in Figure 4.13, there are three 4-cliques. These are summarised in Table 4.2, where we can observe that the clique constructed from Hino Motors, Mitsubishi Motors, Nissan Diesel Motor and Isuzu Motors is regarded as the truck-making group. In addition, the clique constructed from Hino Motors, Toyota Motor, Kanto Auto Works and Daihatsu Motor is regarded as the Toyota group. These two cliques are connected by Hino Motors, so we can conclude that Hino Motors is the gatekeeper. The other clique is constructed from Nissan Motor, Aichi Machine Industry, Fuji Heavy Industries and Suzuki Motor, and is regarded as the Nissan group. As we can see in Figure 4.13 there are no cliques constructed from five or more nodes.

If we calculate the sum of the weight of links within each clique (the results are shown in the third column of Table 4.2), we observe that the Toyota group has the largest value for the total sum of link weights, and we can infer that the Toyota group is a more tightly connected group than other groups.

4.5   Statistical properties of network indices

In the previous section, as an example, we investigated a small network constructed only from automobile companies, and calculated some indices and considered the overall characteristics of the network. In this section, we will investigate some large networks and consider the statistical characteristics of network indices.

4.5.1   Comparison of industries by using network indices

Before we calculate network indices, as explained in the previous section, it should be noted that if the number of nodes becomes large then disconnected parts may

Table 4.3. *Network indices for the whole network and the electrical and electronics and automobile industries.*

Index		Whole network	Electrical and electronics	Automobile
N		3,576	285	85
K		55,332	2,196	568
$\langle k \rangle$		30.95	15.41	13.37
$\langle L \rangle$		2.78	2.32	1.98
$\langle C \rangle$		0.24	0.65	0.89
$\langle C^{\mathrm{w}} \rangle$		0.19	0.45	0.46
C^{b}	1	Japanese Securities Finance	Hitachi	Honda
	2	Mitsui	Toshiba	Nissan
	3	Mitsubishi Co.	Panasonic	Suzuki
	4	Hitachi	Mitsubishi Electric	Toyota
	5	Panasonic	Sharp	Fuji Heavy

appear. If we regard these disconnected parts as islands, the whole network looks like a world map. That is, although each node in an island is connected, there are no links connecting the islands. Consequently, we must calculate network indices for the largest island, which we call the *largest connected component*.

Firstly, we will investigate the whole network described so far. As shown in the second column of Table 4.3, this network contains $N = 3,576$ nodes and $K = 55,332$ links. This network comprises one connected component, i.e. the largest connected component is the network itself. In addition, the average degree, the average path length, the average clustering coefficient and the average weighted clustering coefficient are $\langle k \rangle = 30.95$, $\langle L \rangle = 2.78$, $\langle C \rangle = 0.24$ and $\langle C^{\mathrm{w}} \rangle = 0.19$, respectively. If we calculate betweenness centrality C^{b} for each node, we can list the top five companies, namely Japanese Securities Finance Co. Ltd., Mitsui & Co. Ltd., Mitsubishi Corporation, Hitachi Ltd. and Panasonic Corporation, as shown in the second column of Table 4.3.[11] The first company, Japanese Securities Finance, has a large number of links concerned with shareholding; therefore it has a large value of betweenness centrality. The second and third companies, Mitsui and Mitsubishi, have many links concerned with shareholding and transactions. The fourth and fifth companies, Hitachi and Panasonic, have many links concerned with shareholding, transactions and innovation.

The analysed results for the electrical and electronics industry are summarised in the third column of Table 4.3. This industry contains 285 companies and 2,196 links. In this case, again, the largest connected component is the network itself. However, if we

---

[11] Note that banks were not included in this investigation.

compare the value of $\langle k \rangle$ for this industry with that for the whole network, we find it is approximately half. However, the value of $\langle L \rangle$ is almost the same in both the electrical and electronics industry and the whole network. On the other hand, $\langle C \rangle$ and $\langle C^w \rangle$ for the electrical and electronics industry are larger than the corresponding values for the whole network, meaning that companies in the electrical and electronics industry are densely connected with each other.

The results for the automobile industry are summarised in the fourth column of Table 4.3. This industry contains the electrical and electronics (automobile-related), automobile (automobile), automobile (auto body and others) and automobile (auto parts) categories. The network for this industry contains 87 nodes and 569 links and is constructed from two connected components, the largest connected component containing 85 nodes and 568 links. In the largest connected component the average degree is $\langle k \rangle = 13.37$, which is almost the same as the average degree in the electrical and electronics industry. On the other hand, the average shortest path length $\langle L \rangle$ in this industry is smaller than that in the electrical and electronics industry. Thus, companies in the automobile industry are connected by a smaller number of steps than companies in the electrical and electronics industry. In addition, though the clustering coefficient $\langle C \rangle$ of the automobile industry is larger than that of the electrical and electronics industry, its weighted clustering coefficient $\langle C^w \rangle$ is almost the same.

We have now compared the companies constituting the whole network with those in the electrical and electronics and automobile industries. However, the numbers of nodes and links in these industries are very different, so let us compare the pharmaceuticals and steel industries, which have almost the same numbers of nodes and links, as shown in the second and third column of Table 4.4. Comparing these two industries, we find that the values of $\langle C \rangle$ and $\langle C^w \rangle$ are very different, namely, the pharmaceuticals industry has very small values compared to the values calculated for the whole network. On the other hand, the values of $\langle C \rangle$ and $\langle C^w \rangle$ in the steel industry are much larger than those for the pharmaceuticals industry. From this we can infer that companies in the steel industry are densely and tightly connected to each other compared to companies in the pharmaceuticals industry.

4.5.2   Degree distribution

As stated in subsection 2.1.1, the coverage of data is important when considering degree distribution. Though this book concentrates on investigation of the shareholding network, the interlocking directors' network, the transaction network and the innovation network, it is not necessarily possible to investigate the precise degree distribution for these networks. For example, in the case of the transaction network the data contains only the main suppliers and customers and this coverage of data is insufficient. However, we can examine the shareholding and innovation networks because data for these networks satisfies the coverage requirement.

As explained in subsection 4.3.1, the data useful to an investigation of the shareholding network is major shareholder and stockholding information. Major shareholder data

Table 4.4. *Network indices for the pharmaceuticals and steel industries.*

Index		Pharmaceuticals	Steel
N		49	47
K		126	119
$\langle k \rangle$		5.14	5.06
$\langle L \rangle$		2.53	2.30
$\langle C \rangle$		0.22	0.57
$\langle C^{\mathrm{w}} \rangle$		0.16	0.42
C^{b}	1	Mitsubishi Pharma	Nippon Steel
	2	Takeda Pharmaceutical	Sumitomo Metal
	3	Seikagaku	Kobe Steel
	4	Yamanouchi Pharmaceutical	Hitachi Metals
	5	Tanabeseiyaku	Daido Steel

contains the total number of shareholders (the total number of incoming degrees) and the list of the top thirty major shareholders (incoming links) for each listed company. In addition, stockholding data contains the total number of stocks (the total number of outgoing degrees) and the list of the top ten major investing companies (outgoing links) for each listed company.

We will now turn to an investigation of the distribution of outgoing degrees in the shareholding network. As stated above, because of the limitation of stockholding data we cannot know precisely which listed companies are connected to outgoing links, but we can to some extent determine the total number of outgoing links. On the other hand, if we use major shareholder data we can find companies with large outgoing degrees, even among unlisted companies, because companies with large outgoing degrees appear frequently in the major shareholder data. Thus we can approximately determine that the number of times a company appears in the major shareholder data corresponds to the number of outgoing degrees of unlisted companies.

We will use the total number of outgoing degrees, which is listed in stockholding data, since this number is a precise value. The black circles in Figure 4.14 correspond to the degree distribution of companies contained in this data. The abscissa corresponds to degree and the ordinate to rank. This figure is a log-log plot of the rank-size plot, which is explained in section 2.1.2. Figure 4.14 is also a kind of rank-size plot; however, we will simply call it the degree distribution. In addition, for unlisted companies we can consider the number of appearances in major shareholder data as being approximately equal to the number of outgoing degrees. The open squares

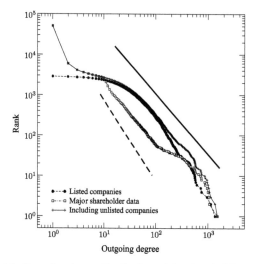

Figure 4.14. Outgoing degree distribution of the shareholding network.

in Figure 4.14 correspond to the degree distribution obtained by this latter method. Unification of these two types of outgoing degree distribution generates the outgoing degree distribution with some precision. However, some companies appear in both outgoing degree distributions, so we will adopt the larger value as the true outgoing degree. The crosses in Figure 4.14 are obtained by the method explained here, and the solid line and dashed line correspond to power-law distributions with power-law exponents $\gamma (= \nu - 1) = 1.5$ and 2.0, respectively. In network science if we denote degree as k and consider the degree distribution, the power-law exponent γ is generally represented using a probability density function:

$$p(k) = Ak^{-\gamma},$$

where A is a normalisation constant. In short, although γ is the same as α defined in subsection 2.1.2, in network science it is customary to denote it as γ. From this figure, we can see that the shareholding network is approximately a scale-free network because the tail part of the outgoing degree distribution follows a power-law distribution.

On the other hand, for the innovation network, i.e. the network of joint patent applications, we can investigate a database that covers all joint patent applications up until 2002, and so analyse the degree distribution. This is the TamadaDB, which contains information relating to all the 4,998,464 patents applied for in Japan over the period 1993 to 2002. The largest connected component of the network of joint patent applications constructed from the TamadaDB contains 34,840 nodes and 84,840 links. The degree distribution of this component is shown in Figure 4.15.[12] This figure is a log-log plot of degree distribution, with the abscissa corresponding to degree and

---

[12] This result was obtained in collaboration with Prof. S. Tamada of Kwansei Gakuin University and Dr H. Inoue of Osaka Sangyo University.

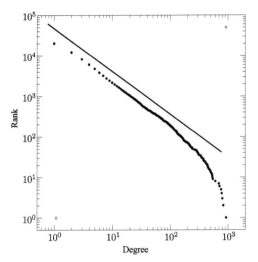

Figure 4.15. Degree distribution of the network of joint patent applications.

the ordinate to rank. The solid line in this figure is a power-law distribution with an exponent equal to 2. We can see in this figure that the distribution follows the power-law distribution over a wide range of degrees; therefore, the network of joint patent applications is a scale-free network.

4.5.3 Correlations related to degree

At this stage we can consider the correlation related to degree. We assume that the node with degree k' is adjacent to the node with degree k. In addition, we define the conditional probability density $p_c(k'|k)$, which is the probability of selecting nodes with degree k' when we select a node with degree k. Thus, the average degree of a node adjacent to a node with degree k is given by

$$\langle k_{nn} \rangle = \sum_{k'} k' p_c(k'|k).$$

Here, $\langle k_{nn} \rangle$ is called the *nearest neighbour's average connectivity*.

If we calculate $\langle k_{nn} \rangle$ for the shareholding network in 2002 and plot it on a log-log graph, we obtain Figure 4.16. The abscissa corresponds to k and the ordinate to $\langle k_{nn} \rangle$. This figure displays *degree–degree correlation*. The solid line in Figure 4.16 is given by

$$\langle k_{nn} \rangle (k) = A k^{-\eta}, \quad \eta \simeq 0.8,$$

where A is a proportionality coefficient. This result shows that the average degree of nodes adjacent to a node with a large degree is small. In short, the probability of connecting between hubs is very low.

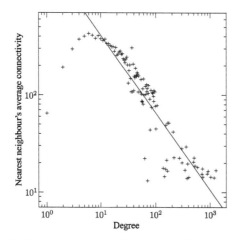

Figure 4.16. Degree correlation of the shareholding network.

It is known that the degree–degree correlation in the study of gene networks and the World Wide Web is represented by a power-law function with an exponent of $\eta \simeq 0.5$ (Pastor-Satorras *et al.*, 2001). Thus, the degree–degree correlation of the shareholding network is almost the same as that of the gene network and the World Wide Web.

In a friendship network, we know experimentally that the probability of connecting persons with many friends is very high. In short, there is a high probability of connecting hubs in a human network. In such a case the scatterplot is not similar to Figure 4.16, in which distribution is diagonally right downwards. Such a distribution pattern is also found in the case of the gene network and the World Wide Web.

We will next consider the correlation between the degree and clustering coefficients of each node. If we investigate the case of the shareholding network in 2002, we obtain the result shown in Figure 4.17. In this figure, the abscissa corresponds to degree k and the ordinate to the clustering coefficient C. The solid line in this figure is given by

$$C(k) = A'k^{-\xi}, \quad \xi \simeq 1,$$

where A' is the proportionality coefficient. From this figure, we can see that nodes with a large degree have a small clustering coefficient. However, we should note that the nodes with a large degree have many clusters. To calculate the clustering coefficient, the number of actual clusters is divided by the possible number of combinations of clusters, i.e. $C(k_i, 2) = k_i(k_i - 1)/2$. In the case of a node with large degree, $C(k_i, 2) = k_i(k_i - 1)/2$ is very large. Thus, the clustering coefficient of such a node is small.

It is also noted that for the gene network and the World Wide Web, the nodes with a large degree have a small clustering coefficient (Ravasz *et al.*, 2002). Thus, the shareholding network has similar characteristics to the gene network and the World Wide

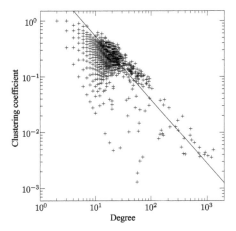

Figure 4.17. Correlation between the degree and the clustering coefficient in the shareholding network.

Web. To explain the relation between degree and clustering coefficients, the concepts of *network motif* and *hierarchy* have been proposed (Milo *et al.*, 2002; Shen-Orr *et al.*, 2002; Barabási and Oltvai, 2004). Network motif is the minimal unit constructing a network, and has a typical shape. Some network motifs construct a *module*, and some modules construct another module. It is considered that such a hierarchical structure in a network realises the relation $C(k) \propto k^{-\xi}$.

4.5.4   The shareholding network and company size

In this subsection, we will construct a network by using only major shareholder data, and then calculate the outgoing degree. In addition, we will consider the correlation between outgoing degree and the total assets of a company and the correlation between outgoing degree and the company's age. Figure 4.18 is a rank-size plot of the total assets of listed companies at the end of March 2002. In this figure, the abscissa corresponds to total assets and the ordinate corresponds to rank. The solid line in this figure is a power-law distribution with an exponent of $\mu = 0.6$. From this figure, we can see that total company assets follow an approximate power-law distribution.

At this point we are only considering listed companies at the end of March 2002. Thus, this data does not contain every company having total assets greater than some value, so it does not cover the distribution of total assets in detail. Because of this defect the complete power law shown in Chapter 2 does not appear in Figure 4.18. However, in Chapter 2, we have shown that the distributions of income, sales and profits of Japanese companies follow the power law. In addition, we have also shown that the distribution of total assets and sales of European companies follows the power law. Thus, it is reasonable to assume that if we can obtain the complete list of total assets for Japanese companies, we can probably show that they also follow a power-law distribution over a wide range of total assets.

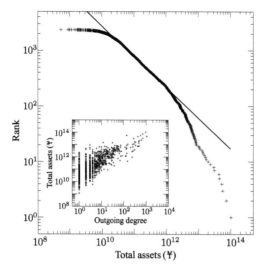

Figure 4.18. Distribution of total assets, and correlation between degree and total assets.

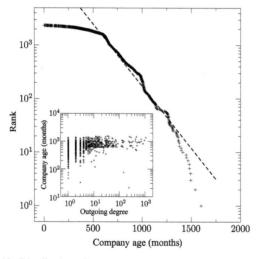

Figure 4.19. Distribution of company age, and correlation between outgoing degree and age.

The small panel in Figure 4.18 is a log-log plot of the correlation between outgoing degree and the total assets of listed companies at the end of March 2002. From this figure, we can see that the outgoing degree and total assets have a strong and positive correlation. In fact, Kendall's τ (see subsection 3.1.7) is equal to 0.53.

In the present study we define a company's age by counting the months from its foundation day to the end of March 2002, the date of the company data we used. The semi-log plot of the rank distribution of company age is shown in Figure 4.19. In this figure, the abscissa corresponds to company age and the ordinate corresponds to rank.

The dashed line in this figure is an exponential distribution. From this figure, we can see that company age follows an approximately exponential distribution. In subsection 3.4.2, we discussed the lifespan of companies, and showed that the distribution of company lifespans follows an exponential distribution. Thus, it is to be expected that company age and lifespan will follow the same distribution.

The small panel in Figure 4.19 shows the log-log plot of the correlation between outgoing degree and company age for listed companies at the end of March 2002. From this figure, we can see that outgoing degree and company age have a weak and positive correlation. In fact, Kendall's τ (see subsection 3.1.7) is equal to 0.20.

 Map constructed by four mega-banks and listed companies in 2002

So far we have drawn several networks, but we have not given any meaning to the positions of companies in those networks. The study of graph drawing has a long history, and international conferences on this subject are held every year. Elementary physics might be useful in determining the relative positions of companies in the entire network of the shareholding relationship.

To do so, we first establish the initial positions of companies as shown at the foot of this box. Note that banks and non-financial listed companies are randomly arranged in a two-dimensional plane, with the *four mega-banks*, Mizuho Bank, Sumitomo Mitsui Banking, the Bank of Tokyo-Mitsubishi and UFJ Bank all marked as solid circles in this figure. Our data lists the top ten major shareholders for each bank and each company. The list of the top ten major shareholders includes stockbroking companies, trust companies and insurance companies. However, we are interested in a network constructed from banks and non-financial listed companies, so we will ignore the other companies.

Let us suppose that a particular company is owned by two shareholders, and that one shareholder has two shares and the other has one share. Now, if we regard the number of shares as a mass, we can set the appropriate position of the company as the *centre of mass*. Thus, in this example, the appropriate position of the company is given by the point at which the line connecting two shareholders is divided in the ratio 2:1. However, these two shareholders are also owned by some shareholders; therefore, these two shareholders also move to an appropriate position. Starting from a randomly arranged initial position shown at the foot of this box and repeating this calculation, we can obtain the stationary state of the distribution of banks and non-financial listed companies, if a stationary state actually exists.

And in fact, if we actually perform this calculation we obtain the stationary state. However, this state is not unique and depends on the initial state of the distribution of banks and non-financial listed companies. The typical stationary state is shown in the right-hand graph below, and from this graph, we can see that most companies are owned by the four mega-banks.

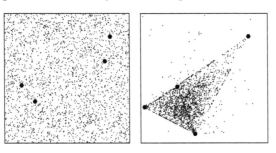

4.6   Dynamics of the company network

Up to this point we have considered networks as snapshots of a certain year, thus these can be termed *static networks*. In this section, we will consider change both in the network and in the correlation between companies in networks; that is to say, we will investigate *dynamic networks*.

4.6.1   Change in the shareholding network

Patent data is extremely useful when discussing change in a network, since we can trace the development from the first patent. Here, a new patent application connects to a network constructed from patents previously applied for. This type of network is referred to as a *growing network*, that is to say one in which the number of nodes and links increases with time.

In many economic networks, growth and collapse of the network, and the rewiring of links, happen frequently. However, as this never occurs in a patent network, we will instead examine the shareholding network since changes are numerous and frequent. We will investigate a shareholding network constructed only from major shareholder data.

Figure 4.20 is the subnetwork extracted from the network constructed from listed companies in 1985. In this subnetwork, shareholders are companies belonging to the transportation equipment industries.[13] In this figure, black nodes correspond to companies belonging to the transportation equipment industries, and white nodes to companies belonging to other industries. We note that four companies, Toyota Motor, Nissan Motor, Honda Motor and Mitsubishi Motors, are hubs in the network. In addition, we can see that these four hubs are not directly connected. As explained in subsection 4.5.3, this sort of network means that the degree–degree correlation is negative. Hubs are connected by companies belonging to both the transportation equipment industries and other industries. These companies generally belong to the

---

[13] Transportation equipment industries comprise the automobile industry and some other industries.

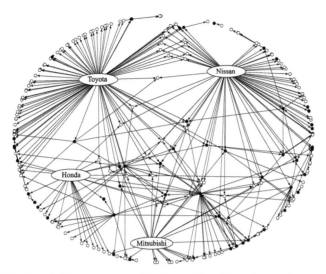

Figure 4.20. Shareholding network with shareholders belonging to the transportation equipment industries (1985).

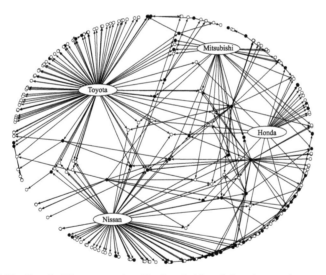

Figure 4.21. Shareholding network with shareholders belonging to the transportation equipment industries (1995).

electrical and electronics industry or to industries in which companies make parts of automobiles.

By applying the same criterion for the shareholding network in 1995, we obtain Figure 4.21. By comparing Figures 4.20 and 4.21, we can see that there is no significant change. If we draw the same type of figure for 2000, we obtain Figure 4.22. This is almost the same as Figures 4.20 and 4.21. However, Figure 4.23 for 2003 is remarkably

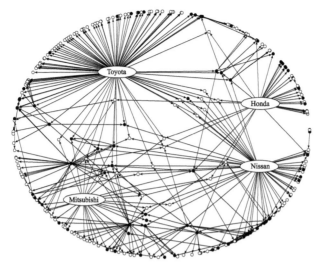

Figure 4.22. Shareholding network with shareholders belonging to the transportation equipment industries (2000).

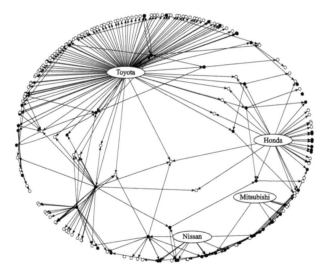

Figure 4.23. Shareholding network with shareholders belonging to the transportation equipment industries (2003).

different from Figures 4.20, 4.21 and 4.22. In this figure, Mitsubishi Motors and Nissan Motor are no longer hubs in the network. In the period between 2000 and 2003, foreign capital was invested in these two companies and the management policy changed significantly, resulting in the drastic change observable in Figure 4.23.

To consider whether a similar change occurred or not in other industries we will investigate the case of the electrical and electronics industry. Figure 4.24 is the subnetwork

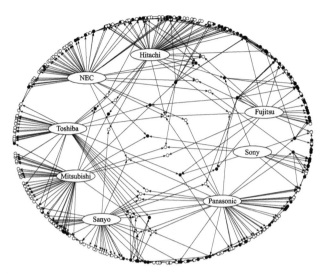

Figure 4.24. Shareholding network with shareholders belonging to the electrical and electronics industry (1985).

extracted from the network constructed from listed companies in 1985. In this subnetwork, shareholders are companies belonging to the electrical and electronics industry. Black nodes correspond to companies belonging to the electrical and electronics industry, and white nodes to companies in other industries. We can see that eight companies, Hitachi Ltd., NEC Corporation, Sony Corporation, Toshiba Corporation, Fujitsu Ltd., Panasonic Corporation, Mitsubishi Electric Corporation and Sanyo Electric Co. Ltd., are hubs in the network. As in the case of the transportation equipment industries, we can see that these eight hubs are not directly connected. As explained in subsection 4.5.3, this type of network means that the degree–degree correlation is negative.

As in the case of the transportation equipment industries, we can draw networks for 1995, 2000 and 2003 (Figures 4.25, 4.26 and 4.27, respectively). By comparing the four figures for the electrical and electronics industry, we can see that there was no significant change, and in fact there was no drastic change of management, such as investment of foreign capital, in the electrical and electronics industry.

4.6.2   Change of degree distribution

We will now consider the change of degree distribution, using only major shareholder data. Originally the shareholding network was drawn as a directed graph. However, as explained in subsection 4.3.1, the major shareholder data provides the list of the top thirty shareholders for each listed company. Thus, if we draw the shareholding network by tracing links from shareholders to listed companies, the incoming degree has an upper bound. However, the outgoing degree does not have an upper bound. Thus, here, we will investigate only the outgoing degree.

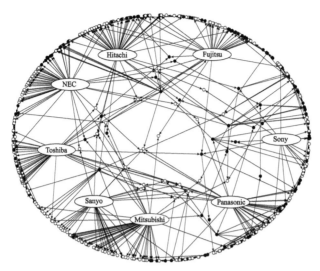

Figure 4.25. Shareholding network with shareholders belonging to the electrical and electronics industry (1995).

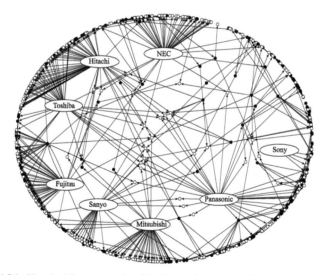

Figure 4.26. Shareholding network with shareholders belonging to the electrical and electronics industry (2000).

Denoting the total number of nodes and links as N and K respectively, the changes of N and K are summarised in Table 4.5. From this table, we can see that N increased rapidly between 1985 and 2002 although more slowly in recent years. This means that the increase of the number of newly listed companies was slow. On the other hand, K peaked in 1995, and decreased rapidly after 1995. This behaviour of K is related to bad-debt disposal after the year 1990, when the so-called Heisei bubble collapsed.

Table 4.5. *Change of shareholding network.*

			Year			
	1985	1990	1995	2000	2002	2003
N	2,078	2,466	3,006	3,527	3,727	3,770
K	23,916	29,054	33,860	32,586	30,000	26,407
γ	1.68	1.67	1.72	1.77	1.82	1.86

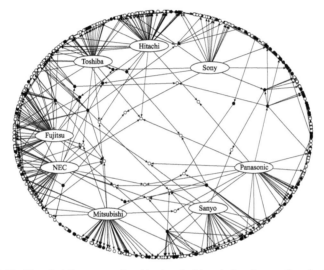

Figure 4.27. Shareholding network with shareholders belonging to the electrical and electronics industry (2003).

Figure 4.28 is a log-log plot of the cumulative distribution of outgoing degrees in 1985, 1990, 1995, 2000, 2002 and 2003. In this figure, the abscissa corresponds to the outgoing degree and the ordinate to the cumulative distribution. From this figure, we can see that all annual distributions can be well fitted by a linear function over a wide range of the distribution, though not in the tail part. In short, the outgoing degree follows a power-law distribution, and the shareholding network is a scale-free network. The change of the power-law exponent γ is summarised in Table 4.5. From this table, we can see that γ is in the range 1.67 to 1.86.

An oligopoly of degree makes the power-law exponent γ small. This characteristic of γ is the same as for the Pareto exponent discussed in section 2.2. As explained in subsection 4.5.2, γ was obtained by fitting the probability density function of degree with a power-law distribution. From Table 4.5, we can see that γ decreased slightly over the period 1985 to 1990, and increased consistently after 1990. This means that shareholding became an oligopoly up to the Heisei bubble, but this oligopoly was eliminated after the collapse of the bubble.

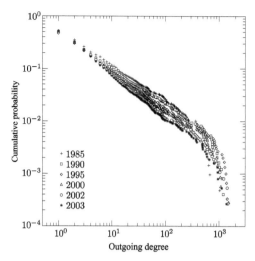

Figure 4.28. Change of degree distribution.

Now, we can consider why the power-law exponent changed. Some years ago, the bad-debt disposal of major banks was a serious problem in Japan. To settle bad debts, banks and non-financial companies sold a portion of their stockholdings. It is believed that these stockholdings were not held by banks and companies for investment, but for cross-shareholding. Thus, it is to be expected that the change of the power-law exponent has a relation with the cross-shareholding rate, i.e. the long-term shareholding rate. Long-term shareholding is not for speculative buying and selling, frequently within one year, but for stable possession for periods greater than a year.

We can now investigate the correlation between the power-law exponent and the shareholding rate with the unit base (long-term shareholding rate and cross-shareholding rate), as reported by Nippon Life Insurance (NLI) Research Institute. The left-hand panel of Figure 4.29 shows the change of the long-term shareholding rate and the cross-shareholding rate. In this figure, solid circles and solid squares correspond to the long-term shareholding rate and the cross-shareholding rate, respectively. In addition, the right-hand panel of Figure 4.29 shows the correlations between the power-law exponent and the long-term shareholding rate and cross-shareholding rates, respectively. From this figure, we can see that the power-law exponent has strong and negative correlations with the long-term shareholding rate and the cross-shareholding rate.

The degree distribution of the shareholding network has also been investigated for companies listed on the Milano Italia Borsa (MIB), the New York Stock Exchange (NYSE) and the National Association of Security Dealers Automated Quotations (NASDAQ) (Garlaschelli *et al.*, 2005). These analyses showed that the degree distribution follows the power law, exactly as is the case in Japan. The power-law exponents of MIB, NYSE and NASDAQ are $\gamma = 1.97$, $\gamma = 1.37$ and $\gamma = 1.22$, respectively. These results are almost identical to those in Japan.

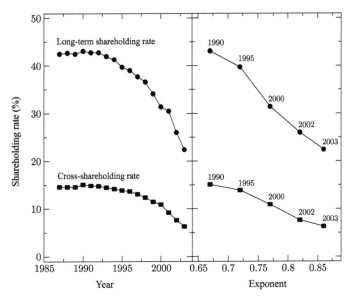

Figure 4.29. Change of the long-term shareholding rate and the cross-shareholding rate, and correlation with the power-law exponent.

Thus, it is to be expected that a degree distribution following a power law is a universal structural feature of shareholding networks, although the value of the power-law exponent, γ, depends on the country and the year. In addition, if we consider that the scale-free characteristic is found in many networks from biological ones to the Internet, it is reasonable to conclude that *the shareholding network in Japan is not special*.

In degree distributions, and also many power-law distribution phenomena, the tail part of the distribution does not follow a power law. In such cases the deviation from a power law is sometimes ignored, because the tail part describes rare events. Nevertheless, detailed investigation is promising, and we will examine this a little further.

If we plot the distribution of outgoing degree in a semi-log graph, we obtain Figure 4.30, and from this figure we can see that the tail part of the distribution is well fitted by a linear function, so the tail part, therefore, follows an exponential distribution. In addition, this tail part mainly comprises financial companies. In contrast, 95 percent of the part following a power-law distribution comprises non-financial companies. Thus, it is expected that the development mechanism of a network of financial companies differs from that for a network of non-financial companies.

4.6.3 *Correlation between companies in networks*
In subsections 4.6.1 and 4.6.2, we considered the change of network topology and the change of degree distribution as the dynamics of a network. However, we can take a different viewpoint and consider the correlation between companies in networks. For

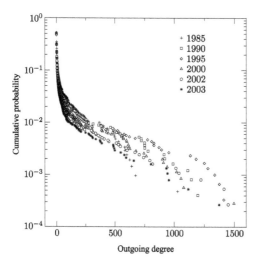

Figure 4.30. Change of degree distribution in a shareholding network.

example, we can consider the correlation between companies by using a correlation coefficient (see the box in section 4.2).

A correlation coefficient has a value in the range −1 to 1. When the correlation coefficient is close to 1, there is said to be a 'strong and positive correlation', while when the correlation coefficient is close to −1, there is said to be a 'strong and negative correlation'. In addition, when the correlation coefficient is close to 0, there is said to be 'no correlation'. However, we should be aware that the correlation coefficient is on an ordinal scale, which represents the relative strength of the correlation. In short, when we compare the correlation coefficients 0.1 and 0.5, we must not conclude that the correlation of the latter is five times stronger than the former.

When considering the correlation between companies in networks, we begin by imagining the correlation between sales and cost in the transaction network. In our analysis up to now we have investigated certain kinds of network, such as shareholding networks and transaction networks, so it is natural to wonder which network accounts for the strong correlation between companies. In addition, from the viewpoint of risk management, the correlation between bankruptcy probabilities is extremely interesting as it is connected with chain bankruptcy.

To investigate the correlation between companies, we need financial and network data for several years. However, for the transaction network we only have data for 2004, so we will assume that the shape (topology) of the transaction network in 2004 was sustained from the past. Hence, we will investigate the correlation between companies by assuming that companies change dynamically in a static network.

Correlation between growth-rates of sales and cost For an adequate description of the growth of each company, we must consider the direct *interaction between companies* through transactions, and we can check this by analysing data on the growth of sales and costs of the company (Ikeda *et al.*, 2008).

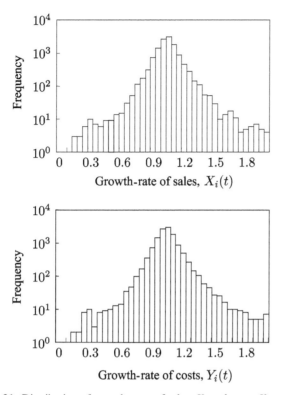

Figure 4.31. Distribution of growth-rates of sales, X, and costs, Y.

Figure 4.31 shows the distribution of the growth of sales, X, and the distribution of the growth of costs, Y, for Japanese companies listed on the First Section of the Tokyo Stock Exchange in 2003. Cost is here defined as approximately equal to the cost of raw materials. In addition, growth-rate is defined as the ratio of realised value in one year to that of the previous year. From Figure 4.31, we can see that the distributions of growth-rates have fat tails on both sides of the distributions, and follow Laplace distributions (double-sided exponential distributions).

Now, we can anticipate that sales and costs (costs of raw materials) for a pair of companies with transactions will have strong correlations. Thus, to check this expectation we will compare the correlation coefficients between the growth-rates of sales and costs for pairs of companies linked by transactions and those of pairs of companies without such connections. The important thing to note is that we are not considering the correlations between sales and costs themselves, but investigating the correlations between the growth-rates of sales and costs. Because a correlation coefficient has meaning only for a *stationary process*, so sales and costs, which are generally considered to be measures of a non-stationary process, must be rendered stationary by calculating the growth rates.

Figure 4.32 shows the correlation coefficient between the growth-rates of sales and costs. From this figure, we can see that the distribution for pairs of companies with

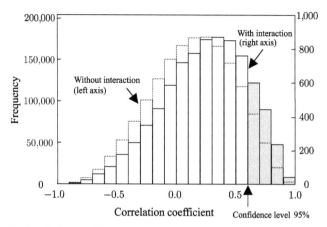

Figure 4.32. Correlation coefficient between growth-rates for sales and costs.

transactions shifts in the direction of a large correlation coefficient, compared to the distribution for pairs of companies without transactions. Although we can find large correlation coefficients for pairs of companies without transactions, we conclude that such large correlation coefficients are effects of correlations with a business partner's business partner. It follows from this that in the discussion of the growth-rate of each company we must consider the direct interaction between companies with transactional relationships. In the discussion of growth-rate given previously we ignored the interaction between companies. Thus, in the next stage we will consider cases which include interaction between companies.

In Figure 4.32, we find that even though we are investigating the correlation coefficient of growth-rate between transacting companies there is an element showing negative correlation. It is reasonable to regard this negative part as noise, and thus, following normal statistical practice, we remove noise by using the *non-correlation test*. The non-correlation test is performed as follows: firstly we assume the null hypothesis that two statistical variables are uncorrelated with each other. If non-correlation is realised the statistical quantity $T = r\sqrt{L-2}/\sqrt{1-r^2}$, which is obtained by using the correlation coefficient r calculated from time-series data, is characterised by the t distribution with $L-2$ degrees of freedom. Here, L is the length of time-series. In addition, P is the area larger than the statistical quantity T in the t distribution with $L-2$ degrees of freedom. In this case, the null hypothesis is rejected with confidence level $(1-P) \times 100$ per cent. In Figure 4.32, the shaded part shows that the correlation coefficient is statistically meaningful with a confidence level larger than 95 per cent.

The transaction network is drawn as a directed graph; therefore, we can calculate the incoming degree k_{in} and outgoing degree k_{out}. If we set the direction of links as the direction of physical distribution, the incoming degree corresponds to the number of suppliers and the outgoing degree corresponds to the number of customers. Figure 4.33 shows the cumulative probability distribution of incoming degree and outgoing degree,

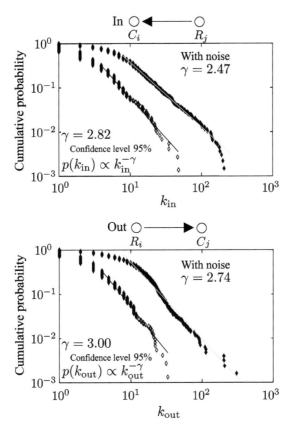

Figure 4.33. Cumulative probability distributions of incoming degree and outgoing degree.

as defined above. The tail part follows an approximate power-law distribution. When we remove noise by using the non-correlation test, the power-law exponent γ is approximately equal to 3, which is the value derived from the growing network model proposed by Barabási and Albert (1999).

If we consider the suppliers in the transaction network, the growth-rate of cost for the i-th company is represented by

$$\delta Y_i(t+1) = \sum_{j=1}^{N_s} k_{ij} \delta X_j(t) + \epsilon_i(t),$$

where $\delta X_i(t)$ and $\delta Y_i(t)$ are the normalised growth rate of sales $(X_i(t) - \langle X_i \rangle_t)/\sigma_i^{(X)}$ and the normalised growth rate of cost $(Y_i(t) - \langle Y_i \rangle_t)/\sigma_i^{(Y)}$, respectively. Here N_s is the number of suppliers, $\langle X_i \rangle_t$ represents the time average of the time-series $X_i(t)$, and $\sigma_i^{(X)}$ represents the standard deviation of the time-series $X_i(t)$. The set of parameters k_{ij} denotes the strength of interaction. See also the upper panel of Figure 4.33 for the cost C_i of i and the revenue R_j of j. The normalised growth-rates are related to each other by the above equation.

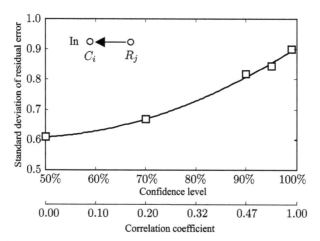

Figure 4.34. Standard deviation of residual error and confidence level.

On the other hand, if we consider the customers in the transaction network, the growth-rate of sales for the i-th company is represented by

$$\delta X_i(t+1) = \sum_{j=1}^{N_c} k_{ij} \delta Y_j(t) + \epsilon_i(t),$$

where the first term on the right-hand side of this equation corresponds to the interaction by transaction between companies. Here, N_c is the number of customers. See also the lower panel of Figure 4.33 for the cost C_j of j and the revenue R_i of i. The normalised growth-rates are related to each other by the above equation.

The parameters k_{ij} are estimated by applying regression analyses with residual error. We performed regression analyses which included k_{ij} for the pairs having statistically significant correlations as explained above. From this analysis we found that the residual error follows a normal distribution with a standard deviation equal to 0.84, which is smaller than that of the normalised growth-rate. This fact means that the introduction of the first term on the right-hand side of the equation above was successful.

It is reasonable to expect that we can make the residual error still smaller by lowering the confidence level and including more interaction terms. Figure 4.34 shows the relation between the standard deviation of residual error and the confidence level, which confirms the validity of our expectation.

Network dependence of the correlation between sales   We will now consider the network dependence of the correlation between companies. To this end, we will consider the shareholding network, the transaction network and the overlapping network. The overlapping network is the network in which nodes are connected by both a shareholding relationship and a transaction relationship. In the previous section we stated that the correlation coefficient only has meaning for a stationary process; however, we will relax this limitation in order to consider the correlation with company sales.

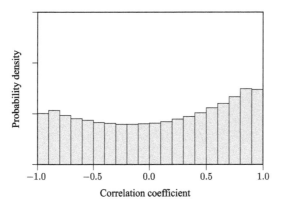

Figure 4.35. Distribution of correlation coefficient for sales.

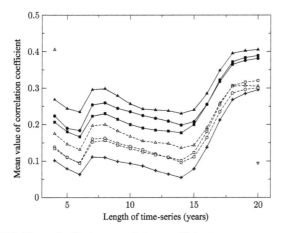

Figure 4.36. Network effect on correlation coefficient.

In graph theory the definition of the correlation coefficient corresponds to a weighted complete graph in which every node connects to every other node. For example, if we calculate correlation coefficients for 1,400 non-financial companies listed on the First Section of the Tokyo Stock Exchange by using sales data over the period 2000–4 (five years), we obtain Figure 4.35. The mean value of this distribution is 0.079. This value is shown in Figure 4.36 as the cross for the 'length of time-series' equal to 5. If we vary the length of time-series from four years (the period 2001–4) to twenty years (the period 1985–2004), and calculate mean values, we obtain the solid line connecting crosses in Figure 4.36.

If we extract the one-link correlation (correlation between companies connected by one link) in the overlapping network from the correlation coefficient calculated by using data over the period 2000–4 (five years), we obtain the distribution shown in Figure 4.37. By comparing Figure 4.35 and Figure 4.37, we can see that the positive correlation in the overlapping network is larger than that of the correlation coefficient.

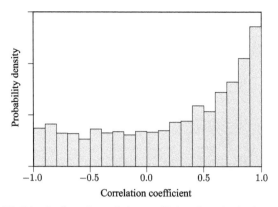

Figure 4.37. Distribution of correlation coefficient for sales in the overlapping network.

The mean value of the correlation coefficient in the overlapping network is equal to 0.244. If we change the length of the time-series we obtain the solid line connecting the solid triangles in Figure 4.36. If we apply the same analysis to the part corresponding to the transaction network, we obtain the solid line connecting the solid circles in Figure 4.36. In addition, the solid line connecting the solid squares in Figure 4.36 is for the part corresponding to the shareholding network.

If we extract the two-link correlation (correlation between companies connected by two links) in the overlapping network and repeat the same calculation used in the case of the one-link correlation, we obtain the dashed line connecting the open triangles in Figure 4.36. In this figure, the dashed lines connecting open circles and open squares correspond to two-link correlations in the transaction network and the shareholding network, respectively. From this figure, we can see, in the case of one-link correlation, that the correlation in the overlapping network is the largest correlation. This is applicable to the case of two-link correlation. In addition, the two-link correlation is smaller than the one-link correlation for every type of network.

Network dependence of correlation between bankruptcy probabilities   We can consider the correlation between bankruptcy probabilities. Although many models for bankruptcy probabilities have been proposed we use the bankruptcy probability model known as *SAF2002* (Simple Analysis of Failure 2002) (Shirata, 2004). SAF2002 is defined by

$$\text{SAF2002} = 0.0104x_1 + 0.0268x_2 - 0.0661x_3 - 0.0237x_4 + 0.7077.$$

Here, x_1, x_2, x_3 and x_4 correspond to retained earnings to total assets, net income before tax to total assets, an inventory turnover period and interest expenses to sales, respectively. This bankruptcy probability was derived by applying non-linear regression for these four financial items, which differ remarkably between bankrupted companies and non-bankrupted companies.

As is obvious from its name, SAF2002 was proposed in 2002, and consequently it is widely supposed that the model is inapplicable to earlier years. However, we assume that this model is so applicable, and we can calculate the correlation coefficient between bankruptcy probabilities over the period 2000–4 (a five-year period). Thus, we obtain the mean value of the correlation coefficient equal to 0.0863. On the other hand, for a one-link correlation the mean values of correlation are 0.1345, 0.1614 and 0.1780 in the transaction network, the shareholding network and the overlapping network, respectively. For a two-link correlation, the mean values of correlation are 0.1136, 0.1334 and 0.1677 in the transaction network, the shareholding network and the overlapping network, respectively.

From these results we can see that the overlapping network has a strong correlation. However, compared with the correlation between sales the network dependence of the correlation between bankruptcy probabilities is weak. In addition, the difference between the one-link correlation and the two-link correlation is small. This finding indicates that chain bankruptcy is unlikely. We can suggest two underlying causes for this fact. One possibility is that SAF2002 is not applicable to network structure phenomena such as chains of bankruptcy, because SAF2002 indexes only the bankruptcy probability of the company itself. Another possibility is that our data covers only listed companies, for which chain bankruptcy is rare.

5 An agent-based model for companies

In Chapters 2 and 3 we investigated various statistical properties of companies by treating them as a statistical ensemble. In the preceding chapter we demonstrated that companies are interconnected through transaction relations, shareholdings, co-operative filing of patents and so on, thus resulting in the formation of a complex network. In this chapter we introduce the results of recent studies elucidating the dynamics of interacting companies using agent-based models.

The agents appearing in economic phenomena comprise consumers, investors, companies and others, and we can regard economic phenomena as many-body systems in which a number of those agents interact. Such an approach is called an *agent-based simulation*. Recently more and more simulations of various economic phenomena have been carried out using computers.

In computer science, an agent means a small piece of software possessing such properties as autonomy (acting with its own 'will'), social nature (collaborating with another) and adaptability (making itself fit to its surroundings). These features of the agent exactly coincide with the agent-based model considered in this chapter.

So we might say that economic agents are the actors and the stage is a network connecting those agents. But what drama is played out in this theatre? We will begin by modelling the dynamics of companies as a stochastic process and then proceed to an explanation of agent-based modelling of companies.

5.1 Gibrat's process

In the present context we refer to the income, assets and number of employees attributed to a company as its complete 'size'. We attempt to model the dynamics of companies on the basis of Gibrat's process (Gibrat, 1931), as has been briefly described in subsection 3.1.4. The size of a company in a certain year t is denoted by $x(t)$; hence $x(t-1)$ represents the size of the company in the preceding year. Gibrat's law is expressed as

$$\frac{x(t)}{x(t-1)} = a(t-1),$$

where $a(t-1)$ is a stochastic variable with some probability distribution which is statistically independent of $x(t-1)$ and plays the role of growth-rate. The law may also be written as

$$x(t) = a(t-1)x(t-1);$$

namely, the size $x(t)$ of a company this year is $x(t-1)$ multiplied by $a(t-1)$. Such a stochastic process, characterised by multiplication of random variables, is generally called a *multiplicative stochastic process*. Since Gibrat's process is the simplest among multiplicative stochastic processes, it may be referred to as a *pure multiplicative stochastic process*.

If we go back one year, Gibrat's law reads

$$x(t-1) = a(t-2)x(t-2),$$

and combination of this with the previous expression for $x(t)$ results in

$$x(t) = a(t-1)x(t-1) = a(t-1)a(t-2)x(t-2).$$

Repeating this process, we reach the original or initial time and obtain

$$x(t) = a(t-1)a(t-2) \cdots a(1)a(0)x(0).$$

Let us take logarithms of both sides of the above equation:

$$\log x(t) = \log a(t-1) + \log a(t-2) + \cdots + \log a(1) + \log a(0) + \log x(0).$$

The right-hand side has been thus converted to additive operations from multiplication. Such a process is called an *additive stochastic process* (Gibrat, 1931; see also Sutton, 1997).

If various instances of $a(t)$ are uncorrelated to each other, then *the central limit theorem* states that the distribution of $\log x(t)$ will asymptotically approach the normal distribution as time passes. Hence the asymptotic distribution of $x(t)$ is given by the log-normal distribution, which is sometimes called Gibrat's distribution. The growth rate $a(t)$ of a company may well depend on the size of the company. However, Gibrat assumed that the size of the company and its growth rate were independent of each other; in other words, that the business chances of a company increased just in proportion to its size. As has been demonstrated by the empirical analyses in Chapter 3, Gibrat's law is certainly satisfied by large companies. The log-normal distribution is skewed with a fat tail on the upper side. But the tail is not particularly fat in comparison with that of the power-law distribution. According to this model, diversity in the size of companies continues to increase without any limitation even if they were of the same size at an initial time. However, the ranking of companies by size is not

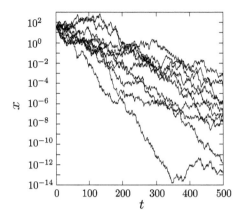

Figure 5.1. Behaviour of companies in Gibrat's process.

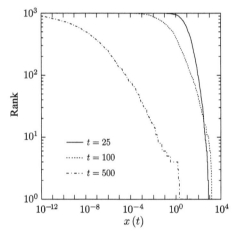

Figure 5.2. Distribution of company sizes in Gibrat's process.

fixed. Figures 5.1 and 5.2 illustrate this interchange of companies. The simulation used 1,000 companies and assumed that $a(t)$ took uniform random numbers such that $\frac{1}{2} < a(t) < \frac{3}{2}$. The initial value for $x(t)$ was set as $x(0) = 40$. Uniform random numbers were generated by selecting numbers in a given range randomly and with equal probability.

5.2   Model of the shareholding network

We can now develop the idea of Gibrat's process to construct a model which reproduces the results in section 3.1 and subsection 4.5.4. And using the model we try to shed light on such phenomena as are characterised by the power-law degree distribution. These phenomena have been demonstrated in subsection 4.6.2.

5.2.1   *Reproduction of size distribution*

How can we derive a power-law distribution on the basis of Gibrat's process? Physicists have already prepared several answers to this question. One of them is to reset the stochastic variable to its initial value with a certain probability q (Manrubia and Zanette, 1999). This can be expressed as

$$x_i(t) = \begin{cases} a_i(t-1)x_i(t-1) & \text{with probability } 1-q \\ x_i(0) & \text{with probability } q \end{cases}$$

where i is an index distinguishing companies. Companies do not interact with each other in this model and they have their own evolutionary paths with differing statistical uncertainties. The process is referred to as a *multiplicative stochastic process with a reset event*.

Suppose that the parameter q represents a bankruptcy probability for companies. In this model, as long as companies do not fall into bankruptcy, they evolve according to Gibrat's process. Once a company becomes bankrupt, it restarts its business under the initial condition or is replaced by a newcomer with the same condition. Actually such a simple process is able to explain the outline facts such as the power-law distribution of the sizes of companies, and the exponential distribution of company lifetimes. Alternative models which can reproduce the power-law distribution include multiplicative stochastic processes with a reflection wall (Solomon and Levy, 1996) or with additive noises (Sornette and Cont, 1997; Takayasu *et al.*, 1997; Sornette, 1998). The reflection wall totally reverses the direction of evolution of a company whose size becomes smaller than some lower limit. The multiplicative stochastic process with additive noises was studied in detail by Kesten (1973), and is sometimes referred to as Kesten's process.

We are now in a position to carry out simulations in the reset-event model described above. It is, however, necessary to specify the simulation parameters. We used 50,000 companies and set $x_i(0) = 1$ as the initial condition. We also adopted $q = 0.005$ for the reset probability. This value arises from the historical fact that Japanese companies went into bankruptcy with annually averaged rates ranging from 0.2 to 1.7 per cent during the period 1970 to 1997. Finally, the growth rate $a_i(t)$ was assumed to take random numbers uniformly distributed in (0.5, 1.5] Figure 5.3 exemplifies the results obtained in the simulation. This is a log-log plot of the size x of companies on the abscissa versus the corresponding rank on the ordinate for results at different times. We can readily observe that the distribution stabilises as time passes. In particular, the distribution is almost stationary beyond $t = 200$. We note that the stable distribution has a power-law tail and its exponent is approximately $\mu = 1$. The inset in Figure 5.3 shows a distribution of the ages of companies at $t = 1000$. This is a linear-log plot of the age T of companies on the abscissa versus the corresponding rank on the ordinate. The linear behaviour of the distribution demonstrates the exponential characteristics of the distribution. We have thus succeeded in explaining half of the results given in subsection 4.5.4.

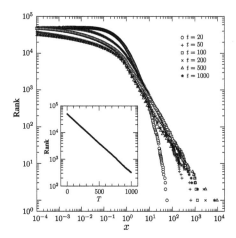

Figure 5.3. Simulated results for sizes and ages of companies.

  The Weber–Fechner law

In 1834 E. H. Weber experimentally established that the perceived intensity of physical stimuli is proportional to the relative change of the magnitudes of the stimuli, not to their absolute change. Further, in 1859 Fechner mathematically formulated Weber's observation by remarking that our perception intensity is proportional to the logarithm of the stimulus intensity. Everybody experiences saturation of perception in response to increasing physical stimuli. The experimental fact is really a characteristic of the logarithmic function. As well as our five senses, our sense of money, if one may call it that, seems to obey the Weber–Fechner law, according to a recent experiment carried out by one of the authors. The modelling of the behaviour of stock prices as a geometric Brownian process may be related to this observation; the rate of return is adopted as a fundamental stochastic variable instead of the stock price itself. Fechner is thus known as a founder of psychophysics. In fact, he also formulated a statistical concept regarding Kendall's τ, introduced in Chapter 3.

5.2.2 Reproduction of degree distribution

To explain all of the results in subsections 4.5.4 and 4.6.2 on the basis of the present model we need an additional creative device. To that end we will try to convert the assets possessed by a company to the degree of its links. Companies possess part of their assets in the form of stocks. The percentage of investment in stocks in the sum of total assets differs from company to company, as does the division of the investment funds into different stocks. We will simply define the degree $k_i(t)$ of company i

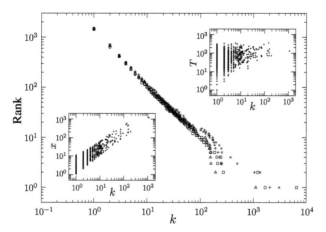

Figure 5.4. Conversion of the simulated results to the degree distribution.

as $k_i(t) := x_i(t)/r_i$ where the assets $x_i(t)$ are divided by a uniform random number $r_i \in [1, 5)$.

Figure 5.4 shows the results for the degree distribution obtained by several simulations at $t = 1000$. This figure plots the simulated results with the degree k on the abscissa and the corresponding rank on the ordinate, both on a logarithmic scale. We see that the distribution shows power-law behaviour over a wide range. Its power-law exponent is estimated as being close to $\gamma = 2$, which is slightly larger than the value in Table 4.5.

The inset placed at the upper-right corner of Figure 5.4 displays a typical example of correlations between the degree k and the age T of companies at $t = 1000$. This figure is a log-log plot of k on the abscissa and T on the ordinate. The correlation is weak, and is quantitatively confirmed by the value $\tau = 0.21$ for Kendall's τ. This agrees well with the result given in subsection 4.5.4. On the other hand, the inset at the lower-left corner of Figure 5.4 exemplifies correlations between the degree k and the assets x of companies at $t = 1000$, both of which are plotted on a logarithmic scale. The correlation, with $\tau = 0.60$, is assessed as rather strong. This is also in good agreement with the result in subsection 4.5.4.

5.2.3 Effects of nodal characteristics

We have proposed a successful model to explain the power-law behaviour of the degree distribution for companies. At this point we will turn to the remaining issue of why the distribution has an exponentially decaying tail, a matter raised at the end of subsection 4.6.2.

In 1999 Barabási and Albert worked out a simple model to reproduce networks with scale-free characteristics, a model which, for brevity, is often referred to as the *BA model* (Barabási and Albert, 1999). The key ingredients in their model are network growth and preferential attachment. By network growth we mean that the number of nodes in the network increases over time, and by preferential attachment we mean that nodes with a higher degree have a larger probability of establishing links with new nodes added to the network; in the original model the attachment probability is proportional to the degree of the existing nodes.

In 2000 Amaral and his collaborators demonstrated that the degree distributions of some networks are characterised by an exponential form instead of a power law (Amaral *et al.*, 2000). They then tried to extend the BA model to explain their finding, and in the process they modified the BA model by setting an upper bound to the number of links that a node can have. They interpreted the upper bound as arising from aging or the limited capacity of nodes. That is, the aging effect prevents old nodes from connecting to a new node. Alternatively nodes with a large degree of connections suffer from the high costs necessary to keep existing links, so that they have no capacity to make a new connection beyond a critical value k_{max} for the degree.

In view of the outline facts of the shareholding network, we will assess the validity of the model due to Amaral *et al.* for studying the tail of the degree distribution. Because the model is a generalised version of the BA model we will initially focus on whether the network is growing with a preferential attachment or not.

Table 4.5 confirms that the network is actually growing although the growth rate is fluctuating over time. Also we note that the tail of the degree distribution mainly stems from contributions by financial institutions, which take positive action in spending their money on investment in new companies. The larger a financial institutions is, the higher the probability it has of acquiring new stocks. This is really a preferential attachment process working for financial institutions. The key postulates in the BA model thus seem to be satisfied in the shareholding network. So how about the effects of aging and limited capacity, which are the new ingredients to the BA model introduced by Amaral *et al.*?

In the case of financial institutions, it is hard to imagine that they tend not to acquire new stocks as they become older. And it is difficult to treat their ages in a systematic way because mergers and acquisitions occur regularly. On the other hand, the total amount of investment money is fixed for financial institutions so that they have a limited capacity to establish shareholding connections. We therefore claim that the model of Amaral and his colleagues can account for the exponential tail in the degree distribution. The next problem is how to estimate the critical value k_{max} from the real data. This is reserved for future study. We expect that k_{max} depends on how much money for investment each financial institution possesses.

5.3   Balance sheet dynamics

An agent-based model can be used to elucidate complex phenomena encountered in a wide variety of social and economic systems, and is a natural extension of the atomic concept worked out for describing physical systems. Agents have internal structures characterised by different parameters. For instance, agents are made sufficiently intelligent as to be autonomous; that is, an agent has the capability to adapt itself to surrounding conditions. In addition, agents interact with each other according to simple rules. A complex system is thus regarded as an assembly of interacting agents.

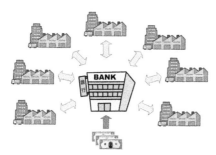

Figure 5.5. Conceptual figure of agent-based model: companies interacting through a single bank.

D. Delli Gatti and M. Gallegati and their collaborators constructed a promising model consisting of interacting economic agents to describe the dynamics of companies (see Delli Gatti *et al.*, 2000 and Gallegati *et al.*, 2003 for the original work; also Delli Gatti *et al.*, 2008). They demonstrated that the model successfully reproduced a set of stylised facts, including the company size distribution with a power-law tail, and the Laplace-type distribution of the growth rate of companies.

A large collection of agents with identical characteristic parameters and a monopolistic bank constitute the model as shown in Figure 5.5. The dynamics of the agents are characterised by their balance sheets. Each company tries to maximise its expected profit against a background of the possible risks in the market. The companies, which are mutually interacting through the bank, become heterogeneous in the course of temporal evolution, and the possibility of bankruptcy is also taken into account. Such a microscopic model, once established, enables us to investigate the interplay between the behaviour of individual companies and the macroscopic trend of the economy. We are now in a position to calibrate the model thanks to the accumulation of results relating to the statistical properties of the dynamics of real companies.

We will initially reconstruct the original model to elucidate the conceptual ingredients. The compromise between the two concepts, *profit maximisation* and maintaining the company as a *going concern*, plays a key role in the decision-making of companies using imperfect information relating to their financial conditions. Simulations based on the model are then carried out for the statistical properties of company dynamics and the results so obtained are discussed in light of observations in the real economy. For more details of the contents given in this section, we refer the reader to Iyetomi *et al.* (2009a).

5.3.1 The basic agent model

The dynamics of the agents are described in terms of balance sheets as shown in Figure 5.6. A company i has total capital $K_i(t)$ and debt $L_i(t)$ from the bank at the beginning of a time period t. Here, $i = 1, \ldots, N$ and N is the total number of companies. According to the accounting equation, the equity capital, $A_i(t)$, of the company must equal the total capital minus the debt. On the other hand, the bank agent has a balance sheet on which its aggregate supply of credit, $L(t) = \sum_i L_i(t)$, is

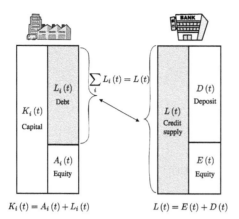

Figure 5.6. Balance sheets for companies and a bank.

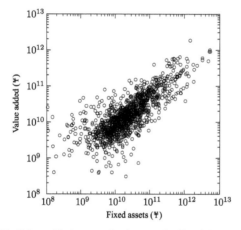

Figure 5.7. Value added versus fixed assets for listed Japanese companies in 2003.

balanced by the sum of total deposits $D(t)$ and equity capital $E(t)$. Stocks and flows are two kinds of basic variable in the construction of models of system dynamics. Balance sheets have only stock variables so they are just snapshots of a company's financial condition. Flow variables such as profit and investment determine the evolution of the economic system.

For the sake of simplicity when we model a company's dynamics we concentrate on the financial aspect of the production function and assume the value added, $Y_i(t)$, linearly scales to the capital input:

$$Y_i(t) = \phi K_i(t)$$

where the proportion ϕ is taken as $\phi = 0.1$. Figure 5.7 validates this modelling for the production function.

At the beginning of a given time period t the i-th company changes its capital $K_i(t)$ to maximise the expected value of profit. This strategic behaviour of the company, called *profit maximisation*, has been a well-known hypothesis in economics since the time of Adam Smith, although it has not yet been confirmed.

The profit of a company is fixed at the end of each period as

$$\pi_i(t) = u_i(t)Y_i(t) - r_i(t)K_i(t) = [u_i(t)\phi - r_i(t)] K_i(t),$$

where $r_i(t)$ is the interest rate for capital. The parameter $u_i(t)$ reflects uncertainty in the market. Since a market consists of a huge number of economic degrees of freedom, the determination of the selling price inevitably becomes stochastic. We also assume that $u_i(t)$ is independent of the company size, in harmony with Gibrat's law. We arbitrarily take $u_i(t)$ as a uniform random number in $(0, 2)$. Expected profit is thus given by setting $u_i(t) = 1$ in the equation for $\pi_i(t)$ as

$$\langle \pi_i(t) \rangle = [\phi - r_i(t)] K_i(t).$$

At the lower limit $u_i(t) = 0$, products are so discounted that they are unable to yield value added, while maximum value added is obtained at a price double the expected price, corresponding to $u_i(t) = 2$.

If a company adopts an aggressive production plan it has a finite probability of bankruptcy. The bankruptcy of a company is defined at the end of a period t by the condition,

$$A_i(t) = A_i(t - 1) + \pi_i(t - 1) < 0.$$

Substitution of the previous equation for $\pi_i(t - 1)$ into the bankruptcy criterion results in the following formula for the bankruptcy probability:

$$P^{\mathrm{B}}(K_i(t)) = \begin{cases} \dfrac{r_i(t)K_i(t) - A_i(t)}{2\phi K_i(t)} & \text{for } K_i(t) > \dfrac{A_i(t)}{r_i(t)}, \\ 0 & \text{otherwise.} \end{cases}$$

We thus see there is an upper bound to the size needed for a company to be free from bankruptcy. The relationship between the increase of expected profit and the emergence of bankruptcy is depicted in Figure 5.8.

Another management policy, known under the label of the *going concern* policy, prevents a company from expanding its size infinitely; a company aims to survive forever. We assume here that companies adopt a solid production plan with a safety factor $\sigma (\leq 1)$:

$$K_i(t) = \sigma \frac{A_i(t)}{r_i(t)}.$$

This choice compromises two directly opposed economic ideas.

The interest rate for each company is then determined through the demand and supply balance in the credit market inhabited by companies and the bank. The company requests the bank to finance the following amount of money derived from the equation

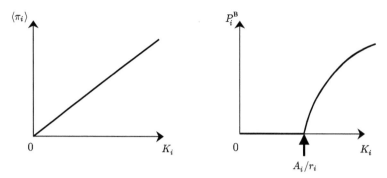

Figure 5.8. Emergence of finite probability of bankruptcy with increase of expected profit.

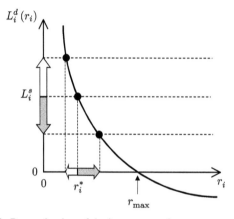

Figure 5.9. Determination of the interest rate for a company.

for $K_i(t)$:

$$L_i^d(t) = K_i(t) - A_i(t) = \left(\frac{\sigma}{r_i(t)} - 1 \right) A_i(t).$$

On the other hand, credit is granted to the company by the bank in proportion to its relative size in the preceding period as

$$L_i^s(t) = L(t) \frac{K_i(t-1)}{\sum_i K_i(t-1)},$$

Balancing $L_i^d(t)$ and $L_i^s(t)$ gives the formula for the interest rate,

$$r_i(t) = \frac{\sigma A_i(t)}{L_i^s(t) + A_i(t)}.$$

Such an equilibrium mechanism to determine the interest rate is depicted in Figure 5.9. The maximum rate is given by $r_{max} = \sigma$. If the company obtains more credit from the bank, the interest rate decreases, and vice versa.

Companies with the above-mentioned behavioural rules would never go bankrupt, but real companies, of course, are always afraid of bankruptcy. To incorporate the possibility of bankruptcy into the model, we will replace the equity capital of the current period by that of the preceding period in the previous equation for $K_i(t)$:

$$K_i(t) = \sigma \frac{A_i(t-1)}{r_i(t)}.$$

Companies thus determine their production plans with delayed information. This replacement overturns the conservative attitude of companies when they are in a recession phase, and the companies incidentally take speculative management actions. We can arbitrarily set $\sigma = \frac{1}{2}$, which enables us to make a smooth connection with the original model. The corresponding equations in Delli Gatti *et al.* (2008) are seamlessly reduced to the present equations by omitting the intensive terms which are independent of the dimensions of the agents.

Delay in information is one of the causes of bankruptcy for companies. Other causes include the existence of unexpected risk and the propagation of bankruptcy akin to a chain reaction. In our analysis so far the possible risk is supposed to be totally predictable by specifying a definite range for the stochastic parameter $u_i(t)$, but nobody can avoid unexpected risk in real business. In fact, companies are linked to each other through transactions and with a supply of credit. If a large company is bankrupted, then a credit risk shock will propagate over the network. The chain reaction bankruptcy arising from such direct interactions among companies is beyond the scope of the present section and will be discussed later in this book.

With regard to the dynamics of the bank we assume that the bank expands its business subject to the minimum requirement of a prudence rule with a risk coefficient α:

$$L(t) = \sum_i L_i(t) = \frac{E(t)}{\alpha}.$$

The Basel Committee of the Bank for International Settlements introduced an international capital adequacy standard called Basel I in 1988.[1] It requires that each bank has capital equivalent to at least 8 per cent of the total assets: $\alpha = 0.08$. The bank derives a profit through investing its money in companies. Here the profit margin is set as 0.2 per cent. However, its net profit Π_t is given by subtracting financial costs from the sum of interest received. The financial costs are interest payments paid to depositors and investors along with additional loss due to bad debts stemming from the bankruptcy of companies.

5.3.2 *Representative agents*
Before discussing the results for multi-agent simulations, we will first study a simple system comprising a single ideal company interacting with the bank agent; companies

---

[1] Basel I is to be replaced by Basel II with more refined rules.

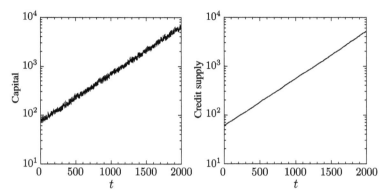

Figure 5.10. Representative company (left panel) and bank (right panel).

are thus represented by a single agent. This representative agent model, neglecting the heterogeneity of agents, is a traditional approach in economics. Figure 5.10 shows that both agents grow exponentially. This is an intrinsic property of the present model. For a market with no fluctuations in the selling price ($u_i(t) = 1$) and in the interest rate ($r_i(t) = r$), one can obtain an analytic solution with exponential growth for each agent. Equating two formulae for the growth rate of the representative agents, one can determine the average interest rate r and hence the growth-rate. The growth-rate derived analytically in this way provides a very good explanation of the results in Figure 5.10.

5.3.3   *Reduction to a multiplicative process*
One can terminate the interaction by assuming

$$r_i(t) = \phi.$$

The profit for companies vanishes on average in such a situation, corresponding to a zero-growth economy without competition between companies. This assumption reduces the present model with ideal companies to a random growth model:

$$A_i(t+1) = \lambda_i(t)A_i(t) = \tfrac{1}{2}[1 + u_i(t)]A_i(t),$$

with

$$\langle \lambda_i(t) \rangle = 1.$$

We thus see that Gibrat's process underlies the present model. If companies do not go into bankruptcy their size distribution approaches the log-normal form, but is ever-growing. The system constituted by companies with finite probability of bankruptcy reaches a stationary state in which the size distribution is represented by the Pareto distribution with $\mu = 1$.

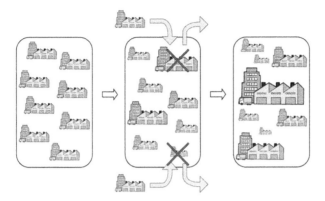

Figure 5.11. Temporal evolution of the agent-based simulation.

5.3.4 Distribution of company sizes

We executed numerical simulations based on the present model with 100,000 companies. This number of companies is still much smaller than the present number of companies in Japan, about 2.5 million. We started the simulations by giving all companies identical initial conditions. When, as time passed, companies went into bankruptcy, they were replaced by new ones with the same initial conditions. That is, the total number of companies was kept constant during the simulations. Although companies were completely equal at the outset, they became differentiated and some of them died and were replaced by new companies. Eventually companies were divided into classes of large, medium and small size. This evolutionary process of companies is depicted in Figure 5.11.

Figure 5.12 exemplifies the temporal behaviour of companies in the present model, and shows results obtained with small numbers of companies ($N = 2, 3, 1,000$). Note that the tracks of companies are very irregular and that there is competition among companies. This is in sharp contrast to the representative agent model in which a single company steadily grows together with the bank. We thus see that heterogeneity of companies is a natural outcome of the competition among companies interacting through the bank.

Figure 5.13 shows how the bank evolves in time. This is the result for a bank dealing with a group of actual companies with possibilities of bankruptcy. Its equity fluctuates appreciably and sometimes encounters large shocks, such idiosyncratic shocks stemming from the bankruptcy of large companies. On the other hand, the growth of the bank is very steady for ideal companies without bankruptcy; its rate is almost indistinguishable from that of the representative company.

In Figure 5.14, we plot the size distribution of ideal companies without bankruptcy. The left-hand panel shows the result obtained when the bank evolves naturally with exponential growth, while the right-hand panel is the result when the size of the bank is artificially fixed, that is a stationary economy is realised. Both distributions are well fitted to the log-normal form, which is in keeping with Gibrat's process in its simple

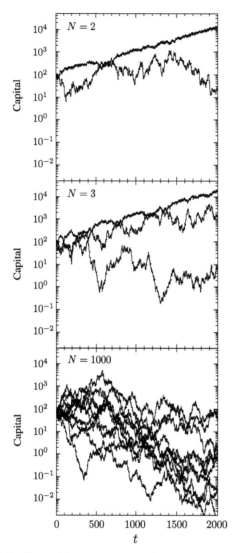

Figure 5.12. Competition among companies.

form. In Figure 5.15, we display the size distributions for actual companies susceptible to bankruptcy, corresponding to the two economic conditions in Figure 5.14. The sizes of those companies are distributed in a power-law form:

$$\text{rank} \propto K_i(t)^{-\mu}.$$

When the bank grows naturally the Pareto exponent is tentatively stabilised around $\mu = 2$ and then approaches $\mu = 1$ as time proceeds. We thus see that the size distribution of companies and the temporal evolution of the bank critically depend on whether companies make full use of available information on their financial conditions or not

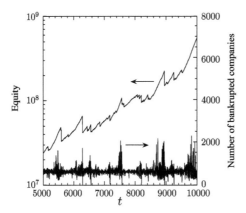

Figure 5.13. Temporal evolution of the bank agent.

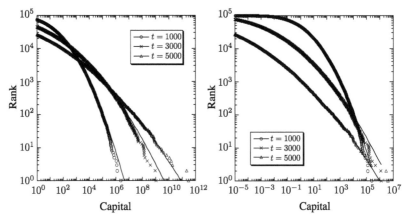

Figure 5.14. Size distribution for companies existing eternally.

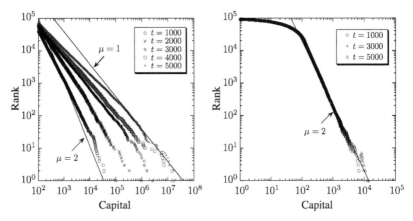

Figure 5.15. Size distribution for companies susceptible to bankruptcy.

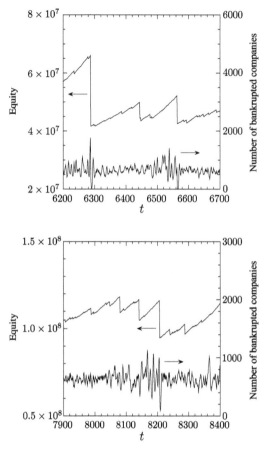

Figure 5.16. Macroscopic shocks originating from synchronised bankruptcy.

in determining a production plan for the next period. If we control the macroscopic economy by keeping the size of the bank fixed, we have a stationary state with a power-law size distribution as shown in the right-hand panel of Figure 5.15. The exponent is close to $\mu = 2$. This value is totally different from the exponent ($\mu = 1$) found for non-interacting companies. The interactions among companies through the bank give rise to profound changes in the statistical properties of companies as manifested by the variation of the Pareto exponent.

5.3.5 *Synchronised bankruptcy*

Bankruptcies of companies take place in a synchronised way with macroscopic shocks reflected in the equity capital of the bank. Figure 5.16 enlarges Figure 5.13 to confirm the emergence of such synchronised bankruptcy. The bankruptcy of a large company triggers a chain of bankruptcies in the present model, which takes into account interactions among companies. The large bankruptcy gives rise to large bad debts for the bank.

Then the equity capital of the bank shrinks and accordingly the bank's credit supply to other companies decreases. This leads to an increase of interest rates for loans from the bank and hence a decrease of profits for companies. Financially fragile companies with a low equity ratio $A_i(t)/K_i(t)$ are thus strongly affected by the bankruptcy of the large company.

 Towards an unequal society

Socioeconomic disparity is growing throughout the world, and is emerging as a serious social problem which should be solved. Equality in every aspect is not a solution, however. As has been demonstrated by the agent-based simulations introduced here, heterogeneity of agents in an economic system is a natural outcome of competition among agents with both growth and failure, giving rise to vitality in the system. Bearing in mind Pareto's law we expect that many readers may be on the 'useless' side of the distribution, but they may be exactly the people to lead society in the near future. Everyone should prepare themselves for taking over the pole position on a routine basis. What must be avoided is a society in which there is no potential for challenge and the current disparity is thereby fixed. A sound society is fluid and continuously promotes the interchange of positions. Having only a single measure for evaluation is one of the major causes of fixing disparities in society. For example, the concentration of research resources is recently observable in the academic world in Japan. This tendency may eventually lead to loss of diversity in research activities. We thus have reason to be concerned that the pursuit of tentative and perhaps illusory efficiency may hamper intellectual progress in the long term.

5.4 Network effects on wealth distribution

Recent development in the means of transport and communication enables companies to connect with each other in spite of physical distances. It is essential to take account of direct interactions among companies arising from such an economic network to elucidate various economic phenomena. For instance, we aim to shed light on the origin of business cycles, the stability of economic systems against external shocks or large bankruptcies and the formation of industrial clusters.

In the previous section, we explained the distributions of company sizes and degrees without taking account of interactions among companies. In the present section we will consider a prototype model for such economic interactions. Although the model may be too simple to be applied to actual economic phenomena, we expect that it will be useful for illuminating the effects of the network on the whole economy. The model described here is not limited to interactions among companies, but is generally applicable to any interactions of agents with entities which can be regarded as constituting wealth

(Bouchaud and Mezard, 2000; Souma et al., 2001). A typical example of wealth is the total asset base of a company. Here $x_i(t)$ denotes the wealth of the i-th agent at time t.

5.4.1 Model construction

Suppose that the i-th and j-th agents are dealing with each other for wealth and their dealing is described by $J_{ij}(t)(\geq 0)$. The interaction coefficients $J_{ij}(t)$ constitute a dealing matrix. The present model is then given by

$$x_i(t+1) = a_i(t)x_i(t) - \sum_j J_{ji}(t)x_i(t) + \sum_j J_{ij}(t)x_j(t).$$

This is a generalisation of Gibrat's process, implemented by incorporating the second and third terms on the right-hand side (Bouchaud and Mezard, 2000). The second term represents the transfer of wealth from the i-th agent to the j-th agent, so that it takes a minus sign. On the other hand, the third term with a plus sign represents the reverse process. Relative magnitudes of these two terms determine the direction of the net flow of wealth. Thus the terms additional to Gibrat's process mimic wealth transactions between agents.

We will now simplify the model so that the dealing matrix $J_{ij}(t)$ is independent of time and given as

$$J_{ij} = \frac{J}{k_j} A_{ij},$$

where A_{ij} is an adjacency matrix which is constituted by values of either 0 or 1. If the i-th and j-th agents are connected (adjacent) to each other through the transaction network, A_{ij} has the value 1 but otherwise 0, and k_j refers to the degree of the j-th agent. In addition, J is a constant and arbitrarily specified. Inclusion of the aforementioned simplifications further reduces the model to

$$x_i(t+1) = a_i(t)x_i(t) - Jx_i(t) + J\sum_{j\in\text{adj}(i)} \frac{x_j(t)}{k_j},$$

where $\text{adj}(i)$ denotes a set of nodes adjacent to the node i in the same way as that in subsection 4.4.1.

5.4.2 Network effects

For our simulation of wealth distribution on a given network let us assume that the total number of agents is 10,000 and $J = 0.01$. Furthermore, the stochastic variable $a_i(t)$ is assumed to obey the normal distribution with an average of 1.01 and a variance of 0.02. Figure 5.17 shows the results so simulated for a regular network of the type depicted by the leftmost panel of Figure 4.1, where the average degree of the network was set to 10. This figure plots magnitudes of wealth, normalized with its average, on the abscissa and the corresponding ranks on the ordinate; both axes are on a logarithmic

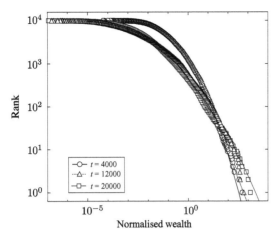

Figure 5.17. Wealth distribution in a regular network.

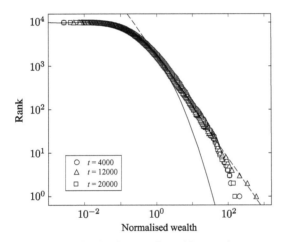

Figure 5.18. Wealth distribution in a small-world network.

scale. Open circles, triangles and squares in the figure show the results at $t = 4,000$, 12,000 and 20,000, respectively. The curves attached to each set of results show the outcome of fitting with the log-normal distribution. We see that the wealth distribution is not stationary and is well described by the log-normal distribution with time-varying average and variance. Also we note that wealth is distributed very unequally over the scale of 10^7.

We will next modify the network structure by keeping the average degree fixed. For instance, the regular network is randomised by rewiring links with the probability of 0.05 as depicted in Figure 4.1. The results in such a network are shown in Figure 5.18. The symbols in the figure share the same meanings as those in Figure 5.17, and the dashed line shows the fitting of the tail part of the distribution with a power-law form, and the solid curve shows fitting of the remaining part of the distribution by a

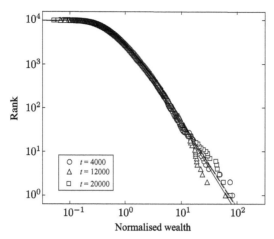

Figure 5.19. Wealth distribution in a random network.

log-normal form. As we clearly see from the figure, the small-world network realises a stationary distribution, which is explained by combining the power-law and the log-normal distributions. In the small-world network wealth is distributed over the scale of 10^5. Addition of even a small amount of randomisation processes to the regular network thus results in a significant improvement over the uneven distribution observed in the network.

So what happens to a completely random network? Figure 5.19 shows the results. The notations in the figure are exactly the same as those in Figure 5.18. The distribution is stationary with a power-law tail and its relative spread is almost confined within the order of 10^3. We see that wealth is distributed much more equally in the random network than in the regular one.

5.4.3   Clustering of wealth

In order to elucidate the origin of different distributions of wealth we will focus our attention on how wealth changes its distribution across agents in a given network as time passes. Figure 5.20 displays the temporal evolution of the distribution of wealth in the regular network used in Figure 5.17. The abscissa of the figure is the agent number, ranging from 1 to 1,000, and the ordinate is the time period, $t = 0 \sim 10^4$. For an agent whose rank as regards magnitude of wealth falls within the top (bottom) 10 per cent, it is depicted by a black (grey) point. We observe those black and grey points make clusters in the figure. Since neighbouring agents are connected to each other in the regular network, this means that linked agents have almost the same magnitude of wealth, i.e. clustering of wealth takes place in the regular network.

What happens to the clustering of wealth if we modify the network structure? Figure 5.21 shows the results in the same small-world network as used in Figure 5.18. Note that the clustering tendency of wealth is significantly depressed. The results for

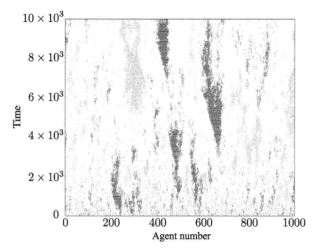

Figure 5.20. Time evolution of distribution of wealth across agents in the regular network, corresponding to Figure 5.17.

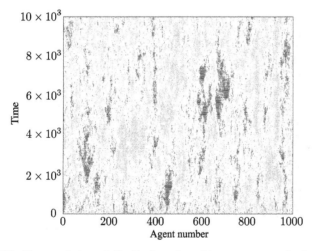

Figure 5.21. Time evolution of distribution of wealth across agents in the small-world network, corresponding to Figure 5.18.

the same random network as used in Figure 5.19 are given in Figure 5.22, where no appreciable clustering tendency of wealth is observed.[2]

We have thus learned that the unequal distribution of wealth stems from clustering of wealth in the case of a regular network. The model given in subsection 5.4.1 has identical values for all k_j in the third term on the right-hand side of the equation, when applied to

---

[2] More strictly speaking, we investigated the correlation between the wealth of the i-th agent, $x_i(t)$, and the mean wealth of agents adj(i), $\overline{x_i}(t)$, i.e. $\langle x_i(t)\overline{x_i}(t)\rangle$ in Souma *et al.* (2001). Such a numerical analysis confirms our present conclusions on the clustering of wealth over the networks.

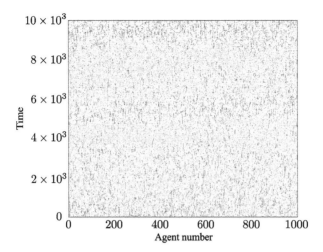

Figure 5.22. Time evolution of distribution of wealth across agents in the random network, corresponding to Figure 5.19.

a regular network, and the number of adj(i) is identical to k_j. In addition $x_i(t) \simeq x_j(t)$ obtains for neighbouring agents owing to the clustering of wealth. Accordingly the second and third terms are almost cancelled out. This cancellation mechanism leads to

$$x_i(t+1) \simeq a_i(t)x_i(t),$$

which is simply Gibrat's process.

On the other hand, the rewiring of links in a network gives rise to a difference between the second and third terms on the right-hand side of the model equation. The model given in subsection 5.4.1 is written as

$$x_i(t+1) = [a_i(t) - J]x_i(t) + J\sum_{j \in \text{adj}(i)} \frac{x_j(t)}{k_j}.$$

Here the first term on the right-hand side amounts to the original with the average of $a_i(t)$ merely shifted by J. If there is no correlation between $x_i(t)$ and the second term on the right-hand side, then this model is reduced to a multiplicative stochastic process with additive noise, and it is well known that the stochastic process is able to reproduce a power-law distribution. We note that the present model is also applicable to any networks other than the small-world network model of Watts and Strogatz. For instance, we applied the model to the scale-free network derived from the BA model and obtained nearly the same results as those in the random network (Souma *et al.*, 2003).

We have introduced a primitive model for interacting agents in this section. However, addressing the real economy requires us to continue to develop the modelling. Subsection 4.6.3 empirically revealed various aspects of interactions between companies. We therefore proceed one step further in the next section to model companies as agents and carry out more realistic simulations.

5.5 Modelling the transaction network

The most fundamental activity of companies is production. Companies build productive facilities and hire employees. They then buy materials to make goods and sell the goods to generate profits. Companies spend the profits generated to expand their productive facilities and increase their number of employees. This is a positive feedback mechanism for the growth of companies. Such production activity apparently requires an individual company to establish connections to other companies for buying materials and selling goods, eventually leading to the formation of a transaction network.

In this section we will consider a model of working interactions between companies over a transaction network (Ikeda *et al.*, 2007a, b). We aim to develop the arguments given in section 5.4. In this model, companies make autonomous decisions as regards investment in capital and labour to make goods, and they buy the necessary materials and sell goods through transaction relations. We refer to this model as a *transaction network model*. We will explain the basic ideas of the model one by one below.

5.5.1 Autonomous companies

As has been demonstrated in subsection 4.6.3, sales grow according to the following formula:

$$\delta X_i(t+1) = \sum_{j=1}^{N} k_{ij} \delta Y_j(t) + \epsilon_i(t),$$

where $\delta X_i(t) = (X_i(t) - \langle X_i \rangle_t)/\sigma_i^{(X)}$ is the standardised sales growth-rate. In the definition of $\delta X_i(t)$, we employed the time-average growth-rate $\langle X_i \rangle_t$. This basically assumes that the economy grows in a constant manner. However, this assumption cannot be valid, because the actual sales of companies depend heavily on the time-varying business trends of competitors and customers and also the consumption trends of individuals. To take account of this situation, we replace $\langle X_i \rangle_t$ by

$$\langle X_i \rangle_t \rightarrow R_i^{(G)}(t+1)/R_i^{(G)}(t),$$

where $R_i^{(G)}(t+1)/R_i^{(G)}(t)$ represents the trend change of the sales growth-rate due to the decision-making of companies as regards capital, $K_i(t)$, and labour, $L_i(t)$. The superscript (G) of $R_i^{(G)}(t)$ stands for *game theory*. The capital is the total amount of expenses for facilities necessary to produce goods, and the labour is the total amount of wages for employees who operate the production facilities. Companies are able to determine $K_i(t)$ and $L_i(t)$ autonomously. On the other hand, the sales $R_i(t)$ and the costs $C_i(t)$ are determined by the transaction relationships between buyers and sellers. A company with such properties is depicted by Figure 5.23. A number of companies thus form a business network through transactions. In passing, we note that $\sigma_i^{(X)}$ takes a small value if the trend of the sales growth-rate changes.

Each company makes decisions about $K_i(t)$ and $L_i(t)$ to maximise its own profit, and accordingly determines $R_i^{(G)}(t)$. So how do companies make their own choices?

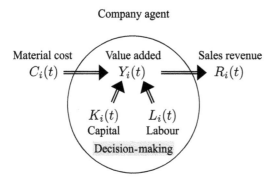

Figure 5.23. Interacting company agents.

To grasp their *autonomy* we can invoke game theory. It should be remembered that companies make decisions about $K_i(t)$ and $L_i(t)$ using game theory in the present model.

Game theory can be traced back to the seminal work of John von Neumann and Oskar Morgenstern in 1944 and is a mathematical theory to describe the decision-making of agents in competition with others (von Neumann and Morgenstern, 1944). Since game theory is full of specific terminologies, many readers may have difficulty understanding it. We will briefly explain the terminology often used in the theory and then describe its basic parts. Readers who are interested in more details of the theory can consult the standard texts (Davis, 1983; Gibbons, 1992; Owen, 1995).

The following paragraphs explain the important terms used in game theory.

Non-cooperative game: This is a game in which agents make their own decisions without any co-operation, leading to a competitive situation. The transaction network model assumes that companies compete against each other to maximise their profits. It is thought that collaboration (co-operation) of companies emerges as a result of the profit maximisation of companies at an individual level.

Pure and mixed strategies: A pure strategy indicates that a player takes only one choice from the available strategies. On the other hand, a mixed strategy means that a player takes multiple choices, randomly, with certain probabilities. The pure strategy is thereby a special case of mixed strategies.

Strategic form: This is a way to define a game in the form of a matrix which shows players, strategies and payoffs. In this case the player stands for an autonomous agent who is able to make a decision; a strategy represents a collection of actions which circumscribes the behaviour of a player in any situation; while payoff indicates an evaluation associated with each action. From now on we will use 'player' as a technical term instead of 'company'. The possible choices for a player about whether to increase or decrease $K_i(t)$ and $L_i(t)$ constitute the strategies of the agent. In this form, all players are assumed to make decisions simultaneously and without knowing other players' choices.

Best response: This is the strategy which leads to the highest payoff for a player, taking other players' strategies as given.

Table 5.1. *Strategic form game 1.*

B \ A	S	T
S	4,4	6,1
T	1,6	2,2

Nash equilibrium: This is a set of the strategies corresponding to the best reactions for every player. In such a state, no player will change his or her strategy unless other players change their strategies. This equilibrium state was named after J. F. Nash, Jr,[3] who first proposed it.

Extensive form: This is a form of game in which the decision-making of players is repeated as time passes. Such a process is depicted using a tree diagram. Each node of the tree represents a point of choice for a player. Branches growing out of the node represent possible actions for the player.

Perfect information: This is the most basic game in extensive-form games. A player can select his or her strategy knowing exactly the past behaviours of other players.

Rationality: This means that a player behaves to maximise his or her own payoff by considering a complete set of the possible strategies which could be adopted by other players in the future. On the other hand, bounded rationality means that a player has to consider other players' future strategies to a limited extent and make an optimum decision with imperfect knowledge.

We will explain the basics of game theory by solving three illustrative examples of strategic form games as shown in Tables 5.1, 5.2 and 5.3. In these examples, players A and B can select one of two strategies, S or T. The left number in each cell of the table refers to the payoff for A and the right number to that for B.

Let us begin with the very simple game shown in Table 5.1. If player A adopts mixed strategy S with probability p, then he or she adopts the other strategy T with probability $1 - p$. The probabilities of player B adopting strategies S and T are given as q and $1 - q$, respectively.

According to Table 5.1, the expectation value of payoff for player A is

$$4pq + 6p(1 - q) + 1(1 - p)q + 2(1 - p)(1 - q) = (4 - q)p - q + 2.$$

The inequality $0 \leq q \leq 1$ guarantees that the prefactor $(4 - q)$ of p is always positive. The more p is increased, therefore, the more payoff player A can obtain. Strategy S $(p = 1)$ is thus the best reaction for player A. The expectation value of payoff for player B is likewise given as

$$4pq + 1p(1 - q) + 6(1 - p)q + 2(1 - p)(1 - q) = (4 - p)q - p + 2.$$

---

[3] Nash won the Nobel Prize for Economics in 1994 and was featured in the film *A Beautiful Mind.*

Table 5.2. *Strategic form game 2.*

A \ B	S	T
S	4,4	1,6
T	6,1	2,2

Table 5.3. *Strategic form game 3.*

A \ B	S	T
S	6,4	0,0
T	0,0	4,6

Since $0 \leq p \leq 1$, the prefactor $(4 - p)$ of q always takes a positive value and hence strategy S $(q = 1)$ is also the best reaction for player B. From the above-mentioned arguments, a set of strategies (S,S) gives a Nash equilibrium solution.

The next example is defined by Table 5.2. The payoffs are slightly different from those in Table 5.1, and the example manifests an interesting phenomenon known as *prisoner's dilemma.*

The expectation value of payoff for player A is calculated as

$$4pq + 1p(1 - q) + 6(1 - p)q + 2(1 - p)(1 - q) = -(1 + q)p + 4q + 2$$

The inequality $0 \leq q \leq 1$ proves that the prefactor $-(1 + q)$ of p is definitely negative. The payoff of player A increases with decreased p, so the best reaction for that player is strategy T $(p = 0)$.

The expectation value of payoff for player B is also calculated as

$$4pq + 6p(1 - q) + 1(1 - p)q + 2(1 - p)(1 - q) = -(1 + p)q + 4p + 2.$$

The prefactor $-(1 + p)$ is likewise negative. Hence the best reaction for player B is the same as that for player A. We thus see that a set (T,T) of strategies is in Nash equilibrium. Let us look at the payoffs in Table 5.2 again. We find the strategy pair (S,S) gives a better choice for both of the players than the Nash equilibrium solution (T,T). Such a phenomenon, called prisoner's dilemma, is a typical example of the way that a combination of the best strategies for individual players does not always result in global optimisation.

The two games so far examined have only one Nash equilibrium solution, but the last game in Table 5.3 has many. The expectation value of payoff for player A is

$$6pq + 4(1 - p)(1 - q) = (10q - 4)p - 4q + 4.$$

Here the positivity of the prefactor $(10q - 4)$ of p is not guaranteed by $0 \leq q \leq 1$. If $(10q - 4)$ is positive $(q > 0.4)$, the best reaction for player A is strategy S $(p = 1)$.

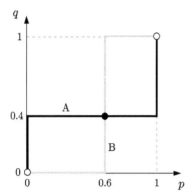

Figure 5.24. Multiple Nash equilibrium solutions.

If $(10q - 4)$ is negative $(q < 0.4)$, on the other hand, the best reaction is strategy T $(p = 0)$. In addition to these two cases, if $(10q - 4)$ is equal to zero $(q = 0.4)$, player A can select any strategy with $0 \le p \le 1$. The expectation value of payoff for player B is given as

$$4pq + 6(1 - p)(1 - q) = (10p - 6)q - 6p + 6.$$

Likewise the prefactor $(10p - 6)$ of q takes either positive or negative values. Therefore, the best reaction for player B is strategy S (T) for $p > 0.6$ $(p < 0.6)$ and any strategy with $0 \le q \le 1$ at $p = 0.6$.

The tracks of the best reactions for players A and B are overlaid on the p-q plane as shown in Figure 5.24. The intersections of the two lines depicted by open and filled circles identify Nash equilibria. Note that there are three such solutions. The open circles corresponding to (S,S) and (T,T) are solutions for pure strategies and the filled circles at $(p, q) = (0.6, 0.4)$ is a solution for mixed strategies.

The three examples discussed so far are all games in which each player makes a single decision. However, managers of actual companies have to make multiple decisions over extended periods of time. This situation corresponds to an extensive form game, which can be graphically represented by way of a game tree diagram. Here we suppose that payoffs of players are calculated in a finite period of time and also that they play with perfect information. In a game of perfect information represented by a tree of finite size we can obtain the exact solution for a pure strategy Nash equilibrium using *backward induction*.

Here is an illustrative example with two terms as shown in Figure 5.25. Players A and B take strategy S or T, and player B makes a decision after player A. Since this is a game of perfect information, each of the information sets depicted by open circles has only a single branching point. The rightmost end points are accompanied by the vectors of payoffs. For instance, let us concentrate on the case where players A and B select strategies S and T, respectively, in the first term, and then take T and S, respectively, in the second term. This series of actions assigns payoffs (7,10) to the players A and

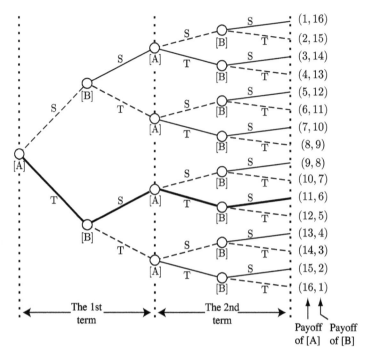

Figure 5.25. Extensive form game.

B. Those payoff values should be regarded as what results when the calculation takes into account interactions between agents. Backward induction proceeds in a direction from end to root by choosing whichever of the upper and lower branches has the larger payoff. We first decide the strategy of player B in the second term. In this example the payoffs of the upper branches (strategy S) are always larger than those of the lower branches (strategy T) for player B, so that player B takes strategy S in the second term; this selection is depicted by solid lines in Figure 5.25. Then player A takes strategy T for all branches in the second term because the lower branches have payoffs larger than the upper branches; this selection is also depicted by solid lines in Figure 5.25. In the next step, player B and then player A decide their strategies in the first term. The decision is made in exactly the same way as that in the second term. The iteration of this procedure enables us to find a Nash equilibrium, which is shown by a connected thick line. We remark that it is not necessarily the case that a player selects the same strategy at every stage in each term, although it is true for this example; the choice of strategies depends on their payoff values.

5.5.2 *Model of bounded rationality*

The number of branches in an extensive game grows exponentially as the numbers of players and terms increase. Accordingly, the computational task based on backward induction becomes heavier, requiring a larger memory region and longer computing

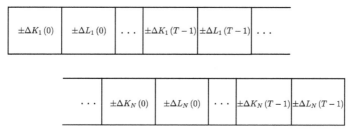

Figure 5.26. Gene.

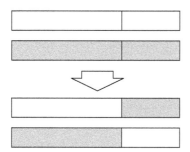

Figure 5.27. Crossover process.

time. When carrying out simulations for a system with many agents, we therefore need an alternative method. One of the candidates is a *genetic algorithm* (Goldberg, 1989) which finds an approximate solution to the Nash equilibrium efficiently with less intensive use of computing resources, thus enabling us to carry out simulations for a large-scale system.

The genetic algorithm is an heuristic optimisation method, and the computational procedure consists of nine steps as outlined below.

Step 1: We input N agents, T terms, M genes, L generations, the probability, p_c, of crossover and the probability, p_m, of mutation. Here the gene is a long tape of the type shown in Figure 5.26. Typical values for p_c and p_m are 0.8 and the inverse of the length of genes, respectively; however, these values may have to be tuned in the light of emergent problems. Each gene site (a separated sector on the tape) inscribes the strategy of each agent. In the t-th period the i-th agent may increase or decrease the capital $K_i(t)$ and the labour $L_i(t)$; that is to say, in total it has four strategies. In Figure 5.26, $+\Delta K_i(t)$ is set to 1 when $K_i(t)$ is increased and $-\Delta K_i(t)$ to 0 when it is decreased. The same is true for $L_i(t)$.

Step 2: We generate initial values for M genes; 1 or 0 is written randomly on each gene site.

Step 3: For each gene, we select another gene randomly with the probability p_c. As displayed in Figure 5.27, the two genes are then cut at a position randomly determined and the two portions are exchanged. This is called a crossover process.

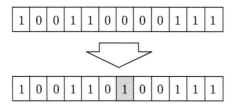

Figure 5.28. Mutation process.

[Payoff]

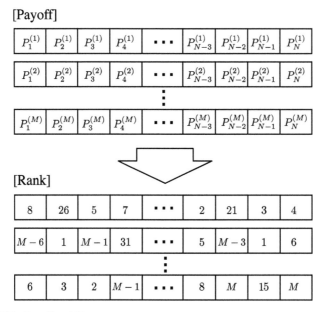

[Rank]

Figure 5.29. Payoff and fitness.

Step 4: For every gene site, the value is flipped with the probability p_m; 0 is converted to 1 or vice versa. This is called a mutation process, and is demonstrated in Figure 5.28.

Step 5: For the j-th gene, we calculate the total sum of profits made by the i-th company during the period $(0, T)$; the payoff is denoted by $P_i^{(j)}$. Then we calculate the payoffs of all of the companies ($i = 1, \ldots, N$) for all of the genes ($j = 1, \ldots, M$). Here we note that the interactions between agents are taken into account in the calculation of the profits.

Step 6: We calculate the individual fitness for M genes. As shown in Figure 5.29, the M genes are ranked for each site. The figure shows that the first agent is ranked eighth in the first gene, $(M - 6)$-th in the second gene, $\ldots$, sixth in the M-th gene. Then we sum up the ranking values assigned at every site for each gene and define the inverse of the sum as the fitness of the gene. If a gene is ranked first at all sites, its fitness is equal to $1/N$, the maximum value that the fitness can take. Since the strategies are best optimised for all of the agents in this case, we have the Nash equilibrium solution.

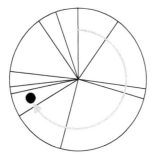

Figure 5.30. Selection by roulette method.

Step 7: Using random numbers, we select M successors from the M genes according to their fitness values, where selection of the same genes is allowed. This selection amounts to M repetitions of a roulette game such as is visualised in Figure 5.30. The roulette wheel is made with M selections corresponding to the M genes and the area of each selection is proportional to the fitness value of the corresponding gene.

Step 8: We repeat the procedure from step 3 to step 7 L times.

Step 9: The genetic information with the highest fitness score is recorded.

A Nash equilibrium solution obtained by a genetic algorithm is different in two ways from that based on backward induction. Firstly we note that the genetic algorithm gives an approximate solution to the Nash equilibrium, not the exact solution. This is true for many complicated problems. Therefore the solution is best understood as decision-making by an agent with bounded rationality. Secondly, each agent makes its decision without knowing strategies adopted by others. This amounts to assuming that agents do not possess perfect information.

The agent-based model sketched here serves as a starting point for building a model of autonomous agents interacting on a transaction network. We believe that this kind of model can and should play an important role in the exploration of business applications, and in the next chapter this perspective will be explored in regard to possible applications of econophysics to the management of companies in the real economy, with illustrative applications of the present model in subsections 6.1.4 and 6.2.6.

6 Perspectives for practical applications

In the previous chapters, we have described various outcomes derived from the basic research, such as a growth theory of companies, business networks and agent simulations. In this chapter, by changing our perspective, we will review what consequences are expected from the research outcomes, in other words the practical applications of econophysics. Real economic data is abundant in Japan compared with other countries, and for this reason alone the Japanese economy is of particular importance in our work. It is also convenient in other ways. The practical applications of our work are currently under development, and the concrete content of these applications is being improved through ongoing conversations with companies in Japan. Indeed, the contents of this chapter should be regarded as an interim statement, which might be greatly altered in the future. However, we think that it is of real interest even at this stage to describe some of our suggested applications. We will concentrate on three topics, namely, the methodology for developing a business strategy, the management of the propagation of credit risk and the encouragement of innovation in business models, and offer them as of potential value to central government civil servants, acquisition specialists, investment bankers, staff working in the management planning division of companies, financial departments, materials departments, credit divisions, and rating companies, as well as business administrators.

6.1 Development of business strategies

In this section we will begin by explaining the elements of *corporate finance theory*, and then move on to discuss issues relating to the practical applications of that theory. Subsequently, we will describe a simulation of company decision-making and business performance in a competitive environment under a given macro-economic trend using the autonomous agent-based model. This approach is not considered in traditional corporate finance theory.

6.1.1 *Valuation of companies*
We need to understand the elements of corporate finance theory in order to estimate corporate value (Brealey *et al.*, 2008). Corporate finance starts by reading financial

statement data, such as income statements, balance sheets and cash flow statements. Although it is hard work to read financial statement data in detail, it is easy to understand their outlines, so a description of these fundamentals is the first step towards an understanding of *corporate valuation*.

When examining a company's operation, sales revenue is decomposed into the following three components:

$$\text{sales revenue} = \text{COGS} + \text{SGA} + \text{operating profit},$$

where COGS is the abbreviated form of 'cost of goods sold', and SGA stands for 'selling, general and administrative expenses'. COGS is the sum of three costs: the cost of raw materials, labour costs and the amortisation cost of premises and equipment. SGA consists of the employment costs of the sales department and administration staff and all sorts of other costs. By rewriting the above relation we can obtain the operating profit,

$$\text{operating profit} = \text{sales revenue} - \text{COGS} - \text{SGA}.$$

Next we calculate the free cash flow from the operating profit. The cash flow, which literally means the flow of money, is a fundamental quantity in corporate valuation, and, more specifically, the net cash flow generated from a company's business operation is called the *free cash flow* (FCF) and is the sum of the operating cash flow and the investment cash flow. It is noted that the sign of cash flow is deemed to be positive when cash flows to the company from other companies, and to be negative when cash flows from the company to other companies. In other words, free cash flow is the money remaining when expenses incurred in a company's operation are deducted from earnings. The word 'free' indicates that a business administrator can distribute this cash flow freely to investors in the company. This quantity is estimated approximately by using both the income statement and the company balance sheet:

$$\begin{aligned} \text{free cash flow} = {}& \text{NOPAT} + \text{amortisation cost of premises and equipment} \\ & - \text{investment of premises and equipment} \\ & - \text{increase in working capital}, \end{aligned}$$

where NOPAT stands for 'net operating profit after tax', although the exact value of free cash flow is usually reported in a cash flow statement with decomposition into two components:

$$\text{free cash flow} = \text{operating cash flow} + \text{investment cash flow}.$$

The correspondence relations of symbols used in corporate finance theory and variables in this book are summarised in Table 6.1.

Table 6.1. *Correspondence between symbols used in corporate finance theory and variables in this book.*

Name of quantity	Corporate finance theory	This book
Free cash flow	FCF	C_t
Net operating profit after tax	NOPAT	O_t
Economic profit	EP	R_t
Corporate value	CV	U
Net present value	NPV	V
Weighted average cost of capital	WACC	r_w
Internal rate of return	IRR	r_0

The corporate value (CV) U at the present time ($t = 0$) is calculated from the time-series of the expected future free cash flow C_t ($t = 1, \ldots, T$) according to

$$U = \sum_{t=1}^{T} \frac{C_t}{(1 + r_w)^t},$$

$$r_w = r_e \frac{E}{E + D} + r_d(1 + \tau)\frac{D}{E + D},$$

where $(1 + r_w)^t$ in the denominator is a factor to reduce C_t for the corresponding value at $t = 0$, namely the *present value*. The weighted average cost of capital (WACC) r_w is sometimes called the *discount rate* for short. In addition, r_e, r_d, E, D, τ are the returns on invested capital, borrowing rate, invested capital, debt payable and tax rate, respectively. The borrowing rate r_d, the invested capital E and the debt payable D are recorded for each company in the relevant financial statements. The expected rate of return μ, which is calculated by using the historical series of stock prices with the *capital asset pricing model* (CAPM), is used as a typical value for the return on invested capital r_e for the companies listed on the stock market.

The corporate value U is also defined as the sum of the present value of economic profit R,

$$U = \sum_{t=1}^{T} \frac{R_t}{(1 + r_w)^t} + E + D,$$

$$R_t = O_t - r_w(E + D),$$

The quantity V, calculated by deducting invested capital $E + D$ from corporate value U, is referred to as the *net present value* (NPV):

$$V(r_w) = U(r_w) - E - D,$$

which plays a very important role in business investment theory for decision-making. If the NPV of the business under consideration is positive, the business will be profitable and is suitable for investment. If r_w is chosen so that $V(r_w)$ is equal to zero:

$$V(r_0) = 0,$$

the discount rate r_0 is called the *internal rate of return* (IRR).

 Capital asset pricing model

In what follows we will try to explain the basics of the capital asset pricing model (CAPM) (Luenberger, 1997). The return $r_i(t)$ of the risk asset i changes from time to time. In CAPM the expected rate of return $\mu_i = \langle r_i \rangle$ of the risk asset i is given by

$$\mu_i = r_f + \beta_i(\mu_M - r_f),$$

where r_f and μ_M are, respectively, the return of a risk-free asset and the expected rate of return of the market portfolio. The coefficient β_i is a proportional factor multiplied by the risk premium $\mu_M - r_f$, and is given by

$$\beta_i = \sigma_{iM}/\sigma_M^2,$$

where σ_{iM} is the covariance (see the box in section 4.2) between the return on the market portfolio and return of the asset i.

Let us assume that the portfolio consists of risk assets $i (= 1, \ldots, n)$ with a ratio x_i. Thus we have $\sum_{i=1}^{n} x_i = 1$. The expected rate μ_p of return and the variance σ_p^2 of the return for this portfolio are written as

$$\mu_p = \sum_{i=1}^{n} x_i \mu_i,$$

$$\sigma_p^2 = \sum_{i=1}^{n} \sum_{j=1}^{n} x_i x_j \sigma_{ij},$$

where σ_{ij} is the covariance between assets i and j. Minimising the variance σ_p^2 with respect to variables $x_i (i = 1, \ldots, n)$ is called portfolio optimisation.

We will now assume that there is no correlation between the returns from the assets ($\sigma_{ij} = 0, i \neq j$). The variance of the return of the risk asset i is

$$\sigma_i^2 = \beta_i^2 \sigma_M^2 + \tilde{\sigma}_i^2, \tag{6.1}$$

and thus the variance of the return of the portfolio σ_p^2 is written as

$$\sigma_p^2 = \sum_{i=1}^{n} x_i^2 (\beta_i^2 \sigma_M^2 + \tilde{\sigma}_i^2). \tag{6.2}$$

The first and second terms of the right-hand side of (6.1) are the market risk and the idiosyncratic risk, respectively. By assuming $x_i = 1/N$, the limit as $N \to \infty$

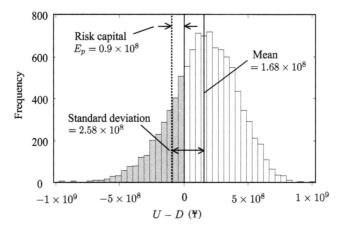

Figure 6.1. Distribution of $U - D$ and risk capital E_p.

of the second term of the right-hand side of (6.2) converges to zero. We could set up the portfolio without idiosyncratic risk by combining a large number of risk assets. It is noted that only market risk brings profit, because β_i is included only in risk. It was recently discovered that the major fraction of the covariance matrix σ_{ij} consists of noise, and noise reduction methodology using the random matrix theory is attracting the attention not only of academic researchers but also of those working in practical business situations.

6.1.2 *Optimum capital structure*

The capital structure of a company is characterised by the ratio of invested capital E and debt payable D. In economics there is a well-known theorem regarding capital structure, namely the *Modigliani–Miller theorem* (Modigliani and Miller, 1958). In this theorem, by assuming a perfect capital market, it is shown that corporate value is independent of the company's capital structure. However, the above assumption is not valid in the real economic system; thus, it is expected that in practice there is an *optimum capital structure* for the maximisation of corporate value.

There are various methods to determine the optimum capital structure; one, for example, calculates a trade-off between opportunity loss and bankruptcy cost, while another proposes a structure designed to minimise agency cost. An alternative method approaches the problem by minimising the cost of financing.

In the following example, the optimum structure is determined from the point of view of risk management, as shown in Figure 6.1. When events of corporate value U are generated using a Monte Carlo simulation about a certain business in due diligence process, we obtain the distribution of $U - D$ by subtracting the debt payable D from the generated corporate value U. If $U - D$ is negative without invested capital E, the company immediately goes bankrupt. On the other hand, if the company is rich in invested capital E to cover the negative deficit $U - D$, the company does not go bankrupt. Thus it is possible to determine the invested capital E required in order to avoid bankruptcy for the large fluctuation of the deficit $U - D$, under the condition that the average net present value is positive $\langle V \rangle > 0$. The invested capital E determined by this method is exposed to risk, that is the fluctuation of cash flow. Therefore the invested capital E determined above is called the risk capital E_p.

α_{β}^{γ} The Modigliani–Miller theorem

Suppose the capital structure of company A is different from that of company B, e.g. company A has only equity as invested capital, whilst company B has both equity and bonds. The question is which company's market value is larger than the other's.

The earnings before interest, the market values of stocks and bonds for company $i(= A, B)$ are $X_i(= X)$, S_i and $D_i(D_A = 0)$, respectively. Thus the market values for the companies are

$$V_A = S_A,$$

$$V_B = S_B + D_B.$$

We have here assumed that the complete capital market satisfies the following conditions:

- There is no tax and no bankruptcy.
- No cost is required for issuance and trading of stocks and bonds.
- Investors can borrow any amount of money with an interest rate equal to that of company B. (Company A has only equity.)
- The differing stakes among financial institutes, companies and investors are harmonised without cost.

Initially, we will assume that the investor's portfolio consists of only stock $\alpha_B S_B$. The coefficient α_i is the fraction of equity of the company i owned by the investor $(0 < \alpha_i < 1)$. The profit of the portfolio is

$$Y_B = \alpha_B (X - r D_B), \tag{6.3}$$

where r is an interest rate of the company B.

If the stock of company A is comparatively low in price $(V_A < V_B)$, investors will sell the stock $\alpha_B S_B$, and buy the stock of company A, $\alpha_A S_A$, by borrowing $d = \alpha_B D_B$. Here it is noted that $\alpha_A = (\alpha_B S_B + d)/S_A$. In this case, the profit of the portfolio is equal to

$$Y_A = \alpha \frac{V_B}{V_A} X - r \alpha D_B. \tag{6.4}$$

If $V_A < V_B$, we have the relation $Y_A > Y_B$ by comparing (6.3) and (6.4). Thus other investors with stock $\alpha_B S_B$ trade in exactly the way described above until the relation $V_A = V_B$ is obtained.

Now, let us consider an investor's portfolio consisting only of stock $\alpha_A S_A$. The profit of the portfolio is

$$Y'_A = \alpha_A X. \tag{6.5}$$

If the stock of company B is comparatively low in price ($V_A > V_B$), the investor will sell the stock, $\alpha_A S_A$, and buy the stock of company B by $\alpha_B S_B = S_B \alpha_A S_A / V_B$ and the bonds of company B by $\beta_B D_B = D_B \alpha_A S_A / V_B$. Here β_i is the fraction of the bonds of company i owned by the investor. It is noted that $\alpha_B S_B + \beta_B D_B = \alpha_A S_A$. In this case, the profit of the portfolio is equal to

$$Y'_B = \alpha_A \frac{V_A}{V_B} X. \tag{6.6}$$

If $V_A > V_B$, we have the relation $Y'_A < Y'_B$ by comparing (6.5) and (6.6). Thus other investors with stock $\alpha_A S_A$ will trade in the way described above until the relation $V_A = V_B$ is obtained.

From the above discussion we can see that the theorem states that a company cannot change its market value V by changing its capital structure, that is the ratio of stock S and debt E (Brealey *et al.*, 2008). This theorem, the Modigliani–Miller theorem, is said to have been shocking to those engaged in finance, and to have caused considerable controversy, as well it might. In actual situations, however, the financial department of a company is responsible for the maximisation of market value V through financing.

6.1.3 *Decision-making for business entry and exit*

We will explain decision-making for business entry and exit using the net present value V calculated by the method described in the previous section. If $V > 0$ we decide to enter into business or continue the business, while if $V < 0$ we will decide not to enter, or to exit from the business. Clearly, the returns from equity r_e have to be evaluated by taking business risks properly into account. However, we have to recall the fact that any evaluation methodology is only an approximation, thus we cannot evaluate the return on equity precisely.

Consequently, the internal rate of return r_0, the rate at which $V = 0$ is obtained, is usually used instead. In this case, the decision-making is guided by a comparison of the internal rate of return r_0 and the target return r_h. If $r_0 > r_h$, we would decide to enter into, or continue with, the business. If $r_0 < r_h$, we would decide not to enter the business, or to exit.

So far we have explained the theoretical basics of corporate finance, and we can now try to apply these methodologies to real problems. Although the evaluation of corporate value V seems to be straightforward, as explained above, there are many difficulties aside from the discount rate. For instance, we might want to forecast the future revenue required for the evaluation of corporate value. The simplest forecast method is to take the expected market size and multiply it by a target share, where the expected market size is a forecast made by a market research company. In this method, the following four issues are immediately cited:

- Issue 1: When the deviation of future trends in economic growth are taken into account, are the expected market size and the target share considered to be a single scenario?
- Issue 2: How many scenarios for the expected market size and the target share should we consider? How should we estimate deviation for each scenario?
- Issue 3: When the future business scenario deviates very widely, how do we achieve flexible decision-making on issues other than the initial investment, such as additional investment to extend the business or to sell out of existing business?
- Issue 4: If we make additional investments to extend the business, or sell out of the existing business, what kind of action will a competitor take in response? How can we make a quantitative estimate of the effect of the competitor's action on our sales revenue and profit?

We now discuss appropriate actions for each of the issues raised above:

- Discussion 1: Decision-making for multiple scenarios is conducted using the decision tree. The probabilities of scenario bifurcations have to be given by the decision-maker as input parameters.
- Discussion 2: If the number of scenarios to be considered is very large, the scenarios are modelled as stochastic processes and simulated by a Monte Carlo method. The width of deviation of a scenario has to be given by the decision-maker as one of the input parameters. The width of deviation could be estimated by analysing the past financial statements for any companies equivalent to the business under consideration.
- Discussion 3: The effect of stochastic deviation of a business scenario on decision-making can be handled using the real option, that is to say a business valuation method based on an analogy between business decision-making and derivative financial instruments. In this method, the business value is estimated as the price of the derivative financial instrument, where its underlying asset is the cash flow of the business. The financial market is assumed to be complete in both economics and financial engineering. The pricing of a European-type option in the complete financial market is given by the Black–Scholes formulae, which are an analytic solution of the Black–Scholes partial differential equation (Black and Scholes, 1973). However, firstly, real options do not satisfy the condition of the complete market, and secondly,

the nature of decision-making in business is of the American type rather than the European type. Thus the Black–Scholes formulae are not appropriate in general for business evaluation.

• Discussion 4: Decision-making in a competitive environment is a very difficult topic to discuss. Indeed, there are still many questions about the quantitative evaluation of the effect of a competitor's action on a company's performance by taking into account transactions between customers and vendors. In order to handle this difficult task, we have offered and explained a new methodology, the transaction network model, in section 5.5.

$\alpha_{\beta}\gamma$ The Black–Scholes formulae

We will attempt to explain the pricing of a derivative financial instrument with stock as its underlying asset. For a plain European-type call option, the Black–Scholes formulae are used (Hull, 2008). The European-type call option is a claim to buy stock in the company by paying the predetermined exercise price K at the maturity date T if the stock price S is higher than the exercise price K at the maturity date T. If the stock price S is higher than the exercise price K at the maturity date T, the option-holder exercises the claim. The option-holder earns a profit $S - K$ by selling the stock at the market price S. On the other hand, if the stock price S is lower than the exercise price K at the maturity date T, the option-holder does not exercise the claim. Therefore the payoff P of the option is

$$P = \max(S - K, 0). \tag{6.7}$$

The stock price S is assumed to be described by the geometric Brownian motion,

$$dS = \mu S dt + \sigma S dz.$$

We obtain the partial differential equation to describe the option price $C = C(S, t)$ at time t,

$$\frac{\partial C}{\partial t} + \frac{\sigma^2 S^2}{2} \frac{\partial^2 C}{\partial S^2} + r \frac{\partial C}{\partial S} S - rC = 0, \tag{6.8}$$

using Ito's lemma,

$$dC = \frac{\partial C}{\partial t} dt + \frac{\partial C}{\partial S} dS + \frac{1}{2} \sigma^2 S^2 \frac{\partial^2 C}{\partial S^2} dt,$$

where r is the return on a risk-free asset. Equation (6.8) is physically interpreted as a drift-diffusion partial differential equation and called the Black–Scholes differential equation. This equation can be solved analytically with the boundary condition of the payoff (6.7). The analytic solution given by

$$C = SN(d_1) - Ke^{-r(T-t)}N(d_2), \tag{6.9}$$

$$d_1 = \frac{\log \frac{S}{K} + (r + \frac{1}{2}\sigma^2)(T-t)}{\sigma\sqrt{T-t}},$$

$$d_2 = \frac{\log \frac{S}{K} + (r - \frac{1}{2}\sigma^2)(T-t)}{\sigma\sqrt{T-t}}.$$

is called the Black–Scholes formulae. Here $N(x)$ is the cumulative probability function for the normal distribution. It is noted that the discount rate used in (6.9) is not the return μ on stock, but the return on the risk-free asset r. This pricing method is called the risk-neutral method. For the pricing of the American-type option, which can be exercised before the maturity date T, the lattice model is often used (Hull, 2008).

In the next subsection we will explain a simple application of the model described in section 5.5.

6.1.4 Decision-making under a given economic trend

In principle the macro-economic trend is determined by aggregating individual company performances. However, at the same time an individual company's investment and performance are affected by the macro-economic trend. This phenomenon is often called the *micro-macro loop*, and here we will examine the effect of a given macro-economic trend on an individual company's investment and performance.

The macro-economic trend is forecast on a periodic basis by many think-tanks, and although these forecasts are not very reliable they can be used practically as possible future scenarios. For this reason it might be invaluable to simulate an individual company's investment and performance under a given macro-economic trend. This simulation could be conducted by using the transaction network model described in section 5.5, where the decision-making of the company takes into account the interactions between companies due to transactions.

Figure 6.2 shows a portion of the Japanese transaction network. This transaction network shows sixteen listed companies belonging to a Japanese industrial group led by a flagship conglomerate (indicated by open circles), and some seventy-nine listed companies with sales revenue of over ¥367 billion (indicated by solid circles). Even this small portion of the transaction network includes companies with widely varying degrees (numbers of links); for example, a small number of the companies have a large degree and many companies have a small degree.

Figure 6.2. Portion of the transaction network in Japan.

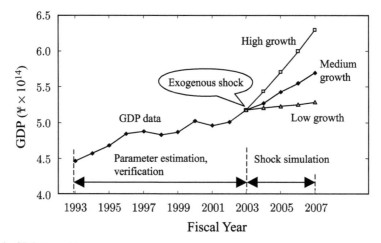

Figure 6.3. GDP scenario.

The gross domestic product (GDP) scenario shown in Figure 6.3 is used as the macro-economic trend input for the simulation. Other model parameters were estimated using financial statement data for individual companies in the period from Japanese fiscal year (JFY) 1993 to JFY 2003. Individual company investment and performance under the given macro-economic trend was then simulated from JFY 1993 to JFY 2003 with the initial values of a company's performance set at JFY 1993. In this case a company's investment means the temporal variation of capital K and labour L. A company's performance means the temporal variation of sales revenue R and cost C.

Each company makes an investment decision for the capital K and the labour L so that the sum of its own operational profit during the period from JFY 1993 to JFY 2003 is maximised. The company's operational profit is determined by sales revenue from customers and cost payments to suppliers, all under the influence of the given

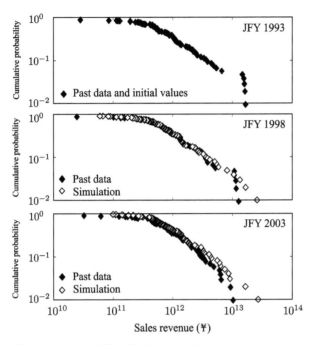

Figure 6.4. Cumulative probability distributions of sales revenues.

macro-economic trend. Therefore a company's decision-making is the best response to another company's strategy, and the results obtained in the simulation are a Nash equilibrium.

In the next stage we will verify the model by comparing the simulation results and the actual data. The cumulative probability distributions of sales revenue at JFY 1993, 1998 and 2003 are shown in Figure 6.4. The solid diamond indicates actual data, and the open diamond, the results of the simulation. The simulation results at JFY 1993 are identical to the actual data because those numbers are initial values, but as time goes by, there is a growing discrepancy between the simulation results and the data. It is, however, notable that the overall characteristics are similar.

Suppose that an exogenous shock is given at JFY 2003 and the subsequent GDP trend presents three divergent scenarios, that is, high (5%), medium (2.5%) and low (0.5%) growth (Figure 6.3). We can simulate the effect of these GDP scenarios on the company's investment and performance up to JFY 2007, and Figure 6.5 shows the relation between GDP scenarios and the cumulative probability distributions of sales revenue. The open diamond indicates the simulation results of the cumulative probability distributions of sales revenue for the low-growth scenario, while the solid diamond plots the results for the high-growth scenario. As expected, the high-growth scenario gives a distribution with a fatter tail.

So far we have shown the simulation results for the cumulative probability distributions of sales revenue for companies belonging to the transaction network. The

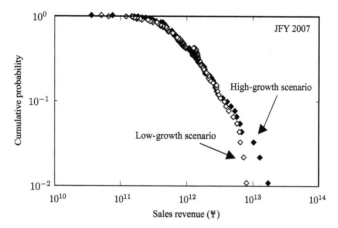

Figure 6.5. GDP scenarios and cumulative probability distributions of sales revenues.

temporal variation of the sales revenue R, the cost C, the capital K and the labour L for an individual company might be used to develop a business strategy. As explained in this section, by using the transaction network model it is possible to simulate an individual company's investment decision-making and resultant performance assuming a particular macro-economic trend forecast. We believe that this is a significant step towards the practical application of the theories we are proposing.

6.2   Chain bankruptcy and credit risk

6.2.1   Transaction network

A *transaction network* is a succession of economic activities where companies buy materials and intermediate goods and services from suppliers located in the 'upstream' area of the network, and add value by making products and services and selling these to customer companies located in the 'downstream' area of the network, and to consumers. The exact definitions of 'upstream' and 'downstream' are interesting problems in themselves. We will here content ourselves with the intuitive meaning of these terms, namely that companies manufacturing interim products from raw materials are located upstream, while companies manufacturing end-products from interim products are located downstream. The process by which production successively adds value is extremely complicated.

For instance, take the automobile industry. An automobile manufacturer buys various mechanical and electrical parts from auto-parts manufacturers, and manufactures automobiles using machine tools. The resulting manufactured cars have an economic value which exceeds that of the materials and parts. On the upstream side of the automobile manufacturer there may be an auto-body manufacturer. The auto-body manufacturer buys steel sheets and manufactures auto-bodies using machine tools. The customer companies of the auto-body manufacturer may include not only the above auto-manufacturer but also other auto-manufacturers and even companies in different industry sectors, such as railway companies. Downstream of the automobile manufacturer we find dealers who sell cars to a large number of consumers located at the outfall of the transaction network; the value added by the dealers is service. So, each individual company buys intermediate goods from upstream companies, and adds value, then sells products to downstream companies and consumers. This cascade of economic activity forms a very complicated network structure with several million Japanese companies engaging in something like 10 million economic relationships.

In complex network theory, each company and the relationship through which value is added are called a node and a link, respectively. The whole structure of the succession of economic activity can be described by a vast directed graph. Each link consists not only of materials and intermediate goods but also two inputs, namely *labour* and *finance*. Most economics textbooks suggest that the production of goods, labour and finance are the most fundamental processes of economic activity, and this idea is intuitively intelligible if we consider the directed graph to describe the cascade of economic activity. In fact, the goods, labour and financial markets play a fundamental role in macro-economics. It is well known that the individual equilibria of each of these three markets are assumed as the grounding concepts of mainstream economics.

Since the aggregation of value added throughout the whole transaction network is equal to GDP, it is clearly important to understand the structural and temporal variation of the transaction network in any study of the various aspects of macro- and micro-economics. Furthermore, it is also important to understand the meaning of the relative position of each individual company on the transaction network. The economic influence of one company on another is determined by the relative position on the transaction network, because the network structure governs the detailed behaviour of the propagation of both positive and negative economic influences. Since the production of goods requires links between companies, no company can be independent of the propagation of both positive and negative economic influences, and it is to this that we will now turn, starting with positive influence.

The propagation of positive economic influence. Suppose that consumers and companies on the downstream side of the transaction network make a sizeable demand for a group of final products and for specific intermediate goods. For instance, the promotion of economic growth in China and India increases orders for construction machinery such as loading shovels and bulldozers. At this time, a positive economic influence is propagated from the construction machinery manufacturer to upstream companies, for example engine-makers selling equipment to the machinery manufacturer. The propagation is continued from the engine manufacturers to electrical parts manufacturers, and so on.

The range and magnitude of this influence may be strongly dependent on the structure of the transaction network. Although the input-output analysis is aimed at the analysis of the strength of correlation between goods, complex network analysis might reveal the propagation of economic influence through microscopic relationships. In fact, the propagation of economic influence affects production as well as the labour market. There is certainly an influence not only on the labour market but also on financial markets via commercial banks. As can be seen in the foregoing example, the network of companies, financial institutions, and workers plays an essential role in the economic system, but it appears that this network of microscopic relationships is little studied. In the next subsection we will try to rectify this, in part by showing the importance of the transaction network when examining the propagation of negative economic influence.

6.2.2 The relationship of debtors and creditors

Why does a company manufacture products? Obviously because the company has the expectation of obtaining profits from selling those products. Note that the word 'expectation' is complex, and heavily loaded with meanings. Accomplishment of an expectation is not guaranteed *a priori*, and in this case the profit is determined by sales revenue and costs that arise *a posteriori*. Sales revenue depends on demand from customer companies and consumers located in the downstream direction, while cost depends on supply from suppliers located in the upstream direction, namely labour and financing costs. Consequently, the expected profit is determined *a posteriori*, depending on the relationship between the upstream and downstream companies.

Each link on the transaction network indicates a deal on credit (Stiglitz and Greenwald, 2003). The payment for goods to suppliers is not made concurrently with the delivery of the goods, and is often only made after a certain period of time on credit. This payment on credit is referred to as accounts payable by a purchasing company, and accounts receivable by a supplier. It should be noted at this point that a purchasing company does not have complete information about the credit status of a supplier. Other examples of payment on credit are finance provided by a bank and payment of worker wages. Each link in the transaction network is also interpreted as the relationship between a *creditor* and a *debtor*, which may bring about the following consequence.

As a company goes into capital deficiency, when its liabilities exceed its capital or it has cash-flow problems, the company may go bankrupt. A company located in the upstream region of the bankrupt company might fail to collect accounts receivable. If an upstream company goes into capital deficiency, this negative economic influence may propagate further upstream in the network. Consequently many companies may go bankrupt simultaneously; this is a collective phenomenon known as *chain bankruptcy*.

As explained in section 3.4, bankruptcy is essentially a cash flow problem. Even if a company does not go into capital deficit, the deterioration of cash flow makes operation difficult for the company in many areas, such as production, employment and finance. In this sense, chain bankruptcy is a serious potential risk not only for individual companies but for an industry as a whole.

Although the loss due to all bankrupt companies exceeds 2 per cent of the nominal GDP in Japan, as has been demonstrated in Figure 3.20, it might be thought that chain bankruptcy is essentially a rare event and thus that the resulting economic loss is not significant. However, empirical data tells us that this naive view of chain bankruptcy is incorrect. The number of chain bankruptcies occurring in each of the last ten years is about 10,000 to 20,000, and the losses amount to some ¥10–25 trillion, as shown in Figure 3.19. In the next subsection we will show that chain bankruptcy accounts for about 20 per cent of the aggregate indebtedness of bankrupt companies, and is a far from negligible economic event (Fujiwara, 2008).

6.2.3   The causes of bankruptcy and the link effect

The data we have analysed was taken from an annual report on business bankruptcy published by the Organisation for Small & Medium Enterprises and Regional Innovation, Japan (SMRJ). This dataset originates from a credit research company, Tokyo Shoko Research Ltd. (TSR), whose headquarters and branch offices survey bankruptcies with debts of more than ¥10 million, and is all but comprehensive in its coverage of Japanese bankruptcies.

The data places the causes of bankruptcy into two main categories, the failure in itself and the link effect:[1]

1. intrinsic failure
    (a) anaemic sales (weak performance)
    (b) irresponsible management (business fiasco)
    (c) accumulated deficit
    (d) excessively small capital (lack of working capital, increase in burden of interest)
    (e) random cause
    (f) build-up of inventory
    (g) excessive business investment
2. link effects
    (a) aftershock of another company's bankruptcy (excess of bad debts)
    (b) non-enforceable accounts receivable

The remaining causes are: 3(a) credit collapse due to suspension of bank transactions; and 3(b) others.

Of the 18,246 bankruptcies in JFY 1997, 8,956 were due to (1a), 2,724 to (1b), 2,002 to (1c), 1,792 to (2a), 1,404 to (1d), 373 to (1g), 358 to (2b), 330 to (1e), 210 to (3a), 89 to (1f), and 8 to (3b). The *link effect* is a negative network effect on credit transactions. It works like this: when company B purchases materials from company A, the transaction is a relation between a lender (A) and a borrower (B). If company B becomes bankrupt, company A might not be able to call in accounts receivable or recover the delivered products. Furthermore, since lender and borrower belong to the same industrial group the relation is rather more complicated than a usual transaction.

---

[1] TSR categorises each bankruptcy in accordance with the origin of the bankruptcy, which is specified by a score determined by an unpublished method. The origin categorisation is mutually exclusive; although bankruptcies usually have more than one cause, the categorisation is based only on the most important of these.

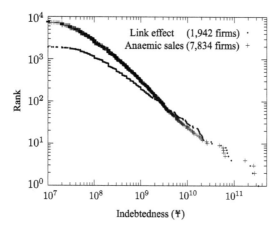

Figure 6.6. Rank-size plots of indebtedness at bankruptcy, comparing origins of bankruptcy.

The next questions are how large the link effect is, and how often it occurs. Whether the effect is dependent on company size is also an interesting question.

6.2.4 Magnitude of link effect

As shown in Figure 3.21, there were 16,526 bankrupt companies in the calendar year 1997. For these, the breakdown of causes was: anaemic sales (1a) 7,834 companies; link effects (2a) and (2b) 1,942 companies. The figure shows a power-law distribution for three orders of magnitude of indebtedness. Figure 6.6 is a rank-size plot of indebtedness at bankruptcy plotted to compare the two causes for bankruptcy, (1a) and (2). The abscissa is the amount of indebtedness at bankruptcy, and the ordinate is the rank of that amount.

Let us compare the probabilities of bankruptcies from the two different origins with indebtedness between x and $x + dx$. The conditional probability of bankruptcy is equal to the number of bankruptcies with two origins divided by the total number of bankruptcies, thus a comparison with rank-size plots is appropriate. Figure 6.6 shows that the shape of the distribution is fat-tailed for both origins, anaemic sales and link effects. It is notable that the slopes of the rank-size plots, that is the power exponents, are different. The plot for link effects exhibits a fatter tail than the plot for anaemic sales, and therefore as indebtedness x increases the conditional probability of bankruptcy due to link effects becomes larger than that due to anaemic sales. This inversion of order is observed in the range of indebtedness between ¥10^9 and ¥10^{10}.

Comparisons for other origins categorised as intrinsic failure show the same tendency for inversion. As indebtedness increases, the conditional probability of bankruptcy due to a link effect becomes larger than that due to intrinsic failure. The same tendency is observed for different periods (see Figure 6.7). In fact, the total number of bankruptcies due to origin (2a) in JFY 2001 was 1,731. Among those bankruptcies with indebtedness

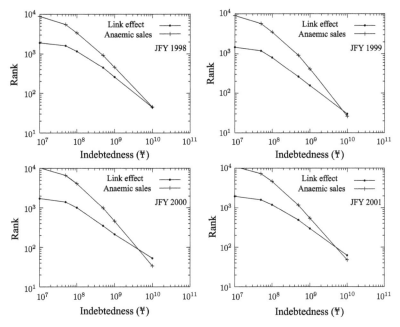

Figure 6.7. Rank-size plots of indebtedness at bankruptcy plotted for comparison between two major causes of bankruptcy.

over ¥10 billion, the number of those due to link effects was 208 and that of those due to anaemic sales, only 48.

Figure 6.8 shows that there was a change in the fraction of bankruptcies due to link effects over the ten years from 1995 to 2004. Panel (a) charts the fraction of bankruptcies due to link effects, where the number of bankruptcies and the level of indebtedness are shown by open triangles and solid squares, respectively. Panel (b) charts the dependence of bankruptcies due to link effects on the level of indebtedness. The fraction of the number of bankruptcies due to link effects is about 10 per cent, and the fraction of indebtedness due to link effects is about 20 per cent. As the indebtedness increases, bankruptcy due to link effects also increases, and in particular the fraction due to indebtedness reaches 30 per cent, a fact indicating the importance of chain bankruptcy as a network effect.

6.2.5 The ripple effect

The question now arises as to what further effects are caused by the bankruptcy of a company; for example, how many creditors are affected by the bankruptcy? As in subsection 6.2.1, bankruptcy will obviously have consequences for workers and banks as well as production, since the propagation paths are not restricted simply to links relating to production but also include employment and finance links. In particular, any direct influence on banks would have a very large effect in terms of the quantity of debt and credit.

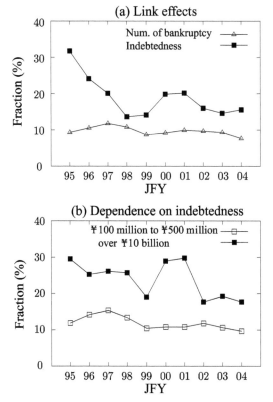

Figure 6.8. (a) Fraction of bankruptcies due to link effects (b) dependence of bankruptcies due to link effects on the amount of indebtedness.

In pursuit of answers to these questions we will study an actual case of bankruptcy in detail (see Table 6.2). This involved a medium-size chain retailer that became bankrupt during 2005 in Japan. The transaction relationships in Table 6.2 can be summarised thus (number of cases in parentheses): accounts receivable (65), leasing receivables (12), deposits received on sale (11), expense (7), cautionary obligation (1). Breaking out the data from the financing relationships we find financial institutions (8), credit associations (2) and debt securities (2).

The indebtedness was about ¥4.7 billion, of which ¥3.4 billion was debt from twelve financial institutions – major commercial and regional banks. Table 6.2 shows that although a large fraction of the indebtedness was debt from financial institutions, the creditors affected by the bankruptcy were mainly companies engaged in goods transactions, especially vendors for the bankrupt retailer. Sixty-five companies among ninety-six transaction goods creditors were creditors through accounts receivable.

As explained before, a link in a transaction network corresponds to a relationship between a debtor (borrower) and a creditor (lender). The effect of a bankruptcy propagates in the upstream direction in a transaction network, because that is where creditors

Table 6.2. *Number of creditors and amount of indebtedness for a bankrupt company.*

Relationship	Number of creditors	Indebtedness (¥'000)
Transaction	96	1,360,592
Financing	12	3,393,976
Total	108	4,754,568

are located. The impact of the propagation depends on the companies affected. For example, a large company would not be seriously disturbed by the loss of one customer and the inability to collect a single account receivable. However, a small company or a company whose major customer is the bankrupt company might be fatally affected. Note that this propagation process is different from the stochastic fluctuations described in section 5.3, which are likely to be jump processes.

If the seriously affected company itself goes bankrupt, this is part of the process of the chain bankruptcy, and it should be noted that there are many companies upstream of a bankrupt company in such a chain. The workers and banks involved with the company are affected through the employment and financing networks. In the event of a bankruptcy the banks must increase the risk premium on the interest rate, thus exposing many other debtors to credit risk. This effect may even cause a credit crunch affecting many other companies further off in the financial network, a matter explained above in section 5.3.

In fact, since almost any company can be affected by a chain bankruptcy, through the transaction, employment and financial networks, it is essential to grasp the structure of the transaction network for effective risk management. In particular, the most important information concerns the financial condition of the customers of a company's customers.

There were about a hundred companies upstream of the bankrupt company in the case considered above. We might ask whether this number is exceptionally large, and to obtain an answer to that question we will examine the degree distribution explained above in subsection 4.5.2. The fact that the degree distribution has a fat tail may yield interesting results about the number of a company's customers' customers.

When company A sells goods to company B, we can postulate a directed link from A to B. Figure 6.9 gives the cumulative distributions of (a) in-degree (vendors) and (b) out-degree (customers) for the directed network consisting of 30,000 companies, including about 3,000 listed companies, in JFY 2003.[2] Both the in-degree and out-degree cumulative distributions have fat tails where the cumulative distribution $P_>(k)$ of degree k shows the power-law behaviour $P_>(k) \propto k^{-\nu}$, and the values of ν are in the range of 1.4 to 1.5 for both in-degree and out-degree.

---

[2] Link data is not available for any listed companies, and it is presumed that distributions of sections with large degree are not affected by the lack of data.

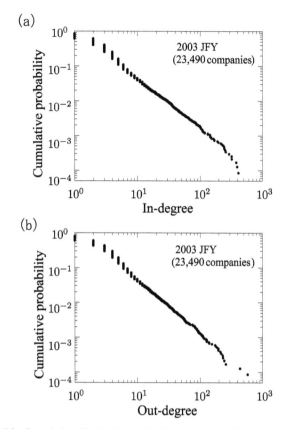

Figure 6.9. Cumulative distributions of (a) in-degree (vendors) (b) out-degree (customers).

As we can see, there are many companies only one link upstream, due to the fat-tail nature of the degree distribution. The number of companies two links away upstream (the friend-of-a-friend, as it were) is larger than might be expected in a rough estimation. If we assume that the average in-degree is 10, then the question is how many vendors are there for the company's vendors. We can estimate this simply by ignoring the possibility of double counting, which would increase the number, and thus calculating $10 \times 10 = 100$.

However, a rigorous estimation shows that in fact the number of companies is much larger than this, because the fat tail of the degree distribution makes the probability of large-degree companies finite.

For clarity, let us assume that all links in the network are non-directed, that is we assume a non-directed graph. The average number of companies upstream by two links, n_2, can be estimated by

$$n_2 = \langle k^2 \rangle - \langle k \rangle,$$

as explained in section 4.2. Here k is the degree and $\langle \cdot \rangle$ is an average over the degree distribution. The average number of vendors is $\langle k \rangle$. Our rigorous estimation of the number of companies, n_2, is thus much larger than the simple estimation $\langle k \rangle^2$, because the first term of the right-hand side of the above equation becomes large for a fat-tail distribution.

For the transaction network, where the number of nodes is 20,601 and the number of links is 66,623, we obtain

$$\langle k \rangle = 6.47, \qquad \langle k^2 \rangle = 287.$$

With these numbers, the simple estimation leads to $\langle k \rangle^2 \simeq 42$. By contrast, the rigorous estimation using the equation for n_2 results in 281. The actual observation is $n_2 = 220$, which is very close to the estimate.[3] See also Fujiwara and Aoyama (2008).

In summary, there are many companies upstream by one link, and the number of companies upstream by two links is much larger than might be imagined from a simple estimation, on account of the fat tail of the degree distribution. At present, only companies upstream by one link are considered in credit exposure management, but this underestimates the risk, an error which we suggest could be corrected by employing the theory explained here.

As noted before, the impact of the propagation of credit risk depends on the character of the affected companies, for example a small company or a company whose major customer is the bankrupt company could well be affected fatally. It is possible to detect these weak paths in the transaction network in advance by examining the relationships in the downstream to upstream direction.

On the other hand, a large company is not affected seriously by an uncollectable account receivable or the loss of a single customer, for the simple reason that a large company has many alternative customers. If the network is studied in the upstream to downstream direction, a different view emerges. There are a great number of companies downstream by one, two or three links from a large company, and since there are many weak paths in this set of links the possibility of a ripple from those companies downstream cannot be ignored.[4] In this way even a large company that is thought unlikely to be affected seriously if the company loses a single customer could not ignore the impact of chain bankruptcy.

Figure 6.10 is a part of the transaction network consisting of a bankrupt company, creditors and creditors of creditors, drawn for transaction data in JFY 2005. Nodes on the inner circle are creditors and nodes on the outer circle are vendors of the creditors.

If we want to be able to issue an alert of the likelihood of chain bankruptcy we need to detect weak paths in the transaction network in advance, and traditional credit exposure management is not sufficient for this purpose. Instead, it is essential to capture the structure of the transaction network, and collaborative work engaging both the business and academic worlds needs to start immediately.

---

[3] Error in the rigorous estimate may arise from two sources. One is where company C is one of the linked companies of company B which are linked by company A, and company C is directly linked to company A. This means there is a triangle $\triangle ABC$ and the cluster coefficient is not equal to 0. The other reason may be that there is a quadrangle where $A \rightarrow B \rightarrow C$, $A \rightarrow D \rightarrow C$, and no link between B and D.

[4] The ripple effect is a general term to indicate the effect of an influence from a secondary factor, a tertiary factor, etc.

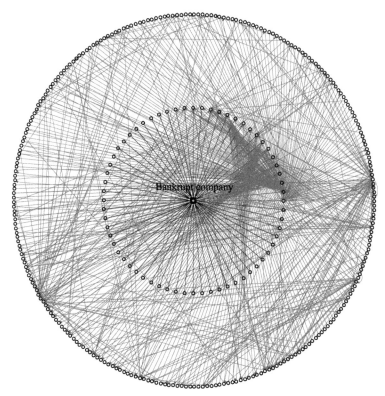

Figure 6.10. A part of the transaction network consisting of a bankrupt company, creditors and creditors of creditors.

6.2.6 *Propagation of credit risk on the transaction network*

We will now explain another practical application of the network model presented in section 5.5, namely the simulation of chain bankruptcy in attempts to grasp the importance of accounts receivable, accounts payable and capital structure.

The concept of chain bankruptcy in the network model is schematically shown in Figure 6.11. An arrow in the figure indicates the direction of the distribution of goods in the transaction network; thus the company shown by a diamond is located at the outfall of the transaction network in the range of this figure. Note that such a company distributes goods to a company located further downstream which is not shown in this figure. We assume that each company manufactured goods and then distributed them to a downstream company, and is waiting to call in accounts receivable. If the company shown by a diamond is bankrupted by an unexpected accident, it cannot pay these accounts to upstream companies. The company i shown by a triangle located at the left of the company shown by a diamond expects to obtain profit Π_i from sales revenue R_i less total cost $C_i + r_i K_i + L_i$, and increases equity $E_i^{(i)}$ at the beginning of the period to equity $E_i^{(f)}$ at the end of the period. Because the company shown by a triangle cannot obtain accounts receivable, the sales revenue decreases from R_i to R_i', that is to say it

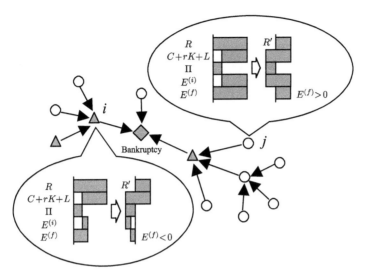

Figure 6.11. Model of chain bankruptcy in a transaction network.

goes into the red. The company makes up for the loss by withdrawing part of its equity, and as a result the equity $E_i^{(f)}$ at the end of the period becomes negative, and of course capital deficit is one of the definitions of bankruptcy. The bankrupt company cannot pay accounts payable, and so some upstream companies may become bankrupt if they do not have sufficient equity to handle the loss of profit. We call this phenomenon the propagation of credit risk through the transaction network. On the other hand, company j, shown by a open circle located at the upper right of the figure, has enough equity $E_j^{(i)}$ at the beginning of the period. This company retains positive equity $E_j^{(f)}$ at the end of the period, even if it makes up for the loss of profit by withdrawing part of equity $E_j^{(i)}$ at the beginning of the period. In this case, the propagation of credit risk on the transaction network is terminated at the company j, because it has sufficient equity to absorb the shock.

We will now put the concept sketched above into a practical simulation and examine the propagation of credit risk. The transaction network used in this simulation consists of about 1,400 companies listed on the Tokyo Stock Exchange. It should, however, be noted that the initial values for sales revenue R_i, cost C_i, equity E_i, capital K_i, labour L_i and interaction parameters k_{ij} were arbitrarily assigned. A company was added to the transaction network and three companies were arbitrarily chosen as suppliers for the additional company. Then we assumed that the additional company became bankrupt as the exogenous trigger of chain bankruptcy. The results obtained from this simulation are shown in Figure 6.12. The network is drawn from the company depicted by a triangle at the centre of the transaction network towards the linked companies in the upstream region in the distribution of goods. The companies which became bankrupt because of the propagation of credit risk are marked by triangles. The basic characteristics of chain bankruptcy are clearly visible, namely a chain of bankrupt

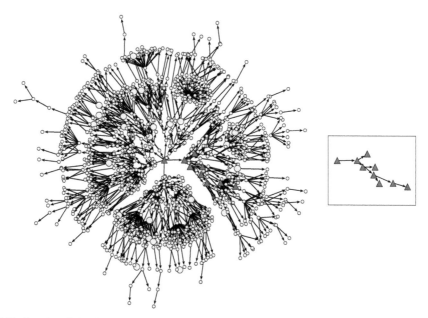

Figure 6.12. Results of the chain bankruptcy simulation.

companies stretching from the outfall towards the upstream region of the transaction network. The companies which terminate the bankruptcy chain are those with a small number of accounts receivable from the bankrupt company or those with sufficiently large capital $E_i^{(i)}$ at the beginning of the period.

While the simulation explained in this subsection remains at a qualitative level, it is nevertheless possible to simulate chain bankruptcy quantitatively if the model parameters are set using actual financial statement data. By selecting an exogenously bankrupt company systematically, a quantitative simulation makes it possible to find weak credit risk links on the real transaction network.

 The world car platform of General Motors Corporation

Most cars are designed, manufactured and sold in order to fit the needs of a specific market, such as that in the United States. Only a few compact cars and a few luxury cars are manufactured in one country and then exported worldwide.

In the 1970s, General Motors Corporation in the USA invented an outstanding business model where cars to fit the various market needs of many countries were designed and manufactured by making minor modifications to a versatile platform. This business model was called the world car platform, and it formed part of General Motors' strategy to dominate the world market.

Starting with the T-car in 1974, General Motors released its X-car in 1979 and then its J-car in 1981. However, their plan to achieve global market supremacy failed, partly because of major drawbacks in the business model itself (Piore and Sabel, 1984). The first drawback was in the distribution of manufacturing to emerging economies. Low-cost and stable labour forces in emerging economies proved to be difficult to obtain, and General Motors suffered serious problems, such as demands for higher wages and various labour disputes immediately after starting to manufacture cars at the newly constructed factories. The second drawback was concerned with global component procurement. This method of component procurement required holding a very large parts inventory in a car manufacturing plant. If faulty parts were delivered from very distant distributed component factories, the company's managers and production engineers could not promptly replace them. This situation was in marked contrast to the just-in-time manufacturing system invented by the Toyota Motor Corporation in Japan.

It is important to note that the world car strategy failed for reasons other than product quality. We know this at first hand, since one of the authors once owned a used J-car, a Pontiac J2000, in the United States in the late 1980s. Although the J-car was never a car to attract enthusiasts, it was a workhorse without serious problems.

6.3   Business model and business information

In Japan there is a kind of industrial group known as a *keiretsu*, which is conventionally understood as an industrial group consisting of a family of companies linked to each other by shareholding. In a narrow sense, the *keiretsu* is a family of companies which are members of a consolidated accounting set. Recently, it has been argued that industrial groups with low profitability need to reactivate their business by changing their fundamental business model through mergers and acquisitions and reconstructing their portfolio of activities. In the last decade the Japanese electrical and electronics sector has used mergers and acquisitions to initiate this sort of reorganisation, and recent cases are shown in Table 6.3. While it is intuitively obvious that one industrial group could record good results at the same time as another group is having a very tough time in the market, it is however difficult to judge their relative success simply by sampling performance at a particular period.

In this section, we will first explain the basic advantages and drawbacks of an industrial group, and then show how the ability to respond to a sudden accident is a very important advantage. Subsequently, we will verify the business synergy expected in an industrial group, and finally we propose to combine business information and computer simulations in order to work out an innovative business model.

6.3.1   The industrial group as a business model

A business model is a scheme used by a company to define how it intends to earn profits in a selected industry sector. In other words, the business model defines the origins of

Table 6.3. *Cases of mergers and acquisitions in the Japanese electronic components industry.*

Year	Merging company	Merged company
1999	Hitachi Plasma Display	PDP divisions of Hitachi and Fujitsu
1999	Elpida Memory	DRAM divisions of Hitachi and NEC
2001	Panasonic	Matsushita Electronics
2001	Sony Ericsson Mobile Communications	Cellphone divisions of Sony and Ericsson
2002	Panasonic	Matsushita Tushin-Kogyo, Kyushu Matsushita, Matsushita Seiko, Matsushita Kotobuki-denshi, Matsushita Densou system
2003	Hitachi Global Storage Technologies	HDD divisions of Hitachi and IBM
2003	Renesas Technology	System LSI divisions of Hitachi and Mitsubishi Electric
2003	PIONEER	PDP division of NEC
2004	S-LCD	LCD divisions of Sony and Samsung Electronics
2005	Sharp	LCD division of Fujitsu

profit, the flows of goods and money, the relationship between customers and vendors and the field of business, and it forms the basis of the business strategy.

Some readers might be familiar with the term 'business model' from the expression 'business model patent', which is a patent relating to a business method using information technology, such as computers and the Internet. The business model patent is infamous for being used to patent the application of a business method even though it is not recognised as an invention. Concerns about the validity of the business model patent do not affect the fact that a business model is essential for well-performed business.

Figure 6.13 is a coarse-grained transaction network in Japan at the industrial sector level of resolution (Ikeda *et al.*, 2008). Arrows in the figure indicate the flow of goods, and the numbers indicate industrial sectors as shown in the table. Industrial sectors related to infrastructure and raw material, such as air transportation, land transportation, warehousing and mining industries, are located in the upstream zone, whilst industrial sectors subject to consumers, such as gas, railways, electricity, telecommunications and retailing industries, are located in the downstream zone. In the central part of the network, which is a so-called 'strongly connected component', we find the electrical and electronics, automobile, chemical, service and wholesale industries.

In the electrical and electronics and automobile industries located in the centre of the coarse-grained transaction network, there are several very large industrial groups employing both vertical integration and a horizontal division of work. Why and how are these industrial groups formed? Let us consider the business model of an industrial group.

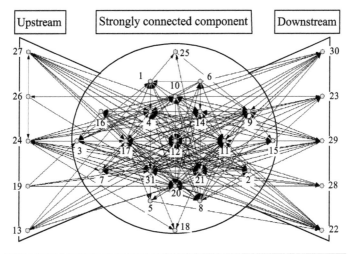

Number	Industrial sector	Number	Industrial sector
1	Food	2	Textiles
3	Paper manufacturing	4	Chemicals
5	Pharmaceutical manufacturing	6	Oil
7	Rubber	8	Ceramics
9	Steel	10	Non-ferrous metal
11	Machinery	12	Electrical and electronics
13	Shipbuilding	14	Automobile
15	Transportation equipment	16	Precision machinery
17	Other manufactures	18	Fishery
19	Mining	20	Construction
21	Wholesale	22	Retail
23	Railways	24	Land transportation
25	Marine transportation	26	Air transportation
27	Warehouse	28	Telecommunications
29	Electric power	30	Gas
31	Service		

Figure 6.13. Coarse-grained transaction network.

By examining their corporate histories we find that many industrial groups were formed as a result of mergers and acquisitions (M&A) or the split-up of companies, actions which are considered to have the advantages described in the following paragraphs.

Management with a long-range perspective. When a company is protected by mutual shareholding, the company is free from the threat of M&A by competitors or investment funds, even if the stock price becomes low. Thus, the managers of the company could take advantage of that security and run the company with a long-range perspective without worrying about imminent M&A drives by competitors or investment funds. In addition, managers could maintain a wage-system policy grounded in seniority and guaranteed lifetime employment.

Augmentation of customers and agility. If a company is split up, a subsidiary company could start to sell goods to competitors of the parent company, and as a result the subsidiary company could enlarge its customer base. In addition, small companies are often more agile in decision and action than larger competitors, and subsidiary companies are, in general, small. Thus in the industry sector, where agility is a requisite for high performance, it is sometimes regarded as advantageous to split a company to reduce overall size.

Ensuring job security and adjustment of cost structure. By relocating personnel from the parent company to important posts in the subsidiary company it is possible to run that company with a management policy consistent with that of the parent. Furthermore, creating new posts in the subsidiary company assists in maintaining a wage system grounded in seniority and guaranteed lifetime employment. In addition, managers save labour costs for the whole industrial group by holding down the wages of the subsidiary companies to fit their profit level. Furthermore, the subsidiary company can maintain friendly relationships with the parent company through straightforward personal acquaintance.

Reduction of transaction costs. The parent company does not need to incur costs when seeking credible companies for outsourcing or other transactions. Savings are also expected on R&D costs because of the collaboration between the parent and the subsidiary companies, and flexible transactions grounded in stable relationships. Moreover, the subsidiary companies can reduce their operating expenses in finding new customers and understanding their needs because of the parent company's broad base of information. Surprisingly, before consolidated accounting was introduced in Japan, subsidiary companies were forced to buy goods from their parent company to reduce the stockpile and increase the revenue of the parent company, and this was almost certainly one of the historical reasons for the success of the industrial group.

Coping with credit risk. It is possible to transact business between members of an industrial group without incurring credit risk. Even if an unforeseeable accident occurs, related companies are expected to make spontaneous arrangements to deal with the emergency without previous agreement, since companies belonging to the same industrial group are strongly tied by common interests. If the transaction is a one-shot sale, arrangements to deal with the emergency must have been designed previously, and unless the arrangements are strangely far-sighted and well designed, it is not likely that they will deal effectively with the emergency.

However, recent changes in the business environment are showing that industrial groups have some drawbacks. As reform of corporate governance rises up the agenda, there is a tendency to attach more importance to short-term profitability in the interests of shareholders. For example, indices of profitability, such as the return on equity (ROE), have been introduced for companies, and capital adequacy requirements, such as those imposed by the Bank for International Settlements (BIS), have been introduced for banks. As a result industrial groups based on mutual shareholding are steadily being dismantled.

Transactions between companies in the same industrial group are stable and cost-saving because credit administration is not required. On the other hand, inefficiency due to a cosy and uncritical relationship gives cause for concern. During Japan's high economic growth period in the 1960s, even if there was inefficient transaction to some extent, most companies could obtain enough profit because of continuous economic growth; but in today's business environment we could not find a leading company willing to predict the direction of general economic movement. Consequently, it is increasingly said that doing business with various companies on a flexible basis is more efficient and profitable than doing so rigidly with related companies in an industrial group.

The drawbacks of the industrial group are apparent even for R&D when it is seen as a source of future profit. Let us consider games as an analogy for business. Victory or defeat in chess is determined largely by the ability to consider an opponent's potential moves. On the other hand, in poker, players have to play their cards in the context of restricted information about their opponents' cards. This distinction resembles that between a traditional business and a new post-Internet business.

For example, in a traditional industry, such as the electrical and electronics sector, a small number of large companies conduct basic research at their own corporate laboratories and apply the research output to their business. The process by which an industrial group moves from R&D to commercialisation of products is called *closed innovation*, or the linear model of product development.

Meanwhile, the product cycles of software products and information technology in the post-Internet information society have become much shorter. A competitor might suddenly introduce a product which is competitive and based on a new and superior technology. Closed innovation does not work well in such a situation.

Consequently, a new method called *open innovation* (Chesbrough, 2006) is attracting attention. This is a method of product development where the boundary between companies is not clearly marked. If a company does not have the technology required for the development of a new product, the company buys the technology from other companies. On the other hand, if a company decides not to use their own technology for the development of a new product, the company sells the technology to another company or to a split-off venture business.

There are several points to keep in mind when initiating open innovation. Firstly, it is important to recognise that there is no intrinsic economic value to technology; a technology can only be evaluated in the context of the business model of a company. Thus, it is necessary to determine the sale price of a technology in the light of the company's own business model. Note, however, that open innovation does not mean that R&D at a company's own laboratory is unnecessary, since they must take on the difficult task of defining systems to integrate the technologies. Furthermore, open innovation is not necessarily a panacea for all new business, and it is extremely important to evaluate which enterprise is suitable for open innovation and which is not. For example, although the effectiveness of open innovation for software development has been proved, in-depth consideration might be required before applying it to hardware development consisting of various complex components.

6.3.2   *Robustness of industrial groups*

One of the outstanding features of the company network for the horizontal division of work is the ability to respond to unexpected accidents.[5] In a business environment with high uncertainty the superiority of the horizontal division of work is becoming apparent when compared with vertical integration. Whereas vertical integration is characterised by the division of labour in each layer of the business process, horizontal division possesses a versatile but specialised strength called *flexible specialisation*.

A company seldom obeys an order from another company in the horizontal division network. Instead, each company exhibits a sort of vague willingness to behave according to the expected demand from other companies, and a tendency to correct that expectation in the light of interactions with other companies in the network. By considering the effect of vagueness, the horizontal division network can be understood as a *hierarchical network* of information-processing nodes.

When load is centralised on a certain node, and consequently the processing speed of the node is decreased, homogenisation of load will result if a bypass link is added to this node. The network generated by adding such bypass links is called a *multi-scale network*. The multi-scale network possesses robustness, which means that the whole network does not break down as the result of a single accident, such as the destruction of a production system due to fire or the bankruptcy of a large company. This robustness is an outstanding feature of the company network, and is not intended or designed by managers.

This feature is dramatically in evidence in the recovery after a serious fire at the Aisin Seiki Co.'s Factory No. 1 in Kariya on 1 February 1997. Aisin Seiki Co. was the exclusive supplier of the p-valve, a part of the brake system used in almost all Toyota's cars. Production was concentrated at the Aisin Seiki Co.'s Factory No. 1, which manufactured more than 30,000 sets of p-valves per day. Since Toyota manufactures 15,000 cars per day, stocks of the p-valve would be consumed within two days. The lack of this tiny part caused the stoppage of the whole production process in Toyota, an astonishing fact.

Even worse, the fire not only stopped the supply of the p-valve but also destroyed the specialised production system for the p-valve. Toyota and Aisin were worried that several months would be required for recovery, a matter of great economic significance even for Toyota. However, the production of the p-valve was restarted on 4 February, just three days after the fire, as the result of the co-operative action of more than 200 companies in the industrial group, and all this without any support from Toyota itself. Toyota restarted car manufacture, and daily production was close to 14,000 on 10 February. It is believed that the key to this dramatic recovery was the robustness of the multi-scale network in the Toyota industrial group. Disaster recovery, then, is a by-product of the network constructed during normal operation.

---

[5] This section is based on chapter 9 of Watts (2003).

From this impressive story we learn that the manager of the flagship conglomerate leading an industrial group should not force business plans on to subsidiary companies, but rather should encourage decision-making in business by exploration of the vaguer aspects of the company network. We believe that a robust industrial group will result from this decision-making strategy.

6.3.3   Synergy in industrial groups

It is widely believed that *synergy* for profit is to be expected in an industrial group. To put this in concrete terms, such synergy means that a company acquiring another company satisfies a certain condition and so makes a larger profit than the sum of profits for each company, in keeping with the definition of synergy which describes it as a phenomenon where the total value of the linked components is larger than the sum of the values of individual components. On superficial examination it might be thought that when company A selling product x and company B selling product y are merged, the sales revenue is increased by selling both products, x and y, through the same salesperson. In addition the merged company might obtain larger profits with the same sales revenue by reducing various costs, e.g. management costs at headquarters. Synergy seems attractive. But is any of this really true?

We can test the hypothesis that the increase of profit is larger than the increase of company size by postulating an industrial group. The company invests the labour L and the capital K and obtains the value-added Y by production activity. Labour and capital are inputs and value-added is the output. In general, multiplying the inputs L and K by a factor of λ increases the output Y by κ times, i.e.

$$\kappa Y = F(\lambda L, \lambda K).$$

Here the function $F(\cdot)$ is the production function explained in subsection 3.5.1. If $\kappa = \lambda$, the size of labour L and capital K is increased by a factor of λ and accordingly the value-added Y is increased by the same factor. This means that there is no synergy at all.

The labour, capital and value-added are calculated using financial statement data for each company belonging to an industrial group. Labour L is the sum of the labour cost, the employment cost and the welfare expenses. Capital K is the sum of the tangible fixed assets and the allowance for depreciation. Value-added Y is the sales revenue less the cost of raw materials and other expenses, such as electricity costs. In this way a number of points equal to the number of companies are obtained in the three-dimensional space (L, K, Y). Parameters A, α and β of the production function

$$F(L, K) = A K^{\alpha} L^{\beta}$$

were estimated in order to reproduce the distribution of data points. Here it should be noted that the condition of 'no synergy' is

$$\alpha + \beta \leq 1,$$

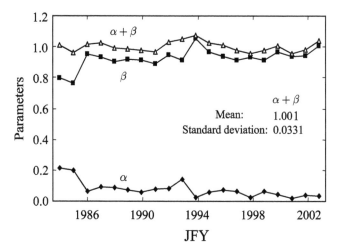

Figure 6.14. Parameters of the production function for companies belonging to a Japanese industrial group.

because the relation

$$F(\lambda L, \lambda K) = \lambda^{\alpha+\beta} F(L, K)$$

holds.

Figure 6.14 shows the result of data analysis for twenty-four companies listed in the first section of the Tokyo Stock Exchange and belonging to a Japanese industrial group. The results of the parameter estimations are statistically significant. The average value in the period 1984–2003 was

$$\alpha + \beta = 1.001 \pm 0.033.$$

Thus, there is no evidence of synergy. Indeed, the data suggests to us that the whole system of linked components is equal to the sum of the individual components. Of course, we cannot deny the existence of small-scale synergy which is undetectable in an analysis using publicly available data, but the result does mean that we cannot expect significant synergy for the existing business model or any extension of it, though it might be possible for us to produce drastically innovative business models which realise large-scale synergy. Time will tell.

6.3.4 Business information systems

The previous section showed that we cannot expect an increase of profitability simply by increasing company size. It rather seems that the most important element in creating high profitability is the business model, and if larger company size is required to realise the business model, the use of mergers and acquisitions might be a pattern for success. We might now ask what the key is to the production of innovative business models. This is a truly hard question, and there are many possible answers. However, the first step necessary for innovation is common to all the answers, namely, that it is necessary to understand the situation of your own company in terms of the relationship between customers and vendors.

Quantitative analysis of the profitability of the business model, based on newly clarified facts about the company's own business, is the deciding factor in predicting success and failure. In particular, complex network analysis and an agent simulation are invaluable tools for understanding the relationships and for a quantitative evaluation of profitability.

The application of business information.   Various tasks are conducted in each division of a company, and these tasks are categorised as routine or non-routine. A routine task is an operation repeated regularly according to predetermined procedures. On the other hand, a non-routine task is an operation which is different on each occasion, occurs irregularly and for which only a rough procedure is given. Business information systems are categorised in the same manner. Conducting routine tasks is associated with the mission-critical system, that is to say the system that processes the information of the company as a whole for material procurement, physical distribution, sales, finance and personnel affairs. The system is characterised by information transactions concerning the relationship between customers and suppliers. On the other hand, the handling of non-routine tasks is associated with business information systems and related software. The business information system processes information for tasks relating to each individual division, and the system is characterised by the linking of many software packages. Of these tasks, decision-making for business strategy is the most important target of the business information system.

There is a long history to company information processing, and many systems were developed in the era of the mainframe computer. Many mission-critical systems are being reconstructed in order to facilitate the interactive transaction of many core corporate functions. It is now becoming common to process information for material procurement, physical distribution, sales, finance and personnel affairs in an integrated manner using an *enterprise resource planning* (ERP) system. In addition, it is also coming to be normal to use *supply chain management* (SCM) in the management of a series of task chains from procurement of materials and components to production, physical distribution and sales, in order to improve efficiency relating to delivery date and inventory management. The SCM is categorised either as an intracompany SCM, which manages material procurement, physical distribution, sales and finance within the same company, or an intercompany SCM, which manages relations between materials companies, manufacturing companies, customers, wholesale companies and retailers.

Initially, we will explain the noticeable advances in mission-critical systems from the perspective of innovation in the business model. Fortunately, electronic disclosure of financial statement data in *eXtensible Business Reporting Language* (XBRL) is now common (Bergeron, 2003). XBRL is a computer language suitable for the exchange of financial statement data, and is based on, and similar in principle to, the *eXtensible Markup Language* (XML).

In XML, flexible information exchange is made possible by tagging each piece of information. XML is a meta language, that is to say it defines a specific language, such as XBRL. Until very recently, the means for obtaining financial statement data were restricted to downloading data for an individual company or buying bulk data from a specialised data provision company. In addition, there were other problems such as the fact that financial data for listed companies was basically annual, while that for unlisted companies was made public only sporadically. As the use of electronic disclosure employing XBRL becomes more widespread these problems are expected to be resolved.

The disclosure of financial statement data on a quarterly or a monthly basis, which is desirable from the point of view of corporate governance, will be made possible by using the ERP system to hold and process data written in XBRL. It is also anticipated that there will be a reduction in paperwork costs and increases in the speed of decision-making for business strategy formation. If disclosure on a monthly basis is widespread for small and medium-sized companies as well as large companies, the credit risk for customer companies will be captured in real time. When that occurs, automatic data acquisition, using spidering programs such as Googlebot, Scooter and MSNbot, will become an effective tool for business. It is noted here that the most important target outcomes for the business information system and coupled software are increases in the rapidity of business strategy decision-making and real-time capturing of credit risk for customer companies.

We will now explain an *electronic commerce* system using XML. Electronic commerce is a business transaction using a computer network intended to reduce transaction costs and improve customer service. Electronic commerce transactions are categorised as business to business (B2B), business to consumer (B2C) or interconsumer (C2C). In particular it is expected that the B2B transaction will lead to the strengthening of the above-mentioned intercompany SCM.

Traditional electronic commerce using electronic data interchange (EDI) has been used only by large companies and their partner companies, because a dedicated program and a dedicated communication line are required. In contrast with traditional electronic commerce, XML-based electronic commerce uses the Internet and this facilitates low cost and flexible transactions. Furthermore, the integration of business processes using XBRL might bring even higher efficiency, as is the case with the ERP system.

According to the Ministry of the Economy, Trade and Industry in Japan, the market size of B2B electronic commerce in Japan was US$1,939 billion in 2005, and the US Department of Commerce reports that the market size of B2B electronic commerce in the USA was US$1,821 billion in 2004. Direct comparison of these two countries is difficult because the timing of aggregation is different and the Japanese statistics include both transactions using the Internet and those using dedicated communication lines. In fact, according to Global Industry Analysis Inc., the market size of electronic commerce in the Asia-Pacific basin was US$1,700 billion in 2004 and US$3,753 billion in 2005. An estimate of the market size of B2B electronic commerce in Japan in 2004 using the above data is therefore $1,939 \times 1,700/3,753 = \text{US\$}0.878$ billion. This means that the market size in Japan is about half the size of that in the USA.

Meanwhile, it is reasonable to expect the advance of business information systems and coupled software as a reflection of the advance of mission-critical systems. An agent simulation based on data analysis of the transaction data of B2B electronic commerce, accompanied by the ERP system and the SCM system, could forecast the demand for goods and the supply of components simultaneously for many companies on the transaction network. This forecasting method could provide more reliable results than the conventional method, which uses data only for a specific company. As a result, benefits will be obtained in the management of business risks such as inventory growth and opportunity loss, the real-time capturing of credit risk for customer companies and the acceleration of decision-making in business strategy.

The application of complex network analysis.   A very large quantity of data on intercompany transactions other than B2B electronic commerce is currently dormant in the files of commercial banks, since individual records of settlement operations for purchase and sales have to be recorded in the mission-critical systems of the relevant banks. Consequently, the details of commercial distribution in the Japanese economy could be revealed by analysing the combined records of settlement operations together with the B2B electronic commerce data. If these data become available, important steps could be taken towards the design of a new high-profitability business model.

As the Aisin Seiki case shows, the manager of a flagship conglomerate leading an industrial group should not force business plans on to subsidiary companies, but rather should encourage decision-making in business by exploring the vaguer aspects of the company network. But studying this requires data covering changing relationships on the transaction network, a matter we refer to as the *reconnection* of the transaction network. We anticipate that relationships in B2B electronic commerce are relatively flexible, and thus that many reconnection events are recorded in the transaction data, a fact that might open up the potential for studying the characteristics of reconnection – research which is currently impossible. If we were able to model reconnection successfully, it is probable that we would observe that the information system itself makes decisions by exploring the vaguer aspects of the company network, thus opening the door for new methods of business risk management.

In the present complex network analysis, several network indices have been calculated for selected industrial sectors. This is rather like studying the tree which happens to be in front of you, even though the ultimate purpose of your research is to clarify the structure of the forest as a whole. Of course, a biased selection of subject matter is not an appropriate approach. It would be better to begin by calculating the various network indices for the whole network, and then select the subject of analysis on the basis of the indices obtained. To go back to our analogy, this would be like drawing a map of the forest at the outset, and then using that map to select which trees within the forest are to be studied. We have no doubt that by using large amounts of real-time data and sophisticated analytical methodologies it will be possible in the near future to capture the flows of money and goods in real time in order to detect economic problems at an early stage.

The application of agent simulation.   The application of agent simulation is growing in importance in the study of innovative business models. In many research areas PC clusters, which are groups of personal computers linked to each other by high-speed networks to form single high-speed virtual computers, are now being widely used. The processing speed is increased in proportion to the number of linked PCs, because the sequence of calculation is divided and the calculation is then performed in parallel. The fastest supercomputer in the world in June 2009 was the Roadrunner set up at the Los Alamos National Laboratory in the USA. Roadrunner consists of 129,600 processors and has a computation speed of over 1 petaFLOPS.[6] The fastest supercomputer in Japan in June 2009 was the Earth Simulator, which consists of 1,280 processors and performs with a peak speed of 0.122 petaFLOPS. The massively parallel type of supercomputer is not only much faster than the vector type with fewer processors, but also cheaper. For this reason, PC-based massively parallel supercomputers are becoming popular.

In the decade ahead, the performance of computers and networks will improve still further, and it will be plausible to study new business models using agent simulations, including financial markets and consumers as well as companies and banks, depending on the problem to be solved. The aim is to study economic activity by simulating the whole economic network consisting of various agents, each behaving autonomously in order to obtain larger profit through the reconnection of the network.

If the business information system described in this section is realised, we will be able to obtain a company's data changes in real time rather than on a yearly basis, and it will therefore be possible to capture flows of money and goods in real time, which will probably have a very significant impact on practical business. This is a remarkable goal, and while there are many problems ahead, none of these are, in our view, insoluble. It is no exaggeration to say that we are at a turning point in applying the theoretical results of econophysics to practical business situations. All that is needed is more hard work.

---

[6] 1 petaFLOPS stands for 1 quadrillion floating-point arithmetical operations per second.

Epilogue

SALVIATI: Greetings, Simplicio, Sagredo. You are both looking very thoughtful; which I hope is a good sign and shows that you have made good progress with econophysics. In any case, I am very eager to hear what kind of impression the book has left upon you?

SIMPLICIO: Well, I thought the most interesting coffee break bit is . . .

SAGREDO: Oh heavens above; I sometimes wonder if you are a serious person, Simplicio. I haven't forgotten that it was you who made our good friend Galileo go down on his knees before the Pope.

SIMPLICIO: That is a long time ago.

SAGREDO: Indeed, and it is still fresh in my memory.

SALVIATI: Now, now, friends, let us keep our eye on the matter in hand. Sagredo, you first; tell me what you think.

SAGREDO: Well, in spite of what you said about it being written as non-technically as possible and for a wide range of readers, I found much of the argument quite complicated. In any case, I learned of many concepts that were new to me, for example the Pareto distribution, the *fat* tail, Gibrat's law, complex networks and open innovations, to name a few.

SALVIATI: Good. At least you are now free from the restrictive view of the normal Gaussian distribution. Incidentally, our good friend Eugene Stanley has a very inspiring thing to say about the current global economic crisis in relation to the Pareto distribution (Stanley, 2009).

SIMPLICIO: Which is . . . ?

SALVIATI: He pointed out that there is a big difference in the way that physicists and traditional economists approach laws and the theory behind them. Our economist is, by and large, unwilling to accept a law if there is no complete theory behind it. But physicists, as Professor Stanley says, 'cannot afford this reluctance'. There is so much that we don't understand that even very useful laws, Newton's for example, or those of Coulomb, are discovered long before the theoretical underpinning exists. The same is probably true of economics.

SAGREDO: Oh, I see. Then he must be implying that economists cannot *afford* their reluctance now; they should overcome this false and unscientific conscience, and be a little lighter on their intellectual feet, as it were, particularly if these laws give you some degree of understanding that returns as power, as the English philosopher Coleridge once said.

SIMPLICIO: Precisely; you see it immediately, and the value could be enormous.

SAGREDO: Quite, if this scientific research could be applied to design of better, more resilient economic systems, those responsible would truly deserve the thanks of mankind.

SIMPLICIO: Forgive my pouring cold water on this little victory parade, but surely what I have seen described in this book is a long way from providing the panacea that you seem to envisage.

SAGREDO: There is indeed more work to do, and the authors wouldn't claim anything else, but that is no reason for failing to see the potential. May I remind you, Simplicio, you refused even to look through Galileo's telescope, and if you don't mind me saying so, I think you are trying to put on your intellectual blindfold again.

SALVIATI: I would prefer not to be so hard on Simplicio. Let us look back and try to persuade him of the rich possibilities here. What have we learned about the networks made by companies and financial institutions?

SAGREDO: That they are made up of multiple layers: trades, stockholding, multiple positions held by executive officers, money-lending, joint patent applications, to name a few aspects. Briefly, we have learned that these interlocking networks are almost unimaginably complex.

SALVIATI: Precisely, and our conclusion must be that the behaviour of such economic agents should be modelled and understood on the basis of the interactions of the complex networks of which they are part.

SIMPLICIO: Easily said, Salviati, but how do you propose to handle and model such a complex system?

SALVIATI: It is data-intensive, but simulation is one option; for example, problems in cosmology, such as the collision of galaxies, are modelled through calculations using very large parallel computers. The same is true in the microscopic world, where quantum chromodynamics placed on a space-time lattice are beginning to replicate a realistic spectrum of elementary particles.

SAGREDO: What a thought, an Economic Simulator.

SALVIATI: Yes, yes, and difficult though all of this will be, there is always the possibility that we will be able to develop new concepts and theories on the way.

SAGREDO: Your enthusiasm is infectious.

SIMPLICIO: Yes, I think he's a bit feverish.

SAGREDO: But you are as cool as ever, I see. The sparks of reason appear to have had no effect on your fireproof intellect.

SIMPLICIO: Well, that's a little uncalled for. I'm just more cautious, that is all.

SALVIATI: Which is commendable, my dear Simplicio, and it is why in spite of all your faults we love you as a friend, and why I shall trust your recommendation for dinner tonight. See the sun has already set, the dew is falling, the cool of the night is coming on, and a day of thought has given me quite an appetite.

SIMPLICIO: Now that is real wisdom, there's a little place down near the river . . .

SAGREDO: Ha, so basic.

SALVIATI: As are we all, Sagredo, though some of us are 'looking at the stars'.

SIMPLICIO: Yes, yes, aren't they beautiful, almost good enough to eat.

SAGREDO: Heavens, he's at it again.

SALVIATI: No, no, I do believe it's a promising sign; wonder is the beginning of curiosity, and in such inquisitive thoughts lie the roots of science.

SIMPLICIO: Well, that's awfully kind of you; perhaps as we walk you will explain the ideas to me again.

SALVIATI: Of course, Simplicio, my patience is infinite. Lead on and I shall start at the beginning.

Exeunt Omnes

Give me a fruitful error any time, full of seeds, bursting with its own corrections. You can keep your sterile truth for yourself. (Vilfredo Pareto commenting on Johannes Kepler)

References

Aitchison, J. and J. A. C. Brown (1957), *The Lognormal Distribution*, Cambridge University Press.

Albert, R., H. Jeong and A.-L. Barabási (1999), 'Internet: diameter of the World Wide Web', *Nature*, 401, 130–1.

Alligood, K. T., T. Sauer and J. A. Yorke (1997), *Chaos: An Introduction to Dynamical Systems*, Springer-Verlag, New York.

Amaral, L. A. N., S. V. Buldyrev, S. Havlin, H. Leschhorn, P. Maass, M. A. Salinger, H. E. Stanley and M. H. R. Stanley (1997), 'Scaling behavior in economics: I. Empirical results for company growth', *Journal de Physique I France*, 7(4), 621–33.

Amaral, L. A. N., S. V. Buldyrev, S. Havlin, M. A. Salinger and H. E. Stanley (1998), 'Power law scaling for a system of interacting units with complex internal structure', *Physical Review Letters*, 80(7), 1385–8.

Amaral, L. A. N., A. Scala, M. Barthelemy and H. E. Stanley (2000), 'Classes of small-world networks', *Proceedings of the National Academy of Sciences*, 97(21), 11149.

Anderson, C. (2006), *The Long Tail: Why the Future of Business Is Selling Less of More*, Hyperion, New York.

Aoki, M. (2002), *Modeling Aggregate Behavior and Fluctuations in Economics: Stochastic Views of Interacting Agents*, Cambridge University Press.

Aoki, M. and H. Yoshikawa (2007), *Reconstructing Macroeconomics: A Perspective from Statistical Physics and Combinatorial Stochastic Processes*, Cambridge University Press.

Aoyama, H., Y. Fujiwara, H. Iyetomi and A.-H. Sato (2009), eds., *Econophysics – Physical Approach to Social and Economic Phenomena* (Progress of Theoretical Physics, Supplement No. 179), Yukawa Institute for Theoretical Physics and the Physical Society of Japan, Kyoto.

Aoyama, H., Y. Fujiwara and W. Souma (2004), 'Kinematics and dynamics of Pareto–Zipf's law and Gibrat's law', *Physica A*, 344, 117–21.

Aoyama, H. and H. Kikuchi (1992), 'A new valley method for instanton deformation', *Nuclear Physics B*, 369, 219–34.

Aoyama, H., H. Kikuchi, I. Okouchi, M. Sato and S. Wada (1999), 'Valley views: instantons, large order behaviors, and supersymmetry', *Nuclear Physics B*, 553, 644–710.

Aoyama, H., Y. Nagahara, M. P. Okazaki, W. Souma, H. Takayasu and M. Takayasu (2000), 'Pareto's law for income of individuals and debt of bankrupt companies', *Fractals*, 8, 293–300.

Aoyama, H., H. Yoshikawa, H. Iyetomi and Y. Fujiwara (2008), 'Productivity dispersion: facts, theory, and implications', Arxiv preprint arXiv:0805.2792, RIETI Discussion Paper 08-E, 35.

Arrow, K. J., H. B. Chenery, B. S. Minhas and R. M. Solow (1961), 'Capital–labor substitution and economic efficiency', *Review of Economics and Statistics*, 43(3), 225–50.

Auerbach, F. (1913), 'Das Gesetz der Bevölkerungskonzentration', *Petermanns Geographische Mitteilungen*, 59, 74–6.

Axtell, R. L. (2001), 'Zipf distribution of US firm sizes', *Science*, 293(5536), 1818–20.

Barabási, A.-L. (2003), *Linked: How Everything Is Connected to Everything Else and What It Means for Business, Science, and Everyday Life*, Plume, New York.

Barabási, A.-L. and R. Albert (1999), 'Emergence of scaling in complex networks', *Science*, 286, 509–12.

Barabási, A.-L. and Z. N. Oltvai (2004), 'Network biology: understanding the cell's functional organization', *Nature Reviews Genetics*, 5(2), 101–13.

Barrat, A., M. Barthelemy, R. Pastor-Satorras and A. Vespignani (2004), 'The architecture of complex weighted networks', *Proceedings of the National Academy of Sciences*, 101(11), 3747–52.

Berger, S. (2005), *How We Compete: What Companies Around the World Are Doing to Make It in Today's Global Economy*, Random House, New York.

Bergeron, B. (2003), *Essentials of XBRL: Financial Reporting in the 21st Century*, Wiley, New York.

Black, F. and M. Scholes (1973), 'The pricing of options and corporate liabilities', *Journal of Political Economy*, 81(3), 637.

Bollobás, B. (1985), *Random Graphs*, Academic Press, New York.

Bottazzi, G. and A. Secchi (2003), 'Why are distributions of firm growth rates tent-shaped?', *Economics Letters*, 80(3), 415–20.

Bouchaud, J. P. and M. Mezard (2000), 'Wealth condensation in a simple model of economy', *Physica A*, 282(3–4), 536–45.

Bouchaud, J. P. and M. Potters (2003), *Theory of Financial Risk and Derivative Pricing: From Statistical Physics to Risk Management*, Cambridge University Press.

Brealey, R., S. Myers and F. Allen (2008), *Principles of Corporate Finance*, McGraw-Hill/Irwin, Boston.

Brin, S. and L. Page (1998), 'The anatomy of a large-scale hypertextual Web search engine', *Computer Networks and ISDN Systems*, 30(1–7), 107–17.

Buchanan, M. (2003), *Nexus: Small Worlds and the Groundbreaking Science of Networks*, W. W. Norton, New York.

Caldarelli, G. (2007), *Scale-free Networks: Complex Webs in Nature and Technology*, Oxford University Press.

Callen, H. B. (1985), *Thermodynamics and an Introduction to Thermostatistics*, 2nd edn, Wiley, New York.

Champernowne, D. G. (1973), *The Distribution of Income Between Persons*, Cambridge University Press.

Chesbrough, H. W. (2006), *Open Innovation*, Harvard Business School Press, Boston.

Christensen, L. R., D. W. Jorgenson and L. J. Lau (1973), 'Transcendental logarithmic production frontiers', *Review of Economics and Statistics*, 55(1), 28–45.

Cobb, C. W. and P. H. Douglas (1928), 'A theory of production', *American Economic Review*, 18(1), 139–65.

Davis, M. D. (1983), *Game Theory*, 2nd edn, Basic Books, New York.

Delli Gatti, D., E. Gaffeo, M. Gallegati, G. Giulioni and A. Palestrini (2008), *Emergent Macroeconomics: An Agent-based Approach to Business Fluctuations*, Springer, New York.

Delli Gatti, D., M. Gallegati and A. Palestrini (2000), 'Agents' heterogeneity, aggregation, and economic fluctuations', in D. Delli Gatti, M. Gallegati and A. Kirman (eds.), *Interaction and Market Structure: Essays on Heterogeneity in Economics* (Lecture Notes in Economics and Mathematical Systems, no. 484), Springer, New York, pp. 133–49.

Dertouzos, M. L., R. K. Lester and R. M. Solow (1989), *Made in America: Regaining the Productive Edge*, MIT Press, Cambridge, Mass.

Erdős, P. and Rényi, A. (1960), 'On the evolution of random graphs', *Publications of the Mathematical Institute of the Hungarian Academy of Science*, 5, 17–61.

Falconer, K. J. (2003), *Fractal Geometry: Mathematical Foundations and Applications*, Wiley, New York.

Farmer, J. D., M. Shubik and E. Smith (2005), 'Is economics the next physical science?', *Physics Today*, 58(September), 37–42.

Freeman, L. C. (2004), *The Development of Social Network Analysis: A Study in the Sociology of Science*, Empirical Press, Vancouver.

Fu, D., F. Pammolli, S. V. Buldyrev, M. Riccaboni, K. Matia, K. Yamasaki and H. E. Stanley (2005), 'The growth of business firms: theoretical framework and empirical evidence', *Proceedings of the National Academy of Sciences*, 102(52), 18801–6.

Fujiwara, Y. (2004), 'Zipf law in firms' bankruptcy', *Physica A*, 337, 219–30.

 (2008), 'Chain of firms' bankruptcy: a macroscopic study of link effect in a production network', *Advances in Complex Systems*, 11(5), 703–17.

Fujiwara, Y. and H. Aoyama (2008), 'Large-scale structure of a nation-wide production network', Arxiv preprint arXiv:0806.4280, KUNS-2178.

Fujiwara, Y., H. Aoyama and W. Souma (2006a), 'Growth and fluctuations for small-business firms', in H. Takayasu (ed.), *Practical Fruits of Econophysics: Proceedings of the Third Nikkei Econophysics Symposium*, Springer, Tokyo, pp. 291–5.

 (2006b), 'Growth of firms and networks', in B. K. Chakrabarti, A. Chakraborti and A. Chatterjee (eds.), *Econophysics and Sociophysics: Trends and Perspectives*, Wiley-VCH, Berlin, pp. 99–129.

Fujiwara, Y., C. Di Guilmi, H. Aoyama, M. Gallegati and W. Souma (2004), "Do Pareto–Zipf and Gibrat laws hold true? An analysis with European firms', *Physica A*, 335, 197–216.

Fujiwara, Y., W. Souma, H. Aoyama, T. Kaizoji and M. Aoki (2003), 'Growth and fluctuations of personal income', *Physica A*, 321, 598–604.

Gabaix, X. (2008), 'The granular origins of aggregate fluctuations', SSRN eLibrary, Working Paper series, http://ssrn.com/paper=1111765.

Galilei, Galileo (1632), *Dialogue Concerning the Two Chief World Systems*.

Gallegati, M., G. Giulioni and N. Kichiji (2003), 'Complex dynamics and financial fragility in an agent based model', in V. Kumar *et al.* (eds.), *Computational Science and Its Applications – ICCSA 2003* (Lecture Notes in Computer Science, no. 2667), Springer, New York, pp. 770–9.

Garlaschelli, D., S. Battiston, M. Castri, V. D. P. Servedio and G. Caldarelli (2005), 'The scale-free topology of market investments', *Physica A*, 350(2–4), 491–9.

Gell-Mann, M. (1995), *The Quark and the Jaguar: Adventures in the Simple and the Complex*, Owl Books, New York.

Gibbons, R. (1992), *Game Theory for Applied Economists*, Princeton University Press.

Gibrat, R. (1931), *Les inégalités économiques*, Librairie du Recueil Sirey, Paris.

Goldberg, D. E. (1989), *Genetic Algorithms in Search, Optimization and Machine Learning*, Addison-Wesley, Cambridge, Mass.

Holland, J. H. (1996), *Hidden Order: How Adaptation Builds Complexity*, Basic Books, New York.

 (1998), *Emergence: From Chaos to Order*, Oxford University Press, 1998.

Hoover, E. M. (1936), 'The measurement of industrial localization', *Review of Economics and Statistics*, 18, 162–71.

Hull, J. C. (2008), *Options, Futures, and Other Derivatives*, 7th edn, Prentice Hall, Upper Saddle River, N. J.

Ijiri, Y. and H. A. Simon (1977), *Skew Distributions and the Sizes of Business Firms*, North-Holland, Amsterdam.

Ikeda, Y., H. Aoyama, H. Iyetomi, Y. Fujiwara and W. Souma (2008), 'Correlated performance of firms in a transaction network', *Journal of Economic Interaction and Coordination*, 3, 73–80.

Ikeda, Y., H. Aoyama, H. Iyetomi, Y. Fujiwara, W. Souma, and T. Kaizoji (2007a), 'Response of firm agent network to exogenous shock', *Physica A*, 382, 138–48.

Ikeda Y., W. Souma, H. Aoyama, H. Iyetomi, Y. Fujiwara and T. Kaizoji (2007b), 'Quantitative agent-based firm dynamics simulation with parameters estimated by financial and transaction data analysis', *Physica A*, 375, 651–67.

Iyetomi, H., H. Aoyama, Y. Fujiwara, Y. Ikeda and W. Souma (2009a), 'Agent-based model approach to complex phenomena in real economy', *Progress of Theoretical Physics Supplement*, 179, 123–33.

(2009b), 'Production copula', Arxiv preprint arXiv:0902.1576.

Kesten, H. (1973), 'Random difference equations and renewal theory for products of random matrices', *Acta Mathematica*, 131(1), 207–48.

Kleiber, C. and S. Kotz (2003), *Statistical Size Distributions in Economics and Actuarial Sciences*, Wiley, New York.

Kleinberg, J. M. (1999), 'Authoritative sources in a hyperlinked environment', *Journal of the ACM*, 46(5), 604–32.

Leontief, W. W. (1941), *The Structure of the American Economy, 1919–1929: An Empirical Application of Equilibrium Analysis*, Harvard University Press, Cambridge, Mass.

Luenberger, D. G. (1997), *Investment Science*, illustrated edn, Oxford University Press.

Mandelbrot, B. B. (1997), *Fractals and Scaling in Finance: Discontinuity, Concentration, Risk*, Springer, New York.

Manrubia, S. C. and D. H. Zanette (1999), 'Stochastic multiplicative processes with reset events', *Physical Review E*, 59(5), 4945–8.

Mantegna, R. N. and H. E. Stanley (2000), *An Introduction to Econophysics: Correlations and Complexity in Finance*, Cambridge University Press.

Milgram, S. (1967), 'The small world problem', *Psychology Today*, 2(1), 60–7.

Milo, R., S. Shen-Orr, S. Itzkovitz, N. Kashtan, D. Chklovskii and U. Alon (2002), 'Network motifs: simple building blocks of complex networks', *Science*, 298(5594), 824–7.

Modigliani, F. and M. H. Miller (1958), 'The cost of capital, corporation finance and the theory of investment', *American Economic Review*, 48, 261–97.

Nelsen, R. B. (2006), *An Introduction to Copulas*, 2nd edn, Springer, New York.

Newman, M. E. J. (2003a), 'Ego-centered networks and the ripple effect', *Social Networks*, 25(1), 83–95.

(2003b), 'Random graphs as models of networks', in S. Bornholdt and H. G. Schuster (eds.), *Handbook of Graphs and Networks*, Wiley-VCH, Weinheim, pp. 35–68.

(2003c), 'The structure and function of complex networks', *SIAM Review*, 45(2), 167–256.

Nirei, M. and W. Souma (2006), 'Income distribution and stochastic multiplicative process with reset events', in M. Gallegati, A. P. Kirman and M. Marsili (eds.), *The Complex Dynamics of Economic Interaction: Essays in Economics and Econophysics*, Springer, New York, pp. 161–8.

Okuyama, K., M. Takayasu and H. Takayasu (1999), 'Zipf's law in income distribution of companies', *Physica A*, 269(1), 125–31.

Ōno, T. (1988), *Toyota Production System: Beyond Large-scale Production*, Productivity Press, New York.

Owen, G. (1995), *Game Theory*, 3rd edn, Academic Press, New York.

Pareto, V. (1896–7), *Cours d'économie politique*, F. Rouge, Lausanne.

Pastor-Satorras, R., A. Vazquez and A. Vespignani (2001), 'Dynamical and correlation properties of the Internet', *Physical Review Letters*, 87(25), 258701.

Piore, M. J. and C. F. Sabel (1984), *The Second Industrial Divide: Possibilities for Prosperity*, Basic Books, New York.

Pratt, J. (2008), *Financial Accounting in an Economic Context*, 7th edn, Wiley, New York.

Press, W. H., S. A. Teukolsky, W. T. Vetterling and B. P. Flannery (1992), *Numerical Recipes in C: The Art of Scientific Computing*, 2nd edn, Cambridge University Press.

Ravasz, E., A. L. Somera, D. A. Mongru, Z. N. Oltvai and A.-L. Barabási (2002), 'Hierarchical organization of modularity in metabolic networks', *Science*, 297(5586), 1551.

Redner, S. (1990), 'Random multiplicative processes: an elementary tutorial', *American Journal of Physics*, 58, 267–73.

Sapolsky, R. (2005), 'Sick of poverty', *Scientific American*, 293(6), 92–9.

Saramäki, J., M. Kivelä, J. P. Onnela, K. Kaski and J. Kértesz (2007), 'Generalizations of the clustering coefficient to weighted complex networks', *Physical Review E*, 75, 027105.

Shen-Orr, S. S., R. Milo, S. Mangan and U. Alon (2002), 'Network motifs in the transcriptional regulation network of Escherichia coli', *Nature Genetics*, 31(1), 64–8.

Shirata, C. Y. (2004), 'An attempt to rate companies based on bankruptcy prediction model', presented at the 16th Asia-Pacific Conference on International Accounting Issues.

Solomon, S. and M. Levy (1996), 'Power laws are logarithmic Boltzmann laws', *International Journal of Modern Physics C*, 74, 595–601.

Sornette, D. (1998), 'Multiplicative processes and power laws', *Physical Review E*, 57(4), 4811–13.

  (2004), *Critical Phenomena in Natural Sciences: Chaos, Fractals, Selforganization, and Disorder: Concepts and Tools*, 2nd edn, Springer, Berlin.

Sornette, D. and R. Cont (1997), 'Convergent multiplicative processes repelled from zero: power laws and truncated power laws', *Journal de Physique I France*, 7(3), 431–44.

Souma, W., Y. Fujiwara, and H. Aoyama (2001), 'Small-world effects in wealth distribution', Arxiv preprint arXiv:0108.482.

  (2003), 'Wealth distribution in scale-free networks', in T. Terano, H. Deguchi and K. Takadama (eds.), *Meeting the Challenge of Social Problems via Agent-based Simulation: Post-proceedings of the Second International Workshop on Agent-Based Approaches in Economic and Social Complex Systems*, Springer, New York, pp. 37–49.

Stanley, Eugene (2008), 'Econophysics and the current economic turmoil', *APS News*, 17(11), 8–9.

Stanley, M. H. R., L. A. N. Amaral, S. V. Buldyrev, S. Havlin, H. Leschhorn, P. Maass, M. A. Salinger and H. E. Stanley (1996), 'Scaling behaviour in the growth of companies', *Nature*, 379, 804–6.

Steindl, J. (1965), *Random Processes and the Growth of Firms: A Study of the Pareto Law*, Griffin, London.

Stiglitz, J. and B. Greenwald (2003), *Towards a New Paradigm in Monetary Economics*, Cambridge University Press.

Sutton, J. (1997), 'Gibrat's legacy', *Journal of Economic Literature*, 35(1), 40–59.

Takayasu, H. (2002), ed., *Empirical Science of Financial Fluctuations: The Advent of Econophysics*, Springer, Tokyo.

  (2004), ed., *The Application of Econophysics*, Springer, Tokyo.

  (2006), ed., *Practical Fruits of Econophysics*, Springer, Tokyo.

Takayasu, H., A.-H. Sato, and M. Takayasu (1997), 'Stable infinite variance fluctuations in randomly amplified Langevin systems', *Physical Review Letters*, 79(6), 966–9.

Tsallis, C. (1988), 'Possible generalization of Boltzmann–Gibbs statistics', *Journal of Statistical Physics*, 52(1), 479–87.

Varian, H. R. (1992), *Microeconomic Analysis*, 3rd edn, W. W. Norton, New York.

  (2005), *Intermediate Microeconomics*, 7th edn, W. W. Norton, New York.

von Neumann, J. and O. Morgenstern (1944), *Theory of Games and Economic Behavior*, Princeton University Press.

Waldrop, M. (1992), *Complexity: The Emerging Science at the Edge of Chaos*, Simon & Schuster, New York.

Watts, D. J. (1999), *Small Worlds: The Dynamics of Networks between Order and Randomness*, Princeton University Press.

(2003), *Six Degrees: The Science of a Connected Age*, W. W. Norton, New York.

Watts, D. J. and S. H. Strogatz (1998), 'Collective dynamics of "small-world" networks', *Nature*, 393(6684), 440.

Zipf, G. K. (1949), *Human Behavior and the Principle of Least Effort: An Introduction to Human Ecology*, Addison-Wesley, Cambridge, Mass.

Index

For EU product safety concerns, contact us at Calle de José Abascal, 56–1°,
28003 Madrid, Spain or eugpsr@cambridge.org.

www.ingramcontent.com/pod-product-compliance
Ingram Content Group UK Ltd.
Pitfield, Milton Keynes, MK11 3LW, UK
UKHW050105190425
457623UK00009B/94